Cover, "Le Thérapeute," by René Magritte
Private Collection, photo Jacqueline Hyde, Paris

Edges of Reality

Shorter Long Fiction

Edges of Reality: Confrontations with the Uncanny, the Macabre, and the Mad

Prepared by the Editorial Staff
Scott, Foresman and Company

Direction   **Leo B. Kneer**

Development   **Ruth S. Cohen**

with   Stephen Ellis
Chiyoko Omachi
Clement Stacy
David Epstein

Design   Barbara Schneider

This is deliberately a "partially edited" book. The marginal notes contain information, directions for thought, and questions which may take you further into the stories than you would go without them. In no sense are they definitive. You may perhaps want to complete the process yourself—making your personal points of emphasis, noting your own allusions, commenting on or questioning matters of special significance to you.

Believing that writers usually introduce their work themselves, we have omitted introductory remarks, headnotes, prefaces, and the like. Such information as might have been given in an introduction will be found in the COMMENT section at the end of the selection, where it is more appropriate.

The editors hope you will approach the selections in this manner:

(1) Read the selection without referring to the marginal notes. Let it reach you as it will. Speculate as to its significance. Then,

(2) read the notes to get a general idea of their import. Finally,

(3) read the text with the notes, taking time to follow whatever directions your own experience and imagination indicate.

At the end of each narrative are remarks or questions under the heading of SYNTHESIS, which bring details into a general focus or show relationships existing among the several pieces. Any work of art is considerably more than the sum of its parts. Considering the whole construction may make the artistic unity underlying the work more apparent.

In any event, do not let the editorial material circumscribe your reading. It is meant to expand—not restrict.

LEO B. KNEER

THE DIAMOND AS BIG AS THE RITZ

F. SCOTT FITZGERALD

John T. Unger came from a family that had been well known in Hades—a small town on the Mississippi River—for several generations. John's father had held the amateur golf championship through many a heated contest; Mrs. Unger was known "from hot-box to hot-bed," as the local phrase went, for her political addresses; and young John T. Unger, who had just turned sixteen, had danced all the latest dances from New York before he put on long trousers. And now, for a certain time, he was to be away from home. That respect for a New England education

Mrs. Unger is well known to many social groups, from railroad workers (**hot-box**) to garden-club members (**hot-bed**), for her civic activities.

Who was Midas in Greek legend? Note the "Midas" figures in the story.

which is the bane of all provincial places, which drains them yearly of their most promising young men, had seized upon his parents. Nothing would suit them but that he should go to St. Midas' School near Boston—Hades was too small to hold their darling and gifted son.

Now in Hades—as you know if you ever have been there—the names of the more fashionable preparatory schools and colleges mean very little. The inhabitants have been so long out of the world that, though they make a show of keeping up to date in dress and manners and literature, they depend to a great extent on hearsay, and a function that in Hades would be considered elaborate would doubtless be hailed by a Chicago beef-princess as "perhaps a little tacky."

John T. Unger was on the eve of departure. Mrs. Unger, with maternal fatuity, packed his trunks full of linen suits and electric fans, and Mr. Unger presented his son with an asbestos pocket-book stuffed with money.

"Remember, you are always welcome here," he said. "You can be sure, boy, that we'll keep the home fires burning."

"I know," answered John huskily.

"Don't forget who you are and where you come from," continued his father proudly, "and you can do nothing to harm you. You are an Unger—from Hades."

What implications do you see in naming a town "Hades"?

So the old man and the young shook hands and John walked away with tears streaming from his eyes. Ten minutes later he had passed outside the city limits, and he stopped to glance back for the last time. Over the gates the old-fashioned Victorian motto seemed strangely attractive to him. His father had tried time and time again to have it changed to something with a little more push and verve about it, such as "Hades—Your Opportunity," or else a plain "Welcome" sign set over a hearty handshake pricked

The Victorian motto is never phrased. What might it have been?

10

out in electric lights. The old motto was a little depressing, Mr. Unger had thought—but now . . .

So John took his look and then set his face resolutely toward his destination. And, as he turned away, the lights of Hades against the sky seemed full of a warm and passionate beauty.

St. Midas' School is half an hour from Boston in a Rolls-Pierce motor-car. The actual distance will never be known, for no one, except John T. Unger, had ever arrived there save in a Rolls-Pierce and probably no one ever will again. St. Midas' is the most expensive and the most exclusive boys' preparatory school in the world.

John's first two years there passed pleasantly. The fathers of all the boys were money-kings and John spent his summers visiting at fashionable resorts. While he was very fond of all the boys he visited, their fathers struck him as being much of a piece, and in his boyish way he often wondered at their exceeding sameness. When he told them where his home was they would ask jovially, "Pretty hot down there?" and John would muster a faint smile and answer, "It certainly is." His response would have been heartier had they not all made this joke—at best varying it with, "Is it hot enough for you down there?" which he hated just as much.

In the middle of his second year at school, a quiet, handsome boy named Percy Washington had been put in John's form. The newcomer was pleasant in his manner and exceedingly well dressed even for St. Midas', but for some reason he kept aloof from the other boys. The only person with whom he was intimate was John T. Unger, but even to John he was entirely uncommunicative concerning his home or his family. That he was wealthy went without saying, but beyond a few such deductions John knew little of his friend, so it promised rich confectionery for his curiosity when Percy invited him to spend the summer at

Summarize the values of the Ungers. Are these values especially American?

What are the fathers of John's friends like? How does John feel about them?

form: grade-level in British and many American private schools.

11

his home "in the West." He accepted, without hesitation.

It was only when they were in the train that Percy became, for the first time, rather communicative. One day while they were eating lunch in the dining-car and discussing the imperfect characters of several of the boys at school, Percy suddenly changed his tone and made an abrupt remark.

"My father," he said, "is by far the richest man in the world."

"Oh," said John, politely. He could think of no answer to make to this confidence. He considered "That's very nice," but it sounded hollow and was on the point of saying "Really?" but refrained since it would seem to question Percy's statement. And such an astounding statement could scarcely be questioned.

"By far the richest," repeated Percy.

"I was reading in the *World Almanac*," began John, "that there was one man in America with an income of over five million a year and four men with incomes of over three million a year, and——"

"Oh, they're nothing," Percy's mouth was a half-moon of scorn. "Catch-penny capitalists, financial small-fry, petty merchants and money-lenders. My father could buy them out and not know he'd done it."

"But how does he——"

"Why haven't they put down *his* income tax? Because he doesn't pay any. At least he pays a little one—but he doesn't pay any on his *real* income."

"He must be very rich," said John simply. "I'm glad. I like very rich people.

"The richer a fella is, the better I like him." There was a look of passionate frankness upon his dark face. "I visited the Schnlitzer-Murphys last Easter. Vivian Schnlitzer-Murphy had rubies as big as hen's eggs, and sapphires that were like globes with lights inside them——"

Note the contrast between the way the two boys speak about wealth. What does this contrast tell you about each?

12

"I love jewels," agreed Percy enthusiastically. "Of course I wouldn't want any one at school to know about it, but I've got quite a collection myself. I used to collect them instead of stamps."

"And diamonds," continued John eagerly. "The Schnlitzer-Murphys had diamonds as big as walnuts——"

"That's nothing." Percy had leaned forward and dropped his voice to a low whisper. "That's nothing at all. My father has a diamond bigger than the Ritz-Carlton Hotel."

II

The Montana sunset lay between two mountains like a gigantic bruise from which dark arteries spread themselves over a poisoned sky. An immense distance under the sky crouched the village of Fish, minute, dismal, and forgotten. There were twelve men, so it was said, in the village of Fish, twelve sombre and inexplicable souls who sucked a lean milk from the almost literally bare rock upon which a mysterious populatory force had begotten them. They had become a race apart, these twelve men of Fish, like some species developed by an early whim of nature, which on second thought had abandoned them to struggle and extermination.

Out of the blue-black bruise in the distance crept a long line of moving lights upon the desolation of the land, and the twelve men of Fish gathered like ghosts at the shanty depot to watch the passing of the seven o'clock train, the Transcontinental Express from Chicago. Six times or so a year the Transcontinental Express, through some inconceivable jurisdiction, stopped at the village of Fish, and when this occurred a figure or so would disembark, mount into a buggy that always appeared from out of the dusk, and drive off toward the bruised sunset. The observation of this pointless and preposterous phenomenon had become a sort of cult among the men of Fish. To observe, that was all; there remained in them none of the vital quality of illusion which would make them wonder or speculate, else a religion might have grown up around these mysterious visitations. But the men of Fish were beyond all religion—the barest and most savage tenets of even Christianity could gain no foothold on that barren rock—so there was no altar, no priest, no sacrifice; only each night at seven the silent concourse by the shanty depot, a congregation who lifted up a prayer of dim, anaemic wonder.

What emotional reaction to the village of Fish do you have after reading these opening paragraphs?

On this June night, the Great Brakeman, whom, had they deified any one, they might well have chosen as their celestial protagonist, had ordained that the seven o'clock train should leave its human (or inhuman) deposit at Fish. At two minutes after seven Percy Washington and John T. Unger disembarked, hurried past the spellbound, the agape, the fearsome eyes of the twelve men of Fish, mounted into a buggy which had obviously appeared from nowhere, and drove away.

After half an hour, when the twilight had coagulated into dark, the silent Negro who was driving the buggy hailed an opaque body somewhere ahead of them in the gloom. In response to his cry, it turned upon them a luminous disk which regarded them like a malignant eye out of the unfathomable night. As they came closer, John saw that it was the tail-light of an immense automobile, larger and more magnificent than any he had ever seen. Its body was of gleaming metal richer than nickel and lighter than silver, and the hubs of the wheels were studded with iridescent geometric figures of green and yellow—John did not dare to guess whether they were glass or jewel.

What suggests that John may be starting to distrust his own sense of reality?

Two Negroes, dressed in glittering livery such as one sees in pictures of royal processions in London, were standing at attention beside the car and as the two young men dismounted from the buggy they were greeted in some language which the guest could not understand, but which seemed to be an extreme form of the Southern Negro's dialect.

"Get in," said Percy to his friend, as their trunks were tossed to the ebony roof of the limousine. "Sorry we had to bring you this far in that buggy, but of course it wouldn't do for the people on the train or those Godforsaken fellas in Fish to see this automobile."

"Gosh! What a car!" This ejaculation was provoked by its interior. John saw that the upholstery consisted of a thousand minute and exquisite tapestries of silk, woven with jewels and embroideries, and set upon a background of cloth of gold. The two armchair seats in which the boys luxuriated were covered with stuff that resembled duvetyn, but seemed woven in numberless colors of the ends of ostrich feathers.

"What a car!" cried John again, in amazement.

"This thing?" Percy laughed. "Why, it's just an old junk we use for a station wagon."

By this time they were gliding along through the darkness toward the break between the two mountains.

"We'll be there in an hour and a half," said Percy, looking at the clock. "I may as well tell you it's not going to be like anything you ever saw before."

If the car was any indication of what John would see, he was prepared to be astonished indeed. The simple piety prevalent in Hades has the earnest worship of and respect for riches as the first article of its creed—had John felt otherwise than radiantly humble before them, his parents would have turned away in horror at the blasphemy.

They had now reached and were entering the break between the two mountains and almost immediately the way became much rougher.

"If the moon shone down here, you'd see that

> duvetyn (dü′və-tēn): soft, woolen cloth with a velvety finish. See the Pronunciation Key on page 295.

15

we're in a big gulch," said Percy, trying to peer out of the window. He spoke a few words into the mouthpiece and immediately the footman turned on a searchlight and swept the hillsides with an immense beam.

"Rocky, you see. An ordinary car would be knocked to pieces in half an hour. In fact, it'd take a tank to navigate it unless you knew the way. You notice we're going uphill now."

They were obviously ascending, and within a few minutes the car was crossing a high rise, where they caught a glimpse of a pale moon newly risen in the distance. The car stopped suddenly and several figures took shape out of the dark beside it—these were Negroes also. Again the two young men were saluted in the same dimly recognizable dialect; then the Negroes set to work and four immense cables dangling from overhead were attached with hooks to the hubs of the great jeweled wheels. At a resounding "Hey-yah!" John felt the car being lifted slowly from the ground—up and up—clear of the tallest rocks on both sides—then higher, until he could see a wavy, moonlit valley stretched out before him in sharp contrast to the quagmire of rocks that they had just left. Only on one side was there still rock—and then suddenly there was no rock beside them or anywhere around.

It was apparent that they had surmounted some immense knife-blade of stone, projecting perpendicularly into the air. In a moment they were going down again, and finally with a soft bump they were landed upon the smooth earth.

"The worst is over," said Percy, squinting out the window. "It's only five miles from here, and our own road—tapestry brick—all the way. This belongs to us. This is where the United States ends, father says."

"Are we in Canada?"

"We are not. We're in the middle of the Montana

Fitzgerald combines credible and incredible details in his description of the journey from Fish to the valley. What do these details accomplish in the story?

16

Rockies. But you are now on the only five square miles of land in the country that's never been surveyed."

"Why hasn't it? Did they forget it?"

"No," said Percy, grinning, "they tried to do it three times. The first time my grandfather corrupted a whole department of the State survey; the second time he had the official maps of the United States tinkered with—that held them for fifteen years. The last time was harder. My father fixed it so that their compasses were in the strongest magnetic field ever artificially set up. He had a whole set of surveying instruments made with a slight defection that would allow for this territory not to appear, and he substituted them for the ones that were to be used. Then he had a river deflected and he had what looked like a village built up on its banks—so that they'd see it, and think it was a town ten miles farther up the valley. There's only one thing my father's afraid of," he concluded, "only one thing in the world that could be used to find us out."

"What's that?"

Percy sank his voice to a whisper.

"Aeroplanes," he breathed. "We've got half a dozen anti-aircraft guns and we've arranged it so far—but there've been a few deaths and a great many prisoners. Not that we mind *that*, you know, father and I, but it upsets mother and the girls, and there's always the chance that some time we won't be able to arrange it."

Shreds and tatters of chinchilla, courtesy clouds in the green moon's heaven, were passing the green moon like precious Eastern stuffs paraded for the inspection of some Tartar Khan. It seemed to John that it was day, and that he was looking at some lads sailing above him in the air, showering down tracts and patent medicine circulars, with their messages of hope for despairing, rockbound hamlets. It seemed to

How have the Washingtons managed to isolate themselves?

What do Percy's remarks suggest about his family's attitude toward themselves? toward other people?

What effect do Percy's remarks have upon John?

him that he could see them look down out of the clouds and stare—and stare at whatever there was to stare at in this place whither he was bound. What then? Were they induced to land by some insidious device there to be immured far from patent medicines and from tracts until the judgment day—or, should they fail to fall into the trap, did a quick puff of smoke and the sharp round of a splitting shell bring them drooping to earth—and "upset" Percy's mother and sisters. John shook his head and the wraith of a hollow laugh issued silently from his parted lips. What a desperate transaction lay hidden here? What a moral expedient of a bizarre Croesus? What terrible and golden mystery? . . .

The chinchilla clouds had drifted past now and outside the Montana night was bright as day. The tapestry brick of the road was smooth to the tread of the great tires as they rounded a still, moonlit lake; they passed into darkness for a moment, a pine grove, pungent and cool, then they came out into a broad avenue of lawn and John's exclamation of pleasure was simultaneous with Percy's taciturn "We're home."

Full in the light of the stars, an exquisite château rose from the borders of the lake, climbed in marble radiance half the height of an adjoining mountain, then melted in grace, in perfect symmetry, in translucent feminine languor, into the massed darkness of a forest of pine. The many towers, the slender tracery of the sloping parapets, the chiselled wonder of a thousand yellow windows with their oblongs and hectagons and triangles of golden light, the shattered softness of the intersecting planes of star-shine and blue shade, all trembled on John's spirit like a chord of music. On one of the towers, the tallest, the blackest at its base, an arrangement of exterior lights at the top made a sort of floating fairyland—and as John gazed up in warm enchantment the faint acciaccare sound of violins drifted down in a rococo harmony that

acciaccare (ä chä-kä/rä) probably meant to be acciaccatura (ä-chä/kə tû/rə): brief discords in a melody.

18

was like nothing he had ever heard before. Then in a moment the car stopped before wide, high marble steps around which the night air was fragrant with a host of flowers. At the top of the steps two great doors swung silently open and amber light flooded out upon the darkness, silhouetting the figure of an exquisite lady with black, high-piled hair, who held out her arms toward them.

"Mother," Percy was saying, "this is my friend, John Unger, from Hades."

Afterward John remembered that first night as a daze of many colors, of quick sensory impressions, of music soft as a voice in love, and of the beauty of things, lights and shadows, and motions and faces. There was a white-haired man who stood drinking a many-hued cordial from a crystal thimble set on a golden stem. There was a girl with a flowery face, dressed like Titania with braided sapphires in her hair. There was a room where the solid, soft gold of the walls yielded to the pressure of his hand, and a room that was like a platonic conception of the ultimate prison—ceiling, floor, and all, it was lined with an unbroken mass of diamonds, diamonds of every size and shape, until, lit with tall violet lamps in the corners, it dazzled the eyes with a whiteness that could be compared only with itself, beyond human wish or dream.

Through a maze of these rooms the two boys wandered. Sometimes the floor under their feet would flame in brilliant patterns from lighting below, patterns of barbaric clashing colors, of pastel delicacy, of sheer whiteness, or of subtle and intricate mosaic, surely from some mosque on the Adriatic Sea. Sometimes beneath layers of thick crystal he would see blue or green water swirling, inhabited by vivid fish and growths of rainbow foliage. Then they would be treading on furs of every texture and color or along corridors of palest ivory, unbroken as though carved

19

complete from the gigantic tusks of dinosaurs extinct before the age of man. . . .

Then a hazily remembered transition, and they were at dinner—where each plate was of two almost imperceptible layers of solid diamond between which was curiously worked a filigree of emerald design, a shaving sliced from green air. Music, plangent and unobtrusive, drifted down through far corridors—his chair, feathered and curved insidiously to his back, seemed to engulf and overpower him as he drank his first glass of port. He tried drowsily to answer a question that had been asked him, but the honeyed luxury that clasped his body added to the illusion of sleep—jewels, fabrics, wines, and metals blurred before his eyes into a sweet mist. . . .

"Yes," he replied with a polite effort, "it certainly is hot enough for me down there."

He managed to add a ghostly laugh; then, without movement, without resistance, he seemed to float off and away, leaving an iced dessert that was pink as a dream. . . . He fell asleep.

When he awoke he knew that several hours had passed. He was in a great quiet room with ebony walls and a dull illumination that was too faint, too subtle, to be called a light. His young host was standing over him.

"You fell asleep at dinner," Percy was saying. "I nearly did, too—it was such a treat to be comfortable again after this year of school. Servants undressed and bathed you while you were sleeping."

"Is this a bed or a cloud?" sighed John. "Percy, Percy—before you go, I want to apologize."

"For what?"

"For doubting you when you said you had a diamond as big as the Ritz-Carlton Hotel."

Percy smiled.

"I thought you didn't believe me. It's that mountain, you know."

plangent: expressing sadness.

"What mountain?"

"The mountain the château rests on. It's not very big for a mountain. But except about fifty feet of sod and gravel on top it's solid diamond. *One* diamond, one cubic mile without a flaw. Aren't you listening? Say——"

But John T. Unger had again fallen asleep.

III

Morning. As he awoke he perceived drowsily that the room had at the same moment become dense with sunlight. The ebony panels of one wall had slid aside on a sort of track, leaving his chamber half open to the day. A large Negro in a white uniform stood beside his bed.

"Good-evening," muttered John, summoning his brains from the wild places.

"Good-morning, sir. Are you ready for your bath, sir? Oh, don't get up—I'll put you in, if you'll just unbutton your pajamas—there. Thank you, sir."

John lay quietly as his pajamas were removed—he was amused and delighted; he expected to be lifted like a child by this black Gargantua who was tending him, but nothing of the sort happened; instead he felt the bed tilt up slowly on its side—he began to roll, startled at first, in the direction of the wall, but when he reached the wall its drapery gave way, and sliding two yards farther down a fleecy incline he plumped gently into water the same temperature as his body.

He looked about him. The runway or rollway on which he had arrived had folded gently back into place. He had been projected into another chamber and was sitting in a sunken bath with his head just above the level of the floor. All about him, lining the walls of the room and the sides and bottom of the bath itself, was a blue aquarium, and gazing through the crystal surface on which he sat, he could see fish

Does Fitzgerald have John fall asleep merely to indicate that he has had a tiring day?

21

swimming among amber lights and even gliding without curiosity past his outstretched toes, which were separated from them only by the thickness of the crystal. From overhead, sunlight came down through sea-green glass.

"I suppose, sir, that you'd like hot rosewater and soapsuds this morning, sir—and perhaps cold salt water to finish."

The Negro was standing beside him.

"Yes," agreed John, smiling inanely, "as you please." Any idea of ordering this bath according to his own meagre standards of living would have been priggish and not a little wicked.

The Negro pressed a button and warm rain began to fall, apparently from overhead, but really, so John discovered after a moment, from a fountain arrangement near by. The water turned to a pale rose color and jets of liquid soap spurted into it from four miniature walrus heads at the corners of the bath. In a moment a dozen little paddle-wheels, fixed to the sides, had churned the mixture into a radiant rainbow of pink foam which enveloped him softly with its delicious lightness, and burst in shining, rosy bubbles here and there about him.

"Shall I turn on the moving-picture machine, sir?" suggested the Negro deferentially. "There's a good one-reel comedy in this machine to-day, or I can put in a serious piece in a moment, if you prefer it."

"No, thanks," answered John, politely but firmly. He was enjoying his bath too much to desire any distraction. But distraction came. In a moment he was listening intently to the sound of flutes from just outside, flutes dripping a melody that was like a waterfall, cool and green as the room itself, accompanying a frothy piccolo, in play more fragile than the lace of suds that covered and charmed him.

After a cold salt-water bracer and a cold fresh finish, he stepped out and into a fleecy robe, and upon

22

a couch covered with the same material he was rubbed with oil, alcohol, and spice. Later he sat in a voluptuous chair while he was shaved and his hair was trimmed.

"Mr. Percy is waiting in your sitting-room," said the Negro, when these operations were finished. "My name is Gygsum, Mr. Unger, sir. I am to see to Mr. Unger every morning."

John walked out into the brisk sunshine of his living-room, where he found breakfast waiting for him and Percy, gorgeous in white kid knickerbockers, smoking in an easy chair.

Note Fitzgerald's use of name and dialogue to indicate that the Washingtons held their servants in low esteem.

IV

This is a story of the Washington family as Percy sketched it for John during breakfast.

The father of the present Mr. Washington had been a Virginian, a direct descendant of George Washington, and Lord Baltimore. At the close of the Civil War he was a twenty-five-year-old Colonel with a played-out plantation and about a thousand dollars in gold.

Fitz-Norman Culpepper Washington, for that was the young Colonel's name, decided to present the Virginia estate to his younger brother and go West. He selected two dozen of the most faithful blacks, who, of course, worshipped him, and bought twenty-five tickets to the West, where he intended to take out land in their names and start a sheep and cattle ranch.

Beginning with Fitz-Norman Culpepper Washington's selection of "faithful" blacks who "of course, worshipped him," this chapter is filled with ironic—even farcical —detail.

When he had been in Montana for less than a month and things were going very poorly indeed, he stumbled on his great discovery. He had lost his way when riding in the hills, and after a day without food he began to grow hungry. As he was without his rifle, he was forced to pursue a squirrel, and in the course of the pursuit he noticed that it was carrying something shiny in its mouth. Just before it vanished into its hole—for Providence did not intend that this squirrel should alleviate his hunger—it dropped its burden. Sitting down to consider the situation Fitz-Norman's eye was caught by a gleam in the grass beside him. In ten seconds he had completely lost his appetite and gained one hundred thousand dollars. The squirrel, which had refused with annoying persistence to become food, had made him a present of a large and perfect diamond.

Late that night he found his way to camp and twelve hours later all the males among his darkies were back by the squirrel hole digging furiously at the side of the mountain. He told them he had discovered a rhinestone mine, and, as only one or two of them had ever seen even a small diamond before, they believed him, without question. When the magnitude of his discovery became apparent to him, he found himself in a quandary. The mountain was *a* diamond—it was literally nothing else but solid diamond. He filled four saddle bags full of glittering samples and started on horseback for St. Paul. There he managed to dispose of half a dozen small stones—when he tried a larger one a storekeeper fainted and Fitz-Norman was arrested as a public disturber. He escaped from jail and caught the train for New York, where he sold a few medium-sized diamonds and received in exchange about two hundred thousand dollars in gold. But he did not dare to produce any exceptional gems—in fact, he left New York just in time. Tremendous excitement had been created in jewelry circles, not so much by the size of his diamonds as by their appearance in the city from mysterious sources. Wild rumors became current that a diamond mine had been discovered in the Catskills, on the Jersey coast, on Long Island, beneath Washington Square. Excursion trains, packed with men carrying picks and shovels began to leave New York hourly, bound for various neighboring El

Dorados. But by that time young Fitz-Norman was on his way back to Montana.

By the end of a fortnight he had estimated that the diamond in the mountain was approximately equal in quantity to all the rest of the diamonds known to exist in the world. There was no valuing it by any regular computation, however, for it was *one solid diamond* —and if it were offered for sale not only would the bottom fall out of the market, but also, if the value should vary with its size in the usual arithmetical progression, there would not be enough gold in the world to buy a tenth part of it. And what could any one do with a diamond that size?

It was an amazing predicament. He was, in one sense, the richest man that ever lived—and yet was he worth anything at all? If his secret should transpire there was no telling to what measures the Government might resort in order to prevent a panic, in gold as well as in jewels. They might take over the claim immediately and institute a monopoly.

There was no alternative—he must market his mountain in secret. He sent South for his younger brother and put him in charge of his colored following—darkies who had never realized that slavery was abolished. To make sure of this, he read them a proclamation that he had composed, which announced that General Forrest had reorganized the shattered Southern armies and defeated the North in one pitched battle. The Negroes believed him implicitly. They passed a vote declaring it a good thing and held revival services immediately.

Fitz-Norman himself set out for foreign parts with one hundred thousand dollars and two trunks filled with rough diamonds of all sizes. He sailed for Russia in a Chinese junk and six months after his departure from Montana he was in St. Petersburg. He took obscure lodgings and called immediately upon the court jeweller, announcing that he had a diamond for the Czar. He remained in St. Petersburg for two weeks, in constant danger of being murdered, living from lodging to lodging, and afraid to visit his trunks more than three or four times during the whole fortnight.

On his promise to return in a year with larger and finer stones, he was allowed to leave for India. Before he left, however, the Court Treasurers had deposited to his credit, in American banks, the sum of fifteen million dollars—under four different aliases.

He returned to America in 1868, having been gone a little over two years. He had visited the capitals of twenty-two countries and talked with five emperors, eleven kings, three princes, a shah, a khan, and a sultan. At that time Fitz-Norman estimated his own wealth at one billion dollars. One fact worked consistently against the disclosure of his secret. No one of his larger diamonds remained in the public eye for a week before being invested with a history of enough fatalities, amours, revolutions, and wars to have occupied it from the days of the first Babylonian Empire.

From 1870 until his death in 1900, the history of Fitz-Norman Washington was a long epic in gold. There were side issues, of course—he evaded the surveys, he married a Virginia lady, by whom he had a single son, and he was compelled, due to a series of unfortunate complications, to murder his brother, whose unfortunate habit of drinking himself into an indiscreet stupor had several times endangered their safety. But very few other murders stained these happy years of progress and expansion.

Just before he died he changed his policy, and with all but a few million dollars of his outside wealth bought up rare minerals in bulk, which he deposited in the safety vaults of banks all over the world, marked as bric-a-brac. His son, Braddock Tarleton Washington, followed this policy on an even more tensive scale. The minerals were converted into the

tensive: probably meant to be *intensive*.

26

rarest of all elements—radium—so that the equivalent of a billion dollars in gold could be placed in a receptacle no bigger than a cigar box.

When Fitz-Norman had been dead three years his son, Braddock, decided that the business had gone far enough. The amount of wealth that he and his father had taken out of the mountain was beyond all exact computation. He kept a note-book in cipher in which he set down the approximate quantity of radium in each of the thousand banks he patronized, and recorded the alias under which it was held. Then he did a very simple thing—he sealed up the mine.

He sealed up the mine. What had been taken out of it would support all the Washingtons yet to be born in unparalleled luxury for generations. His one care must be the protection of his secret, lest in the possible panic attendant on its discovery he should be reduced with all the property-holders in the world to utter poverty.

This was the family among whom John T. Unger was staying. This was the story he heard in his silver-walled living-room the morning after his arrival.

V

After breakfast, John found his way out the great marble entrance, and looked curiously at the scene before him. The whole valley, from the diamond mountain to the steep granite cliff five miles away, still gave off a breath of golden haze which hovered idly above the fine sweep of lawns and lakes and gardens. Here and there clusters of elms made delicate groves of shade, contrasting strangely with the tough masses of pine forest that held the hills in a grip of dark-blue green. Even as John looked he saw three fawns in single file patter out from one clump about a half mile away and disappear with awkward gayety into the black-ribbed half-light of another. John would not have been surprised to see a goat-foot piping his way among the trees or to catch a glimpse of pink nymph-skin and flying yellow hair between the greenest of the green leaves.

In some such cool hope he descended the marble steps, disturbing faintly the sleep of two silky Russian wolfhounds at the bottom, and set off along a walk of white and blue brick that seemed to lead in no particular direction.

Do you agree with Fitzgerald's description of youth?

He was enjoying himself as much as he was able. It is youth's felicity as well as its insufficiency that it can never live in the present, but must always be measuring up the day against its own radiantly imagined future—flowers and gold, girls and stars, they are only prefigurations and prophecies of that incomparable, unattainable young dream.

John rounded a soft corner where the massed rosebushes filled the air with heavy scent, and struck off across a park toward a patch of moss under some trees. He had never lain upon moss, and he wanted to see whether it was really soft enough to justify the use of its name as an adjective. Then he saw a girl coming toward him over the grass. She was the most beautiful person he had ever seen.

She was dressed in a white little gown that came just below her knees, and a wreath of mignonettes clasped with blue slices of sapphire bound up her hair. Her pink bare feet scattered the dew before them as she came. She was younger than John—not more than sixteen.

Read the rest of this chapter as though it were a play—interpreting the roles of John and Kismine. What is Kismine like? How mature is John in his reaction to her?

"Hello," she cried softly, "I'm Kismine."

She was much more than that to John already. He advanced toward her, scarcely moving as he drew near lest he should tread on her bare toes.

"You haven't met me," said her soft voice. Her blue eyes added, "Oh, but you've missed a great deal!" . . . "You met my sister, Jasmine, last night. I was sick with lettuce poisoning," went on her soft voice, and her eyes continued, "and when I'm sick I'm sweet —and when I'm well."

"You have made an enormous impression on me," said John's eyes, "and I'm not so slow myself"— "How do you do?" said his voice. "I hope you're better this morning."—"You darling," added his eyes tremulously.

John observed that they had been walking along the path. On her suggestion they sat down together upon the moss, the softness of which he failed to determine.

He was critical about women. A single defect—a thick ankle, a hoarse voice, a glass eye—was enough to make him utterly indifferent. And here for the first time in his life he was beside a girl who seemed to him the incarnation of physical perfection.

"Are you from the East?" asked Kismine with charming interest.

"No," answered John simply. "I'm from Hades."

Either she had never heard of Hades, or she could think of no pleasant comment to make upon it, for she did not discuss it further.

"I'm going East to school this fall," she said. "D'you think I'll like it? I'm going to New York to Miss Bulge's. It's very strict, but you see over the weekends I'm going to live at home with the family in our New York house, because father heard that the girls had to go walking two by two."

"Your father wants you to be proud," observed John.

"We are," she answered, her eyes shining with dignity. "None of us has ever been punished. Father said we never should be. Once when my sister Jasmine was a little girl she pushed him down-stairs and he just got up and limped away.

"Mother was—well, a little startled," continued Kismine, "when she heard that you were from—from where you *are* from, you know. She said that when she was a young girl—but then, you see, she's a Spaniard and old-fashioned."

"Do you spend much time out here?" asked John, to conceal the fact that he was somewhat hurt by this remark. It seemed an unkind allusion to his provincialism.

"Percy and Jasmine and I are here every summer, but next summer Jasmine is going to Newport. She's coming out in London a year from this fall. She'll be presented at court."

"Do you know," began John hesitantly, "you're much more sophisticated than I thought you were when I first saw you?"

"Oh, no, I'm not," she exclaimed **hurrie**dly. "Oh, I wouldn't think of being. I think that sophisticated young people are *terribly* common, don't you? I'm not at all, really. If you say I am, I'm going to cry."

She was so distressed that her lip was trembling. John was impelled to protest:

"I didn't mean that; I only said it to tease you."

"Because I wouldn't mind if I *were*," she persisted "but I'm *not*. I'm very innocent and girlish. I never smoke, or drink, or read anything except poetry. I know scarcely any mathematics or chemistry. I dress *very* simply—in fact, I scarcely dress at all. I think sophisticated is the last thing you can say about me. I believe that girls ought to enjoy their youths in a wholesome way."

"I do too," said John heartily.

Kismine was cheerful again. She smiled at him, and a still-born tear dripped from the corner of one blue eye.

"I like you," she whispered, intimately. "Are you going to spend all your time with Percy while you're here, or will you be nice to me? Just think—I'm absolutely fresh ground. I've never had a boy in love with me in all my life. I've never been allowed even to

30

see boys alone—except Percy. I came all the way out here into this grove hoping to run into you, where the family wouldn't be around."

Deeply flattered, John bowed from the hips as he had been taught at dancing school in Hades.

"We'd better go now," said Kismine sweetly. "I have to be with mother at eleven. You haven't asked me to kiss you once. I thought boys always did that nowadays."

John drew himself up proudly.

"Some of them do," he answered, "but not me. Girls don't do that sort of thing—in Hades."

Side by side they walked back toward the house.

VI

John stood facing Mr. Braddock Washington in the full sunlight. The elder man was about forty with a proud, vacuous face, intelligent eyes, and a robust figure. In the mornings he smelt of horses—the best horses. He carried a plain walking-stick of gray birch with a single large opal for a grip. He and Percy were showing John around.

"The slaves' quarters are there." His walking-stick indicated a cloister of marble on their left that ran in graceful Gothic along the side of the mountain. "In my youth I was distracted for a while from the business of life by a period of absurd idealism. During that time they lived in luxury. For instance, I equipped every one of their rooms with a tile bath."

"I suppose," ventured John, with an ingratiating laugh, "that they used the bathtubs to keep coal in. Mr. Schnlitzer-Murphy told me that once he——"

"The opinions of Mr. Schnlitzer-Murphy are of little importance, I should imagine," interrupted Braddock Washington, coldly. "My slaves did not keep coal in their bathtubs. They had orders to bathe every day, and they did. If they hadn't I might have

Note the variety of prejudice exposed here and the way it is expressed.

31

ordered a sulphuric acid shampoo. I discontinued the baths for quite another reason. Several of them caught cold and died. Water is not good for certain races—except as a beverage."

John laughed, and then decided to nod his head in sober agreement. Braddock Washington made him uncomfortable.

"All these Negroes are descendants of the ones my father brought North with him. There are about two hundred and fifty now. You notice that they've lived so long apart from the world that their original dialect has become an almost indistinguishable patois. We bring a few of them up to speak English—my secretary and two or three of the house servants.

Why don't the Washingtons let the slaves learn English?

What might the golf course symbolize?

"This is the golf course," he continued, as they strolled along the velvet winter grass. "It's all a green, you see—no fairway, no rough, no hazards."

He smiled pleasantly at John.

"Many men in the cage, father?" asked Percy suddenly.

Braddock Washington stumbled, and let forth an involuntary curse.

"One less than there should be," he ejaculated darkly—and then added after a moment, "We've had difficulties."

"Mother was telling me," exclaimed Percy, "that Italian teacher——"

"A ghastly error," said Braddock Washington angrily. "But of course there's a good chance that we may have got him. Perhaps he fell somewhere in the woods or stumbled over a cliff. And then there's always the probability that if he did get away his story wouldn't be believed. Nevertheless, I've had two dozen men looking for him in different towns around here."

"And no luck?"

"Some. Fourteen of them reported to my agent that they'd each killed a man answering to that descrip-

32

tion, but of course it was probably only the reward they were after——"

He broke off. They had come to a large cavity in the earth about the circumference of a merry-go-round and covered by a strong iron grating. Braddock Washington beckoned to John, and pointed his cane down through the grating. John stepped to the edge and gazed. Immediately his ears were assailed by a wild clamor from below.

"Come on down to Hell!"

"Hello, kiddo, how's the air up there?"

"Hey! Throw us a rope!"

"Got an old doughnut, Buddy, or a couple of second-hand sandwiches?"

"Say, fella, if you'll push down that guy you're with, we'll show you a quick disappearance scene."

"Paste him one for me, will you?"

It was too dark to see clearly into the pit below, but John could tell from the coarse optimism and rugged vitality of the remarks and voices that they proceeded from middle-class Americans of the more spirited type. Then Mr. Washington put out his cane and touched a button in the grass, and the scene below sprang into light.

"These are some adventurous mariners who had the misfortune to discover El Dorado," he remarked.

Below them there had appeared a large hollow in the earth shaped like the interior of a bowl. The sides were steep and apparently of polished glass, and on its slightly concave surface stood about two dozen men clad in the half costume, half uniform, of aviators. Their upturned faces, lit with wrath, with malice, with despair, with cynical humor, were covered by long growths of beard, but with the exception of a few who had pined perceptibly away, they seemed to be a well-fed, healthy lot.

Braddock Washington drew a garden chair to the edge of the pit and sat down.

How does the invitation to "Hell" link John with these prisoners?

33

"Well, how are you, boys?" he inquired genially.

A chorus of execration in which all joined except a few too dispirited to cry out, rose up into the sunny air, but Braddock Washington heard it with unruffled composure. When its last echo had died away he spoke again.

"Have you thought up a way out of your difficulty?"

From here and there among them a remark floated up.

"We decided to stay here for love!"

"Bring us up there and we'll find us a way!"

Braddock Washington waited until they were again quiet. Then he said:

"I've told you the situation. I don't want you here. I wish to heaven I'd never seen you. Your own curiosity got you here, and any time that you can think of a way out which protects me and my interests I'll be glad to consider it. But so long as you confine your efforts to digging tunnels—yes, I know about the new one you've started—you won't get very far. This isn't as hard on you as you make it out, with all your howling for the loved ones at home. If you were the type who worried much about the loved ones at home, you'd never have taken up aviation."

A tall man moved apart from the others, and held up his hand to call his captor's attention to what he was about to say.

"Let me ask you a few questions!" he cried. "You pretend to be a fair-minded man."

"How absurd. How could a man of *my* position be fair-minded toward *you?* You might as well speak of a Spaniard being fair-minded toward a piece of steak."

At this harsh observation the faces of the two dozen steaks fell, but the tall man continued:

"All right!" he cried. "We've argued this out before. You're not a humanitarian and you're not fair-minded, but you're human—at least you say you are—and you ought to be able to put yourself in our

34

place for long enough to think how—how—how——"

"How what?" demanded Washington, coldly.

"—how unnecessary——"

"Not to me."

"Well,—how cruel——"

"We've covered that. Cruelty doesn't exist where self-preservation is involved. You've been soldiers: you know that. Try another."

"Well, then, how stupid."

"There," admitted Washington, "I grant you that. But try to think of an alternative. I've offered to have all or any of you painlessly executed if you wish. I've offered to have your wives, sweethearts, children, and mothers kidnapped and brought out here. I'll enlarge your place down there and feed and clothe you the rest of your lives. If there was some method of producing permanent amnesia I'd have all of you operated on and released immediately, somewhere outside of my preserves. But that's as far as my ideas go."

"How about trusting us not to peach on you?" cried some one.

"You don't proffer that suggestion seriously," said Washington, with an expression of scorn. "I did take out one man to teach my daughter Italian. Last week he got away."

A wild yell of jubilation went up suddenly from two dozen throats and a pandemonium of joy ensued. The prisoners clog-danced and cheered and yodled and wrestled with one another in a sudden uprush of animal spirits. They even ran up the glass sides of the bowl as far as they could, and slid back to the bottom upon the natural cushions of their bodies. The tall man started a song in which they all joined——

> "Oh, we'll hang the kaiser
> On a sour apple tree——"

Braddock Washington sat in inscrutable silence until the song was over.

This is a World War I song about Kaiser Wilhelm, ruler of Germany. Why is the implied comparison apt?

35

"You see," he remarked, when he could gain a modicum of attention. "I bear you no ill-will. I like to see you enjoying yourselves. That's why I didn't tell you the whole story at once. The man—what was his name? Critchtichiello?—was shot by some of my agents in fourteen different places."

Not guessing that the places referred to were cities, the tumult of rejoicing subsided immediately.

"Nevertheless," cried Washington with a touch of anger, "he tried to run away. Do you expect me to take chances with any of you after an experience like that?"

Again a series of ejaculations went up.

"Sure!"

"Would your daughter like to learn Chinese?"

"Hey, I can speak Italian! My mother was a wop."

"Maybe she'd like t'learna speak N'Yawk!"

"If she's the little one with the big blue eyes I can teach her a lot of things better than Italian."

"I know some Irish songs—and I could hammer brass once't."

Mr. Washington reached forward suddenly with his cane and pushed the button in the grass so that the picture below went out instantly, and there remained only that great dark mouth covered dismally with the black teeth of the grating.

Note the suitability of the metaphor for the prison.

"Hey!" called a single voice from below, "you ain't goin' away without givin' us your blessing?"

But Mr. Washington, followed by the two boys, was already strolling on toward the ninth hole of the golf course, as though the pit and its contents were no more than a hazard over which his facile iron had triumphed with ease.

VII

July under the lee of the diamond mountain was a month of blanket nights and of warm, glowing days.

John and Kismine were in love. He did not know that the little gold football (inscribed with the legend *Pro deo et patria et St. Mida*) which he had given her rested on a platinum chain next to her bosom. But it did. And she for her part was not aware that a large sapphire which had dropped one day from her simple coiffure was stowed away tenderly in John's jewel box.

Late one afternoon when the ruby and ermine music room was quiet, they spent an hour there together. He held her hand and she gave him such a look that he whispered her name aloud. She bent toward him—then hesitated.

"Did you say 'Kismine'?" she asked softly, "or——"

She had wanted to be sure. She thought she might have misunderstood.

Neither of them had ever kissed before, but in the course of an hour it seemed to make little difference.

The afternoon drifted away. That night when a last breath of music drifted down from the highest tower, they each lay awake, happily dreaming over the separate minutes of the day. They had decided to be married as soon as possible.

Do you think the purpose of this short chapter is mainly: (1) to extend characterization; (2) to forward the action; (3) to indicate passage of time; or (4) to intensify atmosphere?

VIII

Every day Mr. Washington and the two young men went hunting or fishing in the deep forests or played golf around the somnolent course—games which John diplomatically allowed his host to win—or swam in the mountain coolness of the lake. John found Mr. Washington a somewhat exacting personality—utterly uninterested in any ideas or opinions except his own. Mrs. Washington was aloof and reserved at all times. She was apparently indifferent to her two daughters, and entirely absorbed in her son Percy, with whom she held interminable conversations in rapid Spanish at dinner.

37

Jasmine, the elder daugher, resembled Kismine in appearance—except that she was somewhat bow-legged, and terminated in large hands and feet—but was utterly unlike her in temperament. Her favorite books had to do with poor girls who kept house for widowed fathers. John learned from Kismine that Jasmine had never recovered from the shock and disappointment caused her by the termination of the World War, just as she was about to start for Europe as a canteen expert. She had even pined away for a time, and Braddock Washington had taken steps to promote a new war in the Balkans—but she had seen a photograph of some wounded Serbian soldiers and lost interest in the whole proceedings. But Percy and Kismine seemed to have inherited the arrogant attitude in all its harsh magnificence from their father. A chaste and consistent selfishness ran like a pattern through their every idea.

John was enchanted by the wonders of the château and the valley. Braddock Washington, so Percy told him, had caused to be kidnapped a landscape gardener, an architect, a designer of stage settings, and a French decadent poet left over from the last century. He had put his entire force of Negroes at their disposal, guaranteed to supply them with any materials that the world could offer, and left them to work out some ideas of their own. But one by one they had shown their uselessness. The decadent poet had at once begun bewailing his separation from the boulevards in spring—he made some vague remarks about spices, apes, and ivories, but said nothing that was of any practical value. The stage designer on his part wanted to make the whole valley a series of tricks and sensational effects—a state of things that the Washingtons would soon have grown tired of. And as for the architect and the landscape gardener, they thought only in terms of convention. They must make this like this and that like that.

But they had, at least, solved the problem of what was to be done with them—they all went mad early one morning after spending the night in a single room trying to agree upon the location of a fountain, and were now confined comfortably in an insane asylum at Westport, Connecticut.

"But," inquired John curiously, "who did plan all your wonderful reception rooms and halls, and approaches and bathrooms——?"

"Well," answered Percy, "I blush to tell you, but it was a moving-picture fella. He was the only man we found who was used to playing with an unlimited amount of money, though he did tuck his napkin in his collar and couldn't read or write."

As August drew to a close John began to regret that he must soon go back to school. He and Kismine had decided to elope the following June.

"It would be nicer to be married here," Kismine confessed, "but of course I could never get father's permission to marry you at all. Next to that I'd rather elope. It's terrible for wealthy people to be married in America at present—they always have to send out bulletins to the press saying that they're going to be married in remnants, when what they mean is just a peck of old second-hand pearls and some used lace worn once by the Empress Eugénie."

"I know," agreed John fervently. "When I was visiting the Schnlitzer-Murphys, the eldest daughter, Gwendolyn, married a man whose father owns half of West Virginia. She wrote home saying what a tough struggle she was carrying on on his salary as a bank clerk—and then she ended up by saying that 'Thank God, I have four good maids anyhow, and that helps a little.' "

"It's absurd," commented Kismine. "Think of the millions and millions of people in the world, laborers and all, who get along with only two maids."

One afternoon late in August a chance remark of

Kismine's changed the face of the entire situation, and threw John into a state of terror.

They were in their favorite grove, and between kisses John was indulging in some romantic forebodings which he fancied added poignancy to their relations.

"Sometimes I think we'll never marry," he said sadly. "You're too wealthy, too magnificent. No one as rich as you are can be like other girls. I should marry the daughter of some well-to-do wholesale hardware man from Omaha or Sioux City, and be content with her half-million."

"I knew the daughter of a wholesale hardware man once," remarked Kismine. "I don't think you'd have been contented with her. She was a friend of my sister's. She visited here."

"Oh, then you've had other guests?" exclaimed John in surprise.

Kismine seemed to regret her words.

"Oh, yes," she said hurriedly, "we've had a few."

"But aren't you—wasn't your father afraid they'd talk outside?"

"Oh, to some extent, to some extent," she answered. "Let's talk about something pleasanter."

But John's curiosity was aroused.

"Something pleasanter!" he demanded. "What's unpleasant about that? Weren't they nice girls?"

To his great surprise Kismine began to weep.

"Yes—th—that's the—the whole t-trouble. I grew qu-quite attached to some of them. So did Jasmine, but she kept inv-viting them anyway. I couldn't under*stand* it."

A dark suspicion was born in John's heart.

"Do you mean that they *told,* and your father had them—removed?"

"Worse than that," she muttered brokenly. "Father took no chances—and Jasmine kept writing them to come, and they had *such* a good time!"

She was overcome by a paroxysm of grief.

Stunned with the horror of this revelation, John sat there open-mouthed, feeling the nerves of his body twitter like so many sparrows perched upon his spinal column.

"Now, I've told you, and I shouldn't have," she said, calming suddenly and drying her dark blue eyes.

"Do you mean to say that your father had them *murdered* before they left?"

She nodded.

Contrast Kismine's euphemisms with John's forthright labeling.

"In August usually—or early in September. It's only natural for us to get all the pleasure out of them that we can first."

"How abominable! How—why, I must be going crazy! Did you really admit that——"

"I did," interrupted Kismine, shrugging her shoulders. "We can't very well imprison them like those aviators, where they'd be a continual reproach to us every day. And it's always been made easier for Jasmine and me, because father had it done sooner than we expected. In that way we avoided any farewell scene——"

"So you murdered them! Uh!" cried John.

"It was done very nicely. They were drugged while they were asleep—and their families were always told that they died of scarlet fever in Butte."

"But—I fail to understand why you kept on inviting them!"

"I didn't," burst out Kismine. "I never invited one. Jasmine did. And they always had a very good time. She'd give them the nicest presents toward the last. I shall probably have visitors, too—I'll harden up to it. We can't let such an inevitable thing as death stand in the way of enjoying life while we have it. Think how lonesome it'd be out here if we never had *any* one. Why, father and mother have sacrificed some of their best friends just as we have."

"And so," cried John accusingly, "and so you were

letting me make love to you and pretending to return it, and talking about marriage, all the time knowing perfectly well that I'd never get out of here alive——"

"No," she protested passionately. "Not any more. I did at first. You were here. I couldn't help that, and I thought your last days might as well be pleasant for both of us. But then I fell in love with you, and—and I'm honestly sorry you're going to—going to be put away—though I'd rather you'd be put away than ever kiss another girl."

"Oh, you would, would you?" cried John ferociously.

"Much rather. Besides, I've always heard that a girl can have more fun with a man whom she knows she can never marry. Oh, why did I tell you? I've probably spoiled your whole good time now, and we were really enjoying things when you didn't know it. I knew it would make things sort of depressing for you."

"Oh, you did, did you?" John's voice trembled with anger. "I've heard about enough of this. If you haven't any more pride and decency than to have an affair with a fellow that you know isn't much better than a corpse, I don't want to have any more to do with you!"

"You're not a corpse!" she protested in horror. "You're not a corpse! I won't have you saying that I kissed a corpse!"

"I said nothing of the sort!"

"You did! You said I kissed a corpse!"

"I didn't!"

Their voices had risen, but upon a sudden interruption they both subsided into immediate silence. Footsteps were coming along the path in their direction, and a moment later the rose bushes were parted displaying Braddock Washington, whose intelligent eyes set in his good-looking vacuous face were peering in at them.

"Who kissed a corpse?" he demanded in obvious disapproval.

"Nobody," answered Kismine quickly. "We were just joking."

"What are you two doing here, anyhow?" he demanded gruffly. "Kismine, you ought to be—to be reading or playing golf with your sister. Go read! Go play golf! Don't let me find you here when I come back!"

Then he bowed at John and went up the path.

"See?" said Kismine crossly, when he was out of hearing. "You've spoiled it all. We can never meet any more. He won't let me meet you. He'd have you poisoned if he thought we were in love."

"We're not, any more!" cried John fiercely, "so he can set his mind at rest upon that. Moreover, don't fool yourself that I'm going to stay around here. Inside of six hours I'll be over those mountains, if I have to gnaw a passage through them, and on my way East."

They had both got to their feet, and at this remark Kismine came close and put her arm through his.

"I'm going, too."

"You must be crazy——"

"Of course I'm going," she interrupted impatiently.

"You most certainly are not. You——"

"Very well," she said quietly, "we'll catch up with father now and talk it over with him."

Defeated, John mustered a sickly smile.

"Very well, dearest," he agreed, with pale and unconvincing affection, "we'll go together."

His love for her returned and settled placidly on his heart. She was his—she would go with him to share his dangers. He put his arms about her and kissed her fervently. After all she loved him; she had saved him, in fact.

Discussing the matter, they walked slowly back toward the château. They decided that since Braddock

What are the real factors motivating Kismine? John?

43

Why is Chapter VIII
so crucial to the
structure of the story?
At what point does the
reader become aware
of its significance?

Washington had seen them together they had best
depart the next night. Nevertheless, John's lips were
unusually dry at dinner, and he nervously emptied a
great spoonful of peacock soup into his left lung. He
had to be carried into the turquoise and sable cardroom and pounded on the back by one of the under-
butlers, which Percy considered a great joke.

IX

As you read this
chapter, think of it as a
motion picture.

Long after midnight John's body gave a nervous
jerk, and he sat suddenly upright, staring into the
veils of somnolence that draped the room. Through
the squares of blue darkness that were his open
windows, he had heard a faint far-away sound that
died upon a bed of wind before identifying itself on his
memory, clouded with uneasy dreams. But the sharp
noise that had succeeded it was nearer, was just
outside the room—the click of a turned knob, a
footstep, a whisper, he could not tell; a hard lump
gathered in the pit of his stomach, and his whole body
ached in the moment that he strained agonizingly to
hear. Then one of the veils seemed to dissolve, and he
saw a vague figure standing by the door, a figure only
faintly limned and blocked in upon the darkness,
mingled so with the folds of the drapery as to seem
distorted, like a reflection seen in a dirty pane of glass.

With a sudden movement of fright or resolution
John pressed the button by his bedside, and the next
moment he was sitting in the green sunken bath of
the adjoining room, waked into alertness by the shock
of the cold water which half filled it.

He sprang out, and, his wet pajamas scattering a
heavy trickle of water behind him, ran for the aqua-
marine door which he knew led out onto the ivory
landing of the second floor. The door opened noiselessly. A single crimson lamp burning in a great dome
above lit the magnificent sweep of the carved stair-

44

ways with a poignant beauty. For a moment John hesitated, appalled by the silent splendor massed about him, seeming to envelop in its gigantic folds and contours the solitary drenched little figure shivering upon the ivory landing. Then simultaneously two things happened. The door of his own sitting-room swung open, precipitating three naked Negroes into the hall—and, as John swayed in wild terror toward the stairway, another door slid back in the wall on the other side of the corridor, and John saw Braddock Washington standing in the lighted lift, wearing a fur coat and a pair of riding boots which reached to his knees and displayed, above, the glow of his rose-colored pajamas.

On the instant the three Negroes—John had never seen any of them before, and it flashed through his mind that they must be the professional executioners—paused in their movement toward John, and turned expectantly to the man in the lift, who burst out with an imperious command:

"Get in here! All three of you! Quick as hell!"

Then, within the instant, the three Negroes darted into the cage, the oblong of light was blotted out as the lift door shut, and John was again alone in the hall. He slumped weakly down against an ivory stair.

It was apparent that something portentous had occurred, something which, for the moment at least, had postponed his own petty disaster. What was it? Had the Negroes risen in revolt? Had the aviators forced aside the iron bars of the grating? Or had the men of Fish stumbled blindly through the hills and gazed with bleak, joyless eyes upon the gaudy valley? John did not know. He heard a faint whir of air as the lift whizzed up again, and then, a moment later, as it descended. It was probable that Percy was hurrying to his father's assistance, and it occurred to John that this was his opportunity to join Kismine and plan an immediate escape. He waited until the lift had been silent for several minutes; shivering a little with the night cool that whipped in through his wet pajamas, he returned to his room and dressed himself quickly. Then he mounted a long flight of stairs and turned down the corridor carpeted with Russian sable which led to Kismine's suite.

The door of her sitting-room was open and the lamps were lighted. Kismine, in an angora kimono, stood near the window of the room in a listening attitude, and as John entered noiselessly, she turned toward him.

"Oh, it's you!" she whispered, crossing the room to him. "Did you hear them?"

"I heard your father's slaves in my——"

"No," she interrupted excitedly. "Aeroplanes!"

"Aeroplanes? Perhaps that was the sound that woke me."

"There're at least a dozen. I saw one a few moments ago dead against the moon. The guard back by the cliff fired his rifle and that's what roused father. We're going to open on them right away."

"Are they here on purpose?"

"Yes—it's that Italian who got away——"

Simultaneously with her last word, a succession of sharp cracks tumbled in through the open window. Kismine uttered a little cry, took a penny with fumbling fingers from a box on her dresser, and ran to one of the electric lights. In an instant the entire château was in darkness—she had blown out the fuse.

"Come on!" she cried to him. "We'll go up to the roof garden, and watch it from there!"

Drawing a cape about her, she took his hand, and they found their way out the door. It was only a step to the tower lift, and as she pressed the button that shot them upward he put his arms around her in the darkness and kissed her mouth. Romance had come to John Unger at last. A minute later they had stepped out upon the star-white platform. Above, under the

46

misty moon, sliding in and out of the patches of cloud that eddied below it, floated a dozen dark-winged bodies in a constant circling course. From here and there in the valley flashes of fire leaped toward them, followed by sharp detonations. Kismine clapped her hands with pleasure, which a moment later, turned to dismay as the aeroplanes at some prearranged signal, began to release their bombs and the whole of the valley became a panorama of deep reverberate sound and lurid light.

Before long the aim of the attackers became concentrated upon the points where the anti-aircraft guns were situated, and one of them was almost immediately reduced to a giant cinder to lie smouldering in a park of rose bushes.

"Kismine," begged John, "you'll be glad when I tell you that this attack came on the eve of my murder. If I hadn't heard that guard shoot off his gun back by the pass I should now be stone dead——"

"I can't hear you!" cried Kismine, intent on the scene before her. "You'll have to talk louder!"

"I simply said," shouted John, "that we'd better get out before they begin to shell the château!"

Suddenly the whole portico of the Negro quarters cracked asunder, a geyser of flame shot up from under the colonnades, and great fragments of jagged marble were hurled as far as the borders of the lake.

"There go fifty thousand dollars' worth of slaves," cried Kismine, "at prewar prices. So few Americans have any respect for property."

John renewed his efforts to compel her to leave. The aim of the aeroplanes was becoming more precise minute by minute, and only two of the anti-aircraft guns were still retaliating. It was obvious that the garrison, encircled with fire, could not hold out much longer.

"Come on!" cried John, pulling Kismine's arm, "we've got to go. Do you realize that those aviators

During the air attack does each care about the other? What thoughts mainly concern each?

will kill you without question if they find you?"

She consented reluctantly.

"We'll have to wake Jasmine!" she said, as they hurried toward the lift. Then she added in a sort of childish delight: "We'll be poor, won't we? Like people in books. And I'll be an orphan and utterly free. Free and poor! What fun!" She stopped and raised her lips to him in a delighted kiss.

How has John's role changed? Have his values changed?

"It's impossible to be both together," said John grimly. "People have found that out. And I should choose to be free as preferable of the two. As an extra caution you'd better dump the contents of your jewel box into your pockets."

Ten minutes later the two girls met John in the dark corridor and they descended to the main floor of the château. Passing for the last time through the magnificence of the splendid halls, they stood for a moment out on the terrace, watching the burning Negro quarters and the flaming embers of two planes which had fallen on the other side of the lake. A solitary gun was still keeping up a sturdy popping, and the attackers seemed timorous about descending lower, but sent their thunderous fireworks in a circle around it, until any chance shot might annihilate its Ethiopian crew.

John and the two sisters passed down the marble steps, turned sharply to the left, and began to ascend a narrow path that wound like a garter about the diamond mountain. Kismine knew a heavily wooded spot half-way up where they could lie concealed and yet be able to observe the wild night in the valley—finally to make an escape, when it should be necessary, along a secret path laid in a rocky gully.

X

It was three o'clock when they attained their destination. The obliging and phlegmatic Jasmine fell off to sleep immediately, leaning against the trunk of a large tree, while John and Kismine sat, his arm around her, and watched the desperate ebb and flow of the dying battle among the ruins of a vista that had been a garden spot that morning. Shortly after four o'clock the last remaining gun gave out a clanging sound and went out of action in a swift tongue of red smoke. Though the moon was down, they saw that the flying bodies were circling closer to the earth. When the planes had made certain that the beleaguered possessed no further resources, they would land and the dark and glittering reign of the Washingtons would be over.

With the cessation of the firing the valley grew quiet. The embers of the two aeroplanes glowed like the eyes of some monster crouching in the grass. The château stood dark and silent, beautiful without light as it had been beautiful in the sun, while the woody rattles of Nemesis filled the air above with a growing and receding complaint. Then John perceived that Kismine, like her sister, had fallen sound asleep.

Nemesis: Greek goddess of vengeance.

It was long after four when he became aware of footsteps along the path they had lately followed, and he waited in breathless silence until the persons to whom they belonged had passed the vantage-point he occupied. There was a faint stir in the air now that was not of human origin, and the dew was cold; he knew that the dawn would break soon. John waited until the steps had gone a safe distance up the mountain and were inaudible. Then he followed. About half-way to the steep summit the trees fell away and a hard saddle of rock spread itself over the diamond beneath. Just before he reached this point he slowed down his pace, warned by an animal sense that there was life just ahead of him. Coming to a high boulder, he lifted his head gradually above its edge. His curiosity was rewarded; this is what he saw:

Braddock Washington was standing there motionless, silhouetted against the gray sky without sound or sign of life. As the dawn came up out of the east, lending a cold green color to the earth, it brought the solitary figure into insignificant contrast with the new day.

While John watched, his host remained for a few moments absorbed in some inscrutable contemplation; then he signalled to the two Negroes who crouched at his feet to lift the burden which lay between them. As they struggled upright, the first yellow beam of the sun struck through the innumerable prisms of an immense and exquisitely chiselled diamond—and a white radiance was kindled that glowed upon the air like a fragment of the morning star. The bearers staggered beneath its weight for a moment—then their rippling muscles caught and hardened under the wet shine of the skins and the three figures were again motionless in their defiant impotency before the heavens.

After a while the white man lifted his head and slowly raised his arms in a gesture of attention, as one who would call a great crowd to hear—but there was no crowd, only the vast silence of the mountain and the sky, broken by faint bird voices down among the trees. The figure on the saddle of rock began to speak ponderously and with an inextinguishable pride.

"You out there—" he cried in a trembling voice. "You—there—!" He paused, his arms still uplifted, his head held attentively as though he were expecting an answer. John strained his eyes to see whether there might be men coming down the mountain, but the mountain was bare of human life. There was only sky and a mocking flute of wind along the tree-tops. Could Washington be praying? For a moment John wondered. Then the illusion passed—there was something in the man's whole attitude antithetical to prayer.

"Oh, you above there!"

The voice was become strong and confident. This

antithetical
(an′tə thet′ə kl):
opposite to.

50

was no forlorn supplication. If anything, there was in it a quality of monstrous condescension.

"You there——"

Words, too quickly uttered to be understood, flowing one into the other . . John listened breathlessly, catching a phrase here and there, while the voice broke off, resumed, broke off again—now strong and argumentative, now colored with a slow, puzzled impatience. Then a conviction commenced to dawn on the single listener, and as realization crept over him a spray of quick blood rushed through his arteries. Braddock Washington was offering a bribe to God!

That was it—there was no doubt. The diamond in the arms of his slaves was some advance sample, a promise of more to follow.

That, John perceived after a time, was the thread running through his sentences. Prometheus Enriched was calling to witness forgotten sacrifices, forgotten rituals, prayers obsolete before the birth of Christ. For a while his discourse took the form of reminding God of this gift or that which Divinity had deigned to accept from men—great churches if he would rescue cities from the plague, gifts of myrrh and gold, of human lives and beautiful women and captive armies, of children and queens, of beasts of the forest and field, sheep and goats, harvests and cities, whole conquered lands that had been offered up in lust or blood for His appeasal, buying a meed's worth of alleviation from the Divine wrath—and now he, Braddock Washington, Emperor of Diamonds, king and priest of the age of gold, arbiter of splendor and luxury, would offer up a treasure such as princes before him had never dreamed of, offer it up not in suppliance, but in pride.

He would give to God, he continued, getting down to specifications, the greatest diamond in the world. This diamond would be cut with many more thousand

Prometheus (prə-mē'thē əs): one of the Titans in Greek mythology. He stole fire from heaven and taught men its use. Zeus punished him by chaining him to a rock.

appeasal: probably meant to be *appeasement.*

facets than there were leaves on a tree, and yet the whole diamond would be shaped with the perfection of a stone no bigger than a fly. Many men would work upon it for many years. It would be set in a great dome of beaten gold, wonderfully carved and equipped with gates of opal and crusted sapphire. In the middle would be hollowed out a chapel presided over by an altar of iridescent, decomposing, ever-changing radium which would burn out the eyes of any worshipper who lifted up his head from prayer —and on this altar there would be slain for the amusement of the Divine Benefactor any victim He should choose, even though it should be the greatest and most powerful man alive.

In return he asked only a simple thing, a thing that for God would be absurdly easy—only that matters should be as they were yesterday at this hour and that they should so remain. So very simple! Let but the heavens open, swallowing these men and their aeroplanes—and then close again. Let him have his slaves once more, restored to life and well.

There was no one else with whom he had ever needed to treat or bargain.

He doubted only whether he had made his bribe big enough. God had His price, of course. God was made in man's image, so it had been said: He must have His price. And the price would be rare—no cathedral whose building consumed many years, no pyramid constructed by ten thousand workmen, would be like this cathedral, this pyramid.

He paused here. That was his proposition. Everything would be up to specifications and there was nothing vulgar in his assertion that it would be cheap at the price. He implied that Providence could take it or leave it.

As he approached the end his sentences became broken, became short and uncertain, and his body seemed tense, seemed strained to catch the slightest

52

pressure or whisper of life in the spaces around him. His hair had turned gradually white as he talked, and now he lifted his head high to the heavens like a prophet of old—magnificently mad.

Then, as John stared in giddy fascination, it seemed to him that a curious phenomenon took place somewhere around him. It was as though the sky had darkened for an instant, as though there had been a sudden murmur in a gust of wind, a sound of far-away trumpets, a sighing like the rustle of a great silken robe—for a time the whole of nature round about partook of this darkness: the birds' song ceased; the trees were still, and far over the mountain there was a mutter of dull, menacing thunder.

That was all. The wind died along the tall grasses of the valley. The dawn and the day resumed their place in a time, and the risen sun sent hot waves of yellow mist that made its path bright before it. The leaves laughed in the sun, and their laughter shook the trees until each bough was like a girl's school in fairyland. God had refused to accept the bribe.

For another moment John watched the triumph of the day. Then, turning, he saw a flutter of brown down by the lake, then another flutter, then another, like the dance of golden angels alighting from the clouds. The aeroplanes had come to earth.

John slid off the boulder and ran down the side of the mountain to the clump of trees, where the two girls were awake and waiting for him. Kismine sprang to her feet, the jewels in her pockets jingling, a question on her parted lips, but instinct told John that there was no time for words. They must get off the mountain without losing a moment. He seized a hand of each, and in silence they threaded the tree-trunks, washed with light now and with the rising mist. Behind them from the valley came no sound at all, except the complaint of the peacocks far away and the pleasant undertone of morning.

Braddock's supplication to God appears to be out of character. Why? What details keep the supplication in character?

When they had gone about half a mile, they avoided the park land and entered a narrow path that led over the next rise of ground. At the highest point of this they paused and turned around. Their eyes rested upon the mountainside they had just left—oppressed by some dark sense of tragic impendency.

Clear against the sky a broken, white-haired man was slowly descending the steep slope, followed by two gigantic and emotionless Negroes, who carried a burden between them which still flashed and glittered in the sun. Half-way down two other figures joined them—John could see that they were Mrs. Washington and her son, upon whose arm she leaned. The aviators had clambered from their machines to the sweeping lawn in front of the château, and with rifles in hand were starting up the diamond mountain in skirmishing formation.

But the little group of five which had formed farther up and was engrossing all the watchers' attention had stopped upon a ledge of rock. The Negroes stooped and pulled up what appeared to be a trap-door in the side of the mountain. Into this they all disappeared, the white-haired man first, then his wife and son, finally the two Negroes, the glittering tips of whose jeweled head-dresses caught the sun for a moment before the trap-door descended and engulfed them all.

Kismine clutched John's arm.

"Oh," she cried wildly, "where are they going? What are they going to do?"

"It must be some underground way of escape——"

A little scream from the two girls interrupted his sentence.

"Don't you see?" sobbed Kismine hysterically. "The mountain is wired!"

Even as she spoke John put up his hands to shield his sight. Before their eyes the whole surface of the mountain had changed suddenly to a dazzling burning yellow, which showed up through the jacket of turf as light shows through a human hand. For a moment the intolerable glow continued, and then like an extinguished filament it disappeared, revealing a black waste from which blue smoke arose slowly, carrying off with it what remained of vegetation and of human flesh. Of the aviators there was left neither blood nor bone—they were consumed as completely as the five souls who had gone inside.

Simultaneously, and with an immense concussion, the château literally threw itself into the air, bursting into flaming fragments as it rose, and then tumbling back upon itself in a smoking pile that lay projecting half into the water of the lake. There was no fire—what smoke there was drifted off mingling with the sunshine, and for a few minutes longer a powdery dust of marble drifted from the great featureless pile that had once been the house of jewels. There was no more sound and the three people were alone in the valley.

Why does Fitzgerald have the château destroyed?

XI

At sunset John and his two companions reached the high cliff which had marked the boundaries of the Washingtons' dominion, and looking back found the valley tranquil and lovely in the dusk. They sat down to finish the food which Jasmine had brought with her in a basket.

"There!" she said, as she spread the table-cloth and put the sandwiches in a neat pile upon it. "Don't they look tempting? I always think that food tastes better outdoors."

"With that remark," remarked Kismine, "Jasmine enters the middle class."

"Now," said John eagerly, "turn out your pocket and let's see what jewels you brought along. If you made a good selection we three ought to live comfortably all the rest of our lives."

Obediently Kismine put her hand in her pocket and tossed two handfuls of glittering stones before him.

"Not so bad," cried John, enthusiastically. "They aren't very big, but—Hello!" His expression changed as he held one of them up to the declining sun. "Why, these aren't diamonds! There's something the matter!"

"By golly!" exclaimed Kismine, with a startled look. "What an idiot I am!"

"Why, these are rhinestones!" cried John.

"I know." She broke into a laugh. "I opened the wrong drawer. They belonged on the dress of a girl who visited Jasmine. I got her to give them to me in exchange for diamonds. I'd never seen anything but precious stones before."

"And this is what you brought?"

"I'm afraid so." She fingered the brilliants wistfully. "I think I like these better. I'm a little tired of diamonds."

"Very well," said John gloomily. "We'll have to live in Hades. And you will grow old telling incredulous women that you got the wrong drawer. Unfortunately your father's bank-books were consumed with him."

"Well, what's the matter with Hades?"

"If I come home with a wife at my age my father is just as liable as not to cut me off with a hot coal, as they say down there."

Jasmine spoke up.

"I love washing," she said quietly. "I have always washed my own handkerchiefs. I'll take in laundry and support you both."

"Do they have washwomen in Hades?" asked Kismine innocently.

"Of course," answered John. "It's just like anywhere else."

"I thought—perhaps it was too hot to wear any clothes."

John laughed.

"Just try it!" he suggested. "They'll run you out before you're half started."

"Will father be there?" she asked.

John turned to her in astonishment.

"Your father is dead," he replied somberly. "Why should he go to Hades? You have it confused with another place that was abolished long ago."

After supper they folded up the table-cloth and spread their blankets for the night.

"What a dream it was," Kismine sighed, gazing up at the stars. "How strange it seems to be here with one dress and a penniless fiancé!

"Under the stars," she repeated. "I never noticed the stars before. I always thought of them as great big diamonds that belonged to some one. Now they frighten me. They make me feel that it was all a dream, all my youth."

"It *was* a dream," said John quietly. "Everybody's youth is a dream, a form of chemical madness."

"How pleasant then to be insane!"

"So I'm told," said John gloomily. "I don't know any longer. At any rate, let us love for a while, for a year or so, you and me. That's a form of divine drunkenness that we can all try. There are only diamonds in the whole world, diamonds and perhaps the shabby gift of disillusion. Well, I have that last and I will make the usual nothing of it." He shivered. "Turn up your coat collar, little girl, the night's full of chill and you'll get pneumonia. His was a great sin who first invented consciousness. Let us lose it for a few hours."

So wrapping himself in his blanket he fell off to sleep.

1922

Tales of the Jazz Age

Contrast the ending of this story with the traditional fairy-tale ending.

SYNTHESIS

Wealth, youth, and beauty have long been important facets of man's aspirations. What points does Fitzgerald make about them? Does this 1922 interpretation suggest any valid comments on American society today?

This story deals with reality and the *Edges of Reality*. Evaluate in terms of plausibility and implausibility the action, settings, and the following character relationships: Percy and his parents, John and his parents, John and Percy, Braddock and God, John and Kismine.

In 1887 Lord Acton wrote, "Power tends to corrupt and absolute power corrupts absolutely." Assess the validity of this judgment as applied to the characters in this story who are powerless as well as those who are powerful.

COMMENT

F. Scott Fitzgerald said in a letter that "The Diamond as Big as the Ritz" was written for his own amusement. He was in a mood, he recalled, "characterized by a perfect craving for luxury"; this fantasy was an attempt to feed that craving.

Fitzgerald was disappointed when the story was rejected by six magazines; finally it was sold to *Smart Set* for $300—an inadequate price for what Fitzgerald considered a genuinely remarkable work.

Two of Fitzgerald's novels, *The Great Gatsby* and *Tender Is the Night,* reflect many of the same themes as "The Diamond as Big as the Ritz." His writings earned him great popularity and influence and convinced his readers that he was the spokesman for those handsome, reckless, "flaming-youth" characters of the 1920's.

The Canterville Ghost

OSCAR WILDE

I

When Mr. Hiram B. Otis, the American Minister, bought Canterville Chase, everyone told him he was doing a very foolish thing, as there was no doubt at all that the place was haunted. Indeed, Lord Canterville himself, who was a man of the most punctilious honour, had felt it his duty to mention the fact to Mr. Otis when they came to discuss terms.

Minister: Ambassador to England.

"We have not cared to live in the place ourselves," said Lord Canterville, "since my grand-aunt, the Dowager Duchess of Bolton, was frightened into a fit, from which she never really recovered, by two skeleton hands being placed on her shoulders as she was dressing for dinner, and I feel bound to tell you, Mr. Otis,

61

that the ghost has been seen by several living members of my family, as well as by the rector of the parish, the Rev. Augustus Dampier, who is a Fellow of King's College, Cambridge. After the unfortunate accident to the Duchess, none of our younger servants would stay with us, and Lady Canterville often got very little sleep at night, in consequence of the mysterious noises that came from the corridor and the library."

"My lord," answered the Minister, "I will take the furniture and the ghost at a valuation. I come from a modern country, where we have everything that money can buy; and with all our spry young fellows painting the Old World red, and carrying off your best actresses and prima donnas, I reckon that if there were such a thing as a ghost in Europe, we'd have it at home in a very short time in one of our public museums, or on the road as a show."

"I fear that the ghost exists," said Lord Canterville, smiling, "though it may have resisted the overtures of your enterprising impresarios. It has been well known for three centuries, since 1584 in fact, and always makes its appearance before the death of any member of our family."

"Well, so does the family doctor for that matter, Lord Canterville. But there is no such thing, sir, as a ghost, and I guess the laws of Nature are not going to be suspended for the British aristocracy."

"You are certainly very natural in America," answered Lord Canterville, who did not quite understand Mr. Otis' last ob-

Account for Lord Canterville's and Mr. Otis' contrasting attitudes toward ghosts.

62

servation, "and if you don't mind a ghost in the house, it is all right. Only you must remember I warned you."

A few weeks after this, the purchase was completed, and at the close of the season the Minister and his family went down to Canterville Chase. Mrs. Otis, who, as Miss Lucretia R. Tappan, of West 53rd Street, had been a celebrated New York belle, was now a very handsome, middle-aged woman, with fine eyes, and a superb profile. Many American ladies on leaving their native land adopt an appearance of chronic ill-health, under the impression that it is a form of European refinement, but Mrs. Otis had never fallen into this error. She had a magnificent constitution, and a really wonderful amount of animal spirits. Indeed, in many respects, she was quite English, and was an excellent example of the fact that we have really everything in common with America nowadays, except, of course, language. Her eldest son, christened Washington by his parents in a moment of patriotism, which he never ceased to regret, was a fair-haired, rather good-looking young man, who had qualified himself for American diplomacy by leading the German at the Newport Casino for three successive seasons, and even in London was well known as an excellent dancer. Gardenias and the peerage were his only weaknesses. Otherwise he was extremely sensible. Miss Virginia E. Otis was a little girl of fifteen, lithe and lovely as a fawn, and with a fine freedom in her large blue eyes. She was a wonderful amazon, and had once raced old Lord Bilton on her pony twice round the park, winning by a length and a half, just in front of the Achilles statue, to the huge delight of the young Duke of Cheshire, who proposed for her on the spot, and was sent back to Eton that very night by his guardians, in floods of tears. After Virginia came the twins, who were usually called "The Stars and Stripes," as they were always getting swished. They were delightful boys, and with the exception of the worthy Minister the only true republicans of the family.

As Canterville Chase is seven miles from Ascot, the nearest railway station, Mr. Otis had telegraphed for a waggonette to meet them, and they started on their drive in high spirits. It was a lovely July evening, and the air was delicate with the scent of the pinewoods. Now and then they heard a wood pigeon brooding over its own sweet voice, or saw, deep in the rustling fern, the burnished breast of the pheasant. Little squirrels peered at them from the beech-trees as they went by, and the rabbits scudded away through the brushwood and over the mossy knolls, with their white tails in the air. As they entered the avenue of Canterville Chase, however, the sky became suddenly overcast with clouds, a curious stillness seemed to hold the atmosphere, a great flight of rooks passed silently over their heads, and, before they reached the house, some big drops of rain had fallen.

Standing on the steps to receive them was an old woman, neatly dressed in black silk, with a white cap and apron. This was Mrs. Umney, the housekeeper, whom Mrs. Otis, at

Lady Canterville's earnest request, had consented to keep on in her former position. She made them each a low curtsey as they alighted, and said in a quaint, old-fashioned manner, "I bid you welcome to Canterville Chase." Following her, they passed through the fine Tudor hall into the library, a long, low room, panelled in black oak, at the end of which was a large stained-glass window. Here they found tea laid out for them, and, after taking off their wraps, they sat down and began to look round, while Mrs. Umney waited on them.

Suddenly Mrs. Otis caught sight of a dull red stain on the floor just by the fireplace and, quite unconscious of what it really signified, said to Mrs. Umney, "I am afraid something has been spilt there." "Yes, madam," replied the old housekeeper in a low voice, "blood has been spilt on that spot."

"How horrid," cried Mrs. Otis; "I don't at all care for blood-stains in a sitting-room. It must be removed at once."

The old woman smiled, and answered in the same low, mysterious voice, "It is the blood of Lady Eleanore de Canterville, who was murdered on that very spot by her own husband, Sir Simon de Canterville, in 1575. Sir Simon survived her nine years, and disappeared suddenly under very mysterious circumstances. His body has never been discovered, but his guilty spirit still haunts the Chase. The blood-stain has been much admired by tourists and others, and cannot be removed."

"That is all nonsense," cried Washington

Otis; "Pinkerton's Champion Stain Remover and Paragon Detergent will clean it up in no time," and before the terrified housekeeper could interfere he had fallen upon his knees, and was rapidly scouring the floor with a small stick of what looked like a black cosmetic. In a few moments no trace of the blood-stain could be seen. "I knew Pinkerton would do it," he exclaimed triumphantly, as he looked round at his admiring family; but no sooner had he said these words than a terrible flash of lightning lit up the sombre room, a fearful peal of thunder made them all start to their feet, and Mrs. Umney fainted.

"What a monstrous climate!" said the American Minister calmly, as he lit a long cheroot. "I guess the old country is so over-populated that they have not enough decent weather for everybody. I have always been of the opinion that emigration is the only thing for England."

"My dear Hiram," cried Mrs. Otis, "what can we do with a woman who faints?"

"Charge it to her like breakages," answered the Minister; "she won't faint after that"; and in a few moments Mrs. Umney certainly came to. There was no doubt, however, that she was extremely upset, and she sternly warned Mr. Otis to beware of some trouble coming to the house.

"I have seen things with my own eyes, sir," she said, "that would make any Christian's hair stand on end, and many and many a night I have not closed my eyes in sleep for the awful things that are done here." Mr. Otis,

cheroot: cigar, squared-off at both ends.

What typical ghost-story devices has Wilde used in Chapter I? Is Mrs. Umney's reaction to these devices what you would expect? How do the Otises react?

66

however, and his wife warmly assured the honest soul that they were not afraid of ghosts, and, after invoking the blessings of Providence on her new master and making arrangements for an increase of salary, the old housekeeper tottered off to her own room.

II

The storm raged fiercely all that night, but nothing of particular note occurred. The next morning, however, when they came down to breakfast, they found the terrible stain of blood once again on the floor. "I don't think it can be the fault of the Paragon Detergent," said Washington, "for I have tried it with everything. It must be the ghost." He accordingly rubbed out the stain a second time, but the second morning it appeared again. The third morning also it was there, though the library had been locked up at night by Mr. Otis himself, and the key carried upstairs. The whole family were now quite interested; Mr. Otis began to suspect that he had been too dogmatic in his denial of the existence of ghosts, Mrs. Otis expressed her intention of joining the Psychical Society, and Washington prepared a long letter to Messrs. Myers and Podmore on the subject of the Permanence of Sanguineous Stains When Connected with Crime. That night all doubts about the objective existence of phantasmata were removed forever.

The day had been warm and sunny; and, in the cool of the evening, the whole family

sanguineous (sang-gwin e əs): containing blood.

phantasmata (fan taz'-m ə tə): apparitions; specters.

67

This whole conversation has a satirical tone. Would you guess that Fanny Davenport is an American actress?

went out for a drive. They did not return home till nine o'clock, when they had a light supper. The conversation in no way turned upon ghosts, so there were not even those primary conditions of receptive expectation which so often precede the presentation of psychical phenomena. The subjects discussed, as I have since learned from Mr. Otis, were merely such as form the ordinary conversation of cultured Americans of the better class, such as the immense superiority of Miss Fanny Davenport over Sarah Bernhardt as an actress; the difficulty of obtaining green corn, buckwheat cakes, and hominy, even in the best English houses; the importance of Boston in the development of the world-soul; the advantages of the baggage check system in railway travelling; and the sweetness of the New York accent as compared to the London drawl. No mention at all was made of the supernatural, nor was Sir Simon de Canterville alluded to in any way. At eleven o'clock the family retired, and by half-past all the lights were out. Sometime after, Mr. Otis was awakened by a curious noise in the corridor, outside his room. It sounded like the clank of metal, and seemed to be coming nearer every moment. He got up at once, and struck a match, and looked at the time. It was exactly one o'clock. He was quite calm, and felt his pulse, which was not at all feverish. The strange noise still continued, and with it he heard distinctly the sound of footsteps. He put on his slippers, took a small oblong phial out of his dressing-case, and opened the door. Right in front of him he saw, in the wan moonlight,

68

an old man of terrible aspect. His eyes were as red burning coals; long grey hair fell over his shoulders in matted coils; his garments, which were of antique cut, were soiled and ragged, and from his wrists and ankles hung heavy manacles and rusty gyves.

"My dear sir," said Mr. Otis, "I really must insist on your oiling those chains, and have brought you for that purpose a small bottle of the Tammany Rising Sun Lubricator. It is said to be completely efficacious upon one application, and there are several testimonials to that effect on the wrapper from some of our most eminent native divines. I shall leave it here for you by the bedroom candles, and will be happy to supply you with more should you require it." With these words the United States Minister laid the bottle down on a marble table, and, closing his door, retired to rest.

For a moment the Canterville ghost stood quite motionless in natural indignation; then, dashing the bottle violently upon the polished floor, he fled down the corridor, uttering hollow groans, and emitting a ghastly green light. Just, however, as he reached the top of the great oak staircase, a door was flung open, two little white-robed figures appeared, and a large pillow whizzed past his head! There was evidently no time to be lost, so hastily adopting the Fourth Dimension of Space as a means of escape, he vanished through the wainscotting, and the house became quite quiet.

On reaching a small secret chamber in the left wing, he leaned up against a moonbeam to recover his breath, and began to try and realise

How does Mr. Otis react to the noise and to the sight of the ghost?

native divines: highly respected men.

wainscotting: wood paneling.

his position. Never, in a brilliant and uninterrupted career of three hundred years, had he been so grossly insulted. He thought of the Dowager Duchess, whom he had frightened into a fit as she stood before the glass in her lace and diamonds; of the four housemaids, who had gone off into hysterics when he merely grinned at them through the curtains of one of the spare bedrooms; of the rector of the parish, whose candle he had blown out as he was coming late one night from the library, and who had been under the care of Sir William Gull ever since, a perfect martyr to nervous disorders; and of old Madame de Tremouillac, who, having wakened up one morning early and seen a skeleton seated in an armchair by the fire reading her diary, had been confined to her bed for six weeks with an attack of brain fever, and, on her recovery, had become reconciled to the Church, and broken off her connection with that notorious sceptic Monsieur de Voltaire. He remembered the terrible night when the wicked Lord Canterville was found choking in his dressing-room, with the knave of diamonds halfway down his throat, and confessed, just before he died, that he had cheated Charles James Fox out of £50,000 at Crockford's by means of that very card, and swore that the ghost had made him swallow it. All his great achievements came back to him again, from the butler who had shot himself in the pantry because he had seen a green hand tapping at the windowpane, to the beautiful Lady Stutfield, who was always obliged to wear a black velvet band round her throat to hide

knave: jack.

the mark of five fingers burnt upon her white skin, and who drowned herself at last in the carp-pond at the end of the King's Walk. With the enthusiastic egotism of the true artist he went over his most celebrated performances, and smiled bitterly to himself as he recalled to mind his last appearance as "Red Ruben, or the Strangled Babe," his *debut* as "Gaunt Gibeon, the Blood-Sucker of Bexley Moor," and the *furore* he had excited one lovely June evening by merely playing ninepins with his own bones upon the lawn-tennis ground. And after all this, some wretched modern Americans were to come and offer him the Rising Sun Lubricator, and throw pillows at his head! It was quite unbearable. Besides, no ghosts in history had ever been treated in this manner. Accordingly, he determined to have vengeance, and remained till daylight in an attitude of deep thought.

What are the ghost's reactions to Mr. Otis? Why does the ghost recall his past before planning vengeance?

III

The next morning when the Otis family met at breakfast, they discussed the ghost at some length. The United States Minister was naturally a little annoyed to find that his present had not been accepted. "I have no wish," he said, "to do the ghost any personal injury, and I must say that, considering the length of time he has been in the house, I don't think it is at all polite to throw pillows at him"—a very just remark, at which, I am sorry to say, the twins burst into shouts of laughter. "Upon the other hand," he con-

71

tinued, "if he really declines to use the Rising Sun Lubricator, we shall have to take his chains from him. It would be quite impossible to sleep, with such a noise going on outside the bedrooms."

For the rest of the week, however, they were undisturbed, the only thing that excited any attention being the continual renewal of the blood-stain on the library floor. This certainly was very strange, as the door was always locked at night by Mr. Otis, and the windows kept closely barred. The chameleon-like colour, also, of the stain excited a good deal of comment. Some mornings it was a dull (almost Indian) red, then it would be vermilion, then a rich purple, and once when they came down for family prayers, according to the simple rites of the Free American Reformed Episcopalian Church, they found it a bright emerald-green. These kaleidoscopic changes naturally amused the party very much, and bets on the subject were freely made every evening. The only person who did not enter the joke was little Virginia, who, for some unexplained reason, was always a good deal distressed at the sight of the blood-stain, and very nearly cried the morning it was emerald-green.

The second appearance of the ghost was on Sunday night. Shortly after they had gone to bed they were suddenly alarmed by a fearful crash in the hall. Rushing downstairs, they found that a large suit of old armour had become detached from its stand, and had fallen on the floor, while, seated in a high-backed chair, was the Canterville ghost, rubbing his knees with an expression of acute agony on his face. The twins, having brought their pea-shooters with them, at once discharged two pellets on him, with that accuracy of aim which can only be attained by long and careful practice on a writing-master, while the United States Minister covered him with his revolver, and called upon him, in accordance with Californian etiquette, to hold up his hands! The ghost started up with a wild shriek of rage, and swept through them like a mist, extinguishing Washington Otis' candle as he passed, and so leaving them all in total darkness. On reaching the top of the staircase he recovered himself, and determined to give his celebrated peal of demoniac laughter. This he had on more than one occasion found extremely useful. It was said to have turned Lord Raker's wig grey in a single night, and had certainly made three of Lady Canterville's French governesses give warning before their month was up. He accordingly laughed his most horrible laugh, till the old vaulted roof rang and rang again; but hardly had the fearful echo died away when a door opened, and Mrs. Otis came out in a light blue dressing-gown. "I am afraid you are far from well," she said, "and have brought you a bottle of Dr. Dobell's tincture. If it is indigestion, you will find it a most excellent remedy." The ghost glared at her in fury, and began at once to make preparations for turning himself into a large black dog, an accomplishment for which he was justly renowned, and to which the family doctor always attributed the permanent idiocy of Lord Canterville's uncle, the

How does the ghost account for his inability to frighten the American family?

This refers to the poem "The Skeleton in Armor" written by Henry Wadsworth Longfellow.

barking: scraping the skin.

What qualities of the ghost are held also by human beings?

Hon. Thomas Horton. The sound of approaching footsteps, however, made him hesitate in his fell purpose, so he contented himself with becoming faintly phosphorescent, and vanished with a deep churchyard groan, just as the twins had come up to him.

On reaching his room he entirely broke down, and became a prey to the most violent agitation. The vulgarity of the twins, and the gross materialism of Mrs. Otis, were naturally extremely annoying, but what really distressed him most was that he had been unable to wear the suit of mail. He had hoped that even modern Americans would be thrilled by the sight of a Spectre in Armour, if for no more sensible reason, at least out of respect for their national poet Longfellow, over whose graceful and attractive poetry he himself had whiled away many a weary hour when the Cantervilles were up in town. Besides, it was his own suit. He had worn it with great success at the Kenilworth tournament, and had been highly complimented on it by no less a person than the Virgin Queen herself. Yet when he had put it on, he had been completely overpowered by the weight of the huge breastplate and steel casque, and had fallen heavily on the stone pavement, barking both his knees severely, and bruising the knuckles of his right hand.

For some days after this he was extremely ill, and hardly stirred out of his room at all, except to keep the blood-stain in proper repair. However, by taking great care of himself, he recovered, and resolved to make a third attempt to frighten the United States Minister

74

and his family. He selected Friday, the seventeenth of August, for his appearance, and spent most of that day in looking over his wardrobe, ultimately deciding in favour of a large slouched hat with a red feather, a winding-sheet frilled at the wrists and neck, and a rusty dagger. Towards evening a violent storm of rain came on, and the wind was so high that all the windows and doors in the old house shook and rattled. In fact, it was just such weather as he loved. His plan of action was this. He was to make his way quietly to Washington Otis' room, gibber at him from the foot of the bed, and stab himself three times in the throat to the sound of slow music. He bore Washington a special grudge, being quite aware that it was he who was in the habit of removing the famous Canterville blood-stain, by means of Pinkerton's Paragon Detergent. Having reduced the reckless and foolhardy youth to a condition of abject terror, he was then to proceed to the room occupied by the United States Minister and his wife, and there to place a clammy hand on Mrs. Otis' forehead, while he hissed into her trembling husband's ear the awful secrets of the charnel-house. With regard to little Virginia, he had not quite made up his mind. She had never insulted him in any way, and was pretty and gentle. A few hollow groans from the wardrobe, he thought, would be more than sufficient, or, if that failed to wake her, he might grabble at the counterpane with palsy-twitching fingers. As for the twins, he was quite determined to teach them a lesson. The first thing to be done was, of course, to sit upon

winding-sheet: burial cloth for a dead person.

charnel-house: place in which dead bodies are laid.

The ghost reacts differently to Virginia. Why?

75

their chests, so as to produce the stifling sensation of nightmare. Then, as their beds were quite close to each other, to stand between them in the form of a green, icy-cold corpse, till they became paralysed with fear, and finally, to throw off the winding-sheet, and crawl round the room, with white bleached bones and one rolling eyeball, in the character of "Dumb Daniel, or the Suicide's Skeleton," a *role* in which he had, on more than one occasion, produced a great effect, and which he considered quite equal to his famous part of "Martin the Maniac, or the Masked Mystery."

At half-past ten he heard the family going to bed. For some time he was disturbed by wild shrieks of laughter from the twins, who, with the light-hearted gaiety of schoolboys, were evidently amusing themselves before they retired to rest, but at a quarter past eleven all was still, and, as midnight sounded, he sallied forth. The owl beat against the windowpanes, the raven croaked from the old yew-tree, and the wind wandered moaning round the house like a lost soul; but the Otis family slept unconscious of their doom, and high above the rain and storm he could hear the steady snoring of the Minister for the United States. He stepped stealthily out of the wainscotting, with an evil smile on his cruel, wrinkled mouth; and the moon hid her face in a cloud as he stole past the great oriel window, where his own arms and those of his murdered wife were blazoned in azure and gold. On and on he glided, like an evil shadow, the very darkness seeming to loathe him as he passed. Once he thought he heard something call, and stopped; but it was only the baying of a dog, from the Red Farm, and he went on, muttering strange sixteenth-century curses, and ever and anon brandishing the rusty dagger in the midnight air. Finally he reached the corner of the passage that led to luckless Washington's room. For a moment he paused there, the wind blowing his long grey locks about his head, and twisting into grotesque and fantastic folds the nameless horror of the dead man's shroud. Then the clock struck the quarter, and he felt the time was come. He chuckled to himself, and turned the corner; but no sooner had he done so, than, with a piteous wail of terror, he fell back, and hid his blanched face in his long, bony hands. Right in front of him was standing a horrible spectre, motionless as a carved image, and monstrous as a madman's dream! Its head was bald and burnished; its face round, and fat, and white; and hideous laughter seemed to have writhed its features into an eternal grin. From the eyes streamed rays of scarlet light, the mouth was a wide well of fire, and a hideous garment, like to his own, swathed with its silent snows the Titan form. On its breast was a placard with strange writing in antique characters, some scroll of shame it seemed, some record of wild sins, some awful calendar of crime, and, with its right hand, it bore aloft a falchion of gleaming steel.

falchion (fôl′chən): short, broad, pointed sword with curved edge.

Never having seen a ghost before, he naturally was terribly frightened, and, after a second hasty glance at the awful phantom, he fled back to his room, tripping up in his long

77

winding-sheet as he sped down the corridor, and finally dropping the rusty dagger into the Minister's jackboots, where it was found in the morning by the butler. Once in the privacy of his own apartment, he flung himself down on a small pallet-bed, and hid his face under the clothes. After a time, however, the brave old Canterville spirit asserted itself, and he determined to go and speak to the other ghost as soon as it was daylight. Accordingly, just as the dawn was touching the hills with silver, he returned towards the spot where he had first laid eyes on the grisly phantom, feeling that, after all, two ghosts were better than one, and that, by the aid of his new friend, he might safely grapple with the twins. On reaching the spot, however, a terrible sight met his gaze. Something had evidently happened to the spectre, for the light had entirely faded from its hollow eyes, the gleaming falchion had fallen from its hand, and it was leaning up against the wall in a strained and uncomfortable attitude. He rushed forward and seized it in his arms, when, to his horror, the head slipped off and rolled on the floor, the body assumed a recumbent posture, and he found himself clasping a white dimity bed-curtain, with a sweeping-brush, a kitchen cleaver, and a hollow turnip lying at his feet! Unable to understand this curious transformation, he clutched the placard with feverish haste, and there, in the grey morning light, he read these fearful words:

Ye Otis Ghoste
Ye Onlie True and Original Spook
Beware of Ye Imitationes
All others are Counterfeite

The whole thing flashed across him. He had been tricked, foiled, and outwitted! The old Canterville look came into his eyes; he ground his toothless gums together; and, raising his withered hands high above his head, swore, according to the picturesque phraseology of the antique school, that when Chanticleer had sounded twice his merry horn, deeds of blood would be wrought, and Murder walk abroad with silent feet.

chanticleer: rooster; cock.

Hardly had he finished this awful oath when, from the red-tiled roof of a distant homestead, a cock crew. He laughed a long, low, bitter laugh, and waited. Hour after hour he waited, but the cock, for some strange reason, did not crow again. Finally, at half-past seven, the arrival of the housemaids made him give up his fearful vigil, and he stalked back to his room, thinking of his vain hope and baffled purpose. There he consulted several books of ancient chivalry, of which he was exceedingly fond, and found that, on every occasion on which his oath had been used, Chanticleer had always crowed a second time. "Perdition seize the naughty fowl," he muttered; "I have seen the day when, with my stout spear, I would have run him through the gorge, and made him crow for me as 'twere in death!" He then retired to a comfortable lead coffin, and stayed there till evening.

IV

The next day the ghost was very weak and tired. The terrible excitement of the last four

79

astral bodies: ghostly
substance forming a
person's second body
which survives after
death.

Note the moral
contradiction expressed
here.

Some duties are very
important to the ghost.
What compromises is
he willing to make?

weeks was beginning to have its effect. His nerves were completely shattered, and he started at the slightest noise. For five days he kept to his room, and at last made up his mind to give up the point of the blood-stain on the library floor. If the Otis family did not want it, they clearly did not deserve it. They were evidently people on a low, material plane of existence, and quite incapable of appreciating the symbolic value of sensuous phenomena. The question of phantasmic apparitions, and the development of astral bodies, was of course quite a different matter, and really not under his control. It was his solemn duty to appear in the corridor once a week, and to gibber from the large oriel window on the first and third Wednesday in every month, and he did not see how he could honourably escape from his obligations. It is quite true that his life had been very evil, but, upon the other hand, he was most conscientious in all things connected with the supernatural. For the next three Saturdays, accordingly, he traversed the corridor as usual between midnight and three o'clock, taking every possible precaution against being either heard or seen. He removed his boots, trod as lightly as possible on the old worm-eaten boards, wore a large black velvet cloak, and was careful to use the Rising Sun Lubricator for oiling his chains. I am bound to acknowledge that it was with a good deal of difficulty that he brought himself to adopt this last mode of protection. However, one night, while the family were at dinner, he slipped into Mr. Otis' bedroom and carried off the bottle.

80

He felt a little humiliated at first, but afterwards was sensible enough to see that there was a great deal to be said for the invention, and, to a certain degree, it served his purpose. Still, in spite of everything, he was not left unmolested. Strings were continually being stretched across the corridor, over which he tripped in the dark, and on one occasion, while dressed for the part of "Black Isaac, or the Huntsman of Hogley Woods," he met with a severe fall, through treading on a butter-slide, which the twins had constructed from the entrance of the Tapestry Chamber to the top of the oak staircase. This last insult so enraged him that he resolved to make one final effort to assert his dignity and social position, and determined to visit the insolent young Etonians the next night in his celebrated character of "Reckless Rupert, or the Headless Earl."

He had not appeared in this disguise for more than seventy years; in fact, not since he had so frightened pretty Lady Barbara Modish by means of it, that she suddenly broke off her engagement with the present Lord Canterville's grandfather, and ran away to Gretna Green with handsome Jack Castleton, declaring that nothing in the world would induce her to marry into a family that allowed such a horrible phantom to walk up and down the terrace at twilight. Poor Jack was afterwards shot in a duel by Lord Canterville on Wandsworth Common, and Lady Barbara died of a broken heart at Tunbridge Wells before the year was out, so, in every way, it had been a great success. It was, however, an extremely difficult "make-up," if I may use such a theatrical expression in connection with one of the greatest mysteries of the supernatural, or, to employ a more scientific term, the higher-natural world, and it took him fully three hours to make his preparations. At last everything was ready, and he was very pleased with his appearance. The big leather riding-boots that went with the dress were just a little too large for him, and he could only find one of the two horse-pistols; but, on the whole, he was quite satisfied, and at a quarter past one he glided out of the wainscotting and crept down the corridor. On reaching the room occupied by the twins, which I should mention was called the Blue Bed Chamber, on account of the colour of its hangings, he found the door just ajar. Wishing to make an effective entrance, he flung it wide open, when a heavy jug of water fell right down on him, wetting him to the skin, and just missing his left shoulder by a couple of inches. At the same moment he heard stifled shrieks of laughter proceeding from the four-post bed. The shock to his nervous system was so great that he fled back to his room as hard as he could go, and the next day he was laid up with a severe cold. The only thing that at all consoled him in the whole affair was the fact that he had not brought his head with him, for, had he done so, the consequences might have been very serious.

He now gave up all hope of ever frightening this rude American family, and contented himself, as a rule, with creeping about the passages in list slippers, with a thick red muffler round his throat for fear of draughts, and a small arquebuse, in case he should be attacked by the twins. The final blow he received occurred on the nineteenth of September. He had gone downstairs to the great entrance-hall, feeling sure that there, at any rate, he would be quite unmolested, and was amusing himself by making satirical remarks on the large Saroni photographs of the United States Minister and his wife, which had now taken the place of the Canterville family pictures. He was simply but neatly clad in a long shroud, spotted with churchyard mould, had tied up his jaw with a strip of yellow linen, and carried a small lantern and a sexton's spade. In fact, he was dressed for the character of "Jonas the Graveless, or the Corpse-Snatcher of Chertsey Barn," one of his most remarkable impersonations, and one which the Cantervilles had every reason to remember, as it was the real origin of their quarrel with their neighbour, Lord Rufford. It was about a quarter past two o'clock in the morning, and, as far as he could ascertain, no one was stirring. As he was strolling towards the library, however, to see if there were any traces left of the blood-stain, suddenly there leaped out on him from a dark corner two figures, who waved their arms wildly above their heads, and shrieked out "BOO!" in his ear.

Seized with a panic, which, under the circumstances, was only natural, he rushed for the staircase, but found Washington Otis waiting for him there with the big garden-syringe; and being thus hemmed in by his enemies on

arquebuse (är′kwə bəs): harquebus; small-caliber long gun fired by lighting powder with a wick.

Saroni: Napoleon Sarony, famous photographer.

83

every side, and driven almost to bay, he vanished into the great iron stove, which, fortunately for him, was not lit, and had to make his way home through the flues and chimneys, arriving at his own room in a terrible state of dirt, disorder, and despair.

After this he was not seen again on any nocturnal expedition. The twins lay in wait for him on several occasions, and strewed the passages with nutshells every night to the great annoyance of their parents and the servants, but it was of no avail. It was quite evident that his feelings were so wounded that he would not appear. Mr. Otis consequently resumed his great work on the history of the Democratic Party, on which he had been engaged for some years; Mrs. Otis organized a wonderful clambake, which amazed the whole county; the boys took to lacrosse, euchre, poker, and other American national games; and Virginia rode about the lanes on her pony, accompanied by the young Duke of Cheshire, who had come to spend the last week of his holidays at Canterville Chase. It was generally assumed that the ghost had gone away, and, in fact, Mr. Otis wrote a letter to that effect to Lord Canterville, who, in reply, expressed his great pleasure at the news, and sent his best congratulations to the Minister's worthy wife.

The Otises, however, were deceived, for the ghost was still in the house, and though now almost an invalid, was by no means ready to let matters rest, particularly as he heard that among the guests was the young Duke of Cheshire, whose grand-uncle, Lord Francis

In what ways has the ghost's world been altered since he first encountered the Otises?

84

Stilton, had once bet a hundred guineas with Colonel Carbury that he would play dice with the Canterville ghost, and was found the next morning lying on the floor of the cardroom in such a helpless paralytic state, that though he lived on to a great age, he was never able to say anything again but "Double Sixes." The story was well known at the time, though, of course, out of respect to the feelings of the two noble families, every attempt was made to hush it up; and a full account of all the circumstances connected with it will be found in the third volume of Lord Tattle's *Recollections of the Prince Regent and His Friends.* The ghost, then, was naturally very anxious to show that he had not lost his influence over the Stiltons, with whom, indeed, he was distantly connected, his own first cousin having been married *en secondes noces* to the Sieur de Bulkeley, from whom, as everyone knows, the Dukes of Cheshire are lineally descended. Accordingly, he made arrangements for appearing to Virginia's little lover in his celebrated impersonation of "The Vampire Monk, or the Bloodless Benedictine," a performance so horrible that when old Lady Startup saw it, which she did on one fatal New Year's Eve, in the year 1764, she went off into the most piercing shrieks, which culminated in violent apoplexy, and died in three days, after disinheriting the Cantervilles, who were her nearest relations, and leaving all her money to her London apothecary. At the last moment, however, his terror of the twins prevented his leaving his room, and the little Duke slept in peace under the great feathered

en secondes noces (än sə-gônd nôs): by a second marriage (French).

Sieur (syèr): old title of respect (French).

canopy in the Royal Bedchamber, and dreamed of Virginia.

V

A few days after this, Virginia and her curly-haired cavalier went out riding on Brockley meadows, where she tore her habit so badly in getting through a hedge, that, on their return home, she made up her mind to go up by the back staircase so as not to be seen. As she was running past the Tapestry Chamber, the door of which happened to be open, she fancied she saw someone inside, and thinking it was her mother's maid, who sometimes used to bring her work there, looked in to ask her to mend her habit. To her immense surprise, however, it was the Canterville ghost himself! He was sitting by the window, watching the ruined gold of the yellowing trees fly through the air, and the red leaves dancing madly down the long avenue. His head was leaning on his hand, and his whole attitude was one of extreme depression. Indeed, so forlorn, and so much out of repair did he look, that little Virginia, whose first idea had been to run away and lock herself in her room, was filled with pity, and determined to try and comfort him. So light was her footfall, and so deep his melancholy, that he was not aware of her presence till she spoke to him.

"I am so sorry for you," she said, "but my brothers are going back to Eton tomorrow and then, if you behave yourself, no one will annoy you."

"It is absurd asking me to behave myself," he answered, looking round in astonishment at the pretty little girl who had ventured to address him, "quite absurd. I must rattle my chains, and groan through keyholes, and walk about at night, if that is what you mean. It is my only reason for existing."

"It is no reason at all for existing, and you know you have been very wicked. Mrs. Umney told us, the first day we arrived here, that you had killed your wife."

"Well, I quite admit it," said the ghost petulantly, "but it was a purely family matter, and concerned no one else."

"It is very wrong to kill anyone," said Virginia, who at times had a sweet Puritan gravity, caught from some old New England ancestor.

What does the narrator's satirical tone imply about Virginia's moralizing?

"Oh, I hate the cheap severity of abstract ethics! My wife was very plain, never had my ruffs properly starched, and knew nothing about cookery. Why, there was a buck I had shot in Hogley Woods, a magnificent pricket, and do you know how she had it sent up to table? However, it is no matter now, for it is all over, and I don't think it was very nice of her brothers to starve me to death, though I did kill her."

pricket: male deer, two years old.

"Starve you to death? Oh, Mr. Ghost, I mean Sir Simon, are you hungry? I have a sandwich in my case. Would you like it?"

"No, thank you, I never eat anything now; but it is very kind of you, all the same, and you are much nicer than the rest of your horrid, rude, vulgar, dishonest family."

Why is Virginia the first one in the Otis family to call the ghost Sir Simon?

"Stop!" cried Virginia, stamping her foot, "it is you who are rude, and horrid, and vulgar, and as for dishonesty, you know you stole the paints out of my box to try and furbish up that ridiculous blood-stain in the library. First you took all my reds, including the vermilion, and I couldn't do any more sunsets; then you took the emerald-green and the chrome-yellow; and finally I had nothing left but indigo and Chinese white, and could only do moonlight scenes, which are always depressing to look at, and not at all easy to paint. I never told on you, though I was very much annoyed, and it was most ridiculous, the whole thing; for who ever heard of emerald-green blood?"

"Well, really," said the ghost, rather meekly, "what was I to do? It is a very difficult thing to get real blood nowadays, and, as your brother began it all with his Paragon Detergent, I certainly saw no reason why I should not have your paints. As for colour, that is always a matter of taste: the Cantervilles have blue blood, for instance, the very bluest in England; but I know you Americans don't care for things of this kind."

What are the ghost's values? How does he feel about Americans?

"You know nothing about it, and the best thing you can do is to emigrate and improve your mind. My father will be only too happy to give you a free passage, and though there is a heavy duty on spirits of every kind, there will be no difficulty about the Custom House, as the officers are all Democrats. Once in New York, you are sure to be a great success. I know lots of people there who would give a hundred thousand dollars to have a grandfather, and much more than that to have a family ghost."

"I don't think I should like America."

"I suppose because we have no ruins and no curiosities," said Virginia satirically.

"No ruins! No curiosities!" answered the ghost; "you have your navy and your manners."

"Good evening; I will go and ask papa to get the twins an extra week's holiday."

"Please don't go, Miss Virginia," he cried; "I am so lonely and so unhappy, and I really don't know what to do. I want to go to sleep and I cannot."

"That's quite absurd! You have merely to go to bed and blow out the candle. It is very difficult sometimes to keep awake, especially at church, but there is no difficulty at all about sleeping. Why, even babies know how to do that, and they are not very clever."

"I have not slept for three hundred years," he said sadly, and Virginia's beautiful blue eyes opened in wonder; "for three hundred years I have not slept, and I am so tired."

Virginia grew quite grave, and her little lips trembled like rose-leaves. She came towards him, and kneeling down at his side, looked up into his old withered face.

"Poor, poor ghost," she murmured; "have you no place where you can sleep?"

"Far away beyond the pinewoods," he answered, in a low dreamy voice, "there is a little garden. There the grass grows long and deep; there are the great white stars of the hemlock flower; there the nightingale sings all night long. All night long he sings, and the cold, crystal moon looks down, and the yew-tree spreads out its giant arms over the sleeper."

Virginia's eyes grew dim with tears, and she hid her face in her hands.

"You mean the Garden of Death?" she whispered.

"Yes, Death. Death must be so beautiful. To lie in the soft brown earth, with the grasses waving above one's head, and listen to silence. To have no yesterday, and no tomorrow. To forget time, to forgive life, to be at peace. You can help me. You can open for me the portals of Death's house, for Love is always with you, and Love is stronger than Death is."

Virginia trembled, a cold shudder ran through her, and for a few moments there was silence. She felt as if she was in a terrible dream.

Then the ghost spoke again, and his voice sounded like the sighing of the wind.

"Have you ever read the old prophecy on the library window?"

"Oh, often," cried the little girl, looking up; "I know it quite well. It is painted in curious black letters, and it is difficult to read. There are only six lines:

> "'When a golden girl can win
> Prayer from out the lips of sin,
> When the barren almond bears,
> And a little child gives away its tears,
> Then shall all the house be still
> And peace come to Canterville.'

But I don't know what they mean."

"They mean," he said sadly, "that you must weep with me for my sins, because I have no tears, and pray with me for my soul, because I have no faith; and then, if you have always been sweet, and good, and gentle, the Angel of Death will have mercy on me. You will see fearful shapes in darkness, and wicked voices will whisper in your ear, but they will not harm you, for against the purity of a little child the powers of Hell cannot prevail."

Virginia made no answer, and the ghost wrung his hands in wild despair as he looked down at her bowed golden head. Suddenly she stood up, very pale, and with a strange light in her eyes. "I am not afraid," she said firmly, "and I will ask the Angel to have mercy on you."

He rose from his seat with a faint cry of joy, and taking her hand, bent over it with old-fashioned grace and kissed it. His fingers were as cold as ice, and his lips burned like fire, but Virginia did not falter, as he led her across the dusky room. On the faded green tapestry were embroidered little huntsmen. They blew their tasselled horns and with their tiny hands waved to her to go back. "Go back! Little Virginia," they cried, "go back!" but the ghost clutched her hand more tightly, and she shut her eyes against them. Horrible animals with lizard tails, and goggle eyes, blinked at her from the carved chimney-piece, and murmured "Beware! Little Virginia, beware! We may never see you again," but the ghost glided on more swiftly, and Virginia did not listen. When they reached the end of the room he

What impressions of Sir Simon and Virginia do you get from this scene?

stopped, and muttered some words she could not understand. She opened her eyes, and saw the wall slowly fading away like a mist, and a great black cavern in front of her. A bitter cold wind swept round them, and she felt something pulling at her dress. "Quick, quick," cried the ghost, "or it will be too late," and, in a moment, the wainscotting had closed behind them, and the Tapestry Chamber was empty.

Consider how the mood of this story has changed since page 88.

VI

About ten minutes later, the bell rang for tea, and, as Virginia did not come down, Mrs. Otis sent up one of the footmen to tell her. After a little time he returned and said that he could not find Miss Virginia anywhere. As she was in the habit of going out to the garden every evening to get flowers for the dinner-table, Mrs. Otis was not at all alarmed at first; but when six o'clock struck, and Virginia did not appear, she became really agitated, and sent the boys out to look for her, while she herself and Mr. Otis searched every room in the house. At half-past six the boys came back and said that they could find no trace of their sister anywhere. They were all now in the greatest state of excitement, and did not know what to do, when Mr. Otis suddenly remembered that, some few days before, he had given a band of gypsies permission to camp in the park. He accordingly at once set off for Black-fell Hollow, where he knew they were, accompanied by his eldest son and two of the farm-servants. The little Duke of Cheshire, who was perfectly frantic with anxiety, begged hard to be allowed to go, too, but Mr. Otis would not allow him, as he was afraid there might be a scuffle. On arriving at the spot, however, he found that the gypsies had gone, and it was evident that their departure had been rather sudden, as the fire was still burning, and some plates were lying on the grass. Having sent off Washington and the two men to scour the district, he ran home, and dispatched telegrams to all the police inspectors in the county, telling them to look out for a little girl who had been kidnapped by tramps or gypsies. He then ordered his horse to be brought round, and, after insisting on his wife and the three boys sitting down to dinner, rode off down the Ascot Road with a groom. He had hardly, however, gone a couple of miles when he heard somebody galloping after him, and, looking round, saw the little Duke coming up on his pony, with his face very flushed and no hat. "I'm awfully sorry, Mr. Otis," gasped out the boy, "but I can't eat any dinner as long as Virginia is lost. Please, don't be angry with me; if you had let us be engaged last year, there would never have been all this trouble. You won't send me back, will you? I can't go! I won't go!"

The Minister could not help smiling at the handsome young scapegrace, and was a good deal touched at his devotion to Virginia; so leaning down from his horse, he patted him kindly on the shoulders, and said, "Well, Cecil, if you won't go back I suppose you must come with me, but I must get you a hat at Ascot."

"Oh, bother my hat! I want Virginia!"

cried the little Duke, laughing, and they galloped on to the railway station. There Mr. Otis inquired of the station-master if any one answering the description of Virginia had been seen on the platform, but could get no news of her. The station-master, however, wired up and down the line, and assured him that a strict watch would be kept for her; and, after having bought a hat for the little Duke from a linen-draper, who was just putting up his shutters, Mr. Otis rode off to Bexley, a village about four miles away, which he was told was a well-known haunt of the gypsies, as there was a large common next to it. Here they roused up the rural policeman, but could get no information from him; and, after riding all over the common, they turned their horses' heads homewards, and reached the Chase about eleven o'clock, dead-tired and almost heartbroken. They found Washington and the twins waiting for them at the gate-house with lanterns, as the avenue was very dark. Not the slightest trace of Virginia had been discovered. The gypsies had been caught on Brockley meadows, but she was not with them, and they had explained their sudden departure by saying that they had mistaken the date of Chorton Fair, and had gone off in a hurry for fear they might be late. Indeed, they had been quite distressed at hearing of Virginia's disappearance, as they were very grateful to Mr. Otis for having allowed them to camp in his park, and four of their number had stayed behind to help in the search. The carp-pond had been dragged, and the whole Chase thoroughly gone over, but without any result. It was evident that, for that night at any rate, Virginia was lost to them; and it was in a state of the deepest depression that Mr. Otis and the boys walked up to the house, the groom following behind with the two horses and the pony. In the hall they found a group of frightened servants, and lying on a sofa in the library was poor Mrs. Otis, almost out of her mind with terror and anxiety, and having her forehead bathed with eau-de-cologne by the old housekeeper. Mr. Otis at once insisted on her having something to eat, and ordered up supper for the whole party. It was a melancholy meal, as hardly anyone spoke, and even the twins were awestruck and subdued, as they were very fond of their sister. When they had finished, Mr. Otis, in spite of the entreaties of the little Duke, ordered them all to bed, saying that nothing more could be done that night, and that he would telegraph in the morning to Scotland Yard for some detectives to be sent down immediately. Just as they were passing out of the dining-room, midnight began to boom from the clock tower, and when the last stroke sounded they heard a crash and a sudden shrill cry; a dreadful peal of thunder shook the house, a strain of unearthly music floated through the air, a panel at the top of the staircase flew back with a loud noise, and out on the landing, looking very pale and white, with a little casket in her hand, stepped Virginia. In a moment they had all rushed up to her. Mrs. Otis clasped her passionately in her arms, the Duke smothered her with violent kisses, and the twins executed a wild war-dance round the group.

"Good heavens, child! Where have you been?" said Mr. Otis, rather angrily, thinking that she had been playing some foolish trick on them. "Cecil and I have been riding all over the country looking for you, and your mother has been frightened to death. You must never play these practical jokes any more."

"Except on the ghost! Except on the ghost!" shrieked the twins, as they capered about.

"My own darling, thank God you are found; you must never leave my side again," murmured Mrs. Otis, as she kissed the trembling child, and smoothed the tangled gold of her hair.

"Papa," said Virginia quietly, "I have been with the ghost. He is dead, and you must come and see him. He had been very wicked, but he was really sorry for all that he had done, and he gave me this box of beautiful jewels before he died."

The whole family gazed at her in mute amazement, but she was quite grave and serious; and, turning round, she led them through the opening in the wainscotting down a narrow secret corridor, Washington following with a lighted candle, which he had caught up from the table. Finally, they came to a great oak door, studded with rusty nails. When Virginia touched it, it swung back on its heavy hinges, and they found themselves in a little low room, with a vaulted ceiling, and one tiny grated window. Imbedded in the wall was a huge iron ring, and chained to it was a gaunt skeleton, that was stretched out at full length on the stone floor, and seemed to be trying to grasp with its long fleshless fingers an old-fashioned trencher and ewer, that were placed just out of its reach. The jug had evidently been once filled with water, as it was covered inside with green mould. There was nothing on the trencher but a pile of dust. Virginia knelt down beside the skeleton, and, holding her little hands together, began to pray silently, while the rest of the party looked on in wonder at the terrible tragedy whose secret was now disclosed to them.

trencher and ewer: wooden serving platter and wide-mouthed water pitcher.

"Hallo!" suddenly exclaimed one of the twins, who had been looking out of the window to try and discover in what wing of the house the room was situated. "Hallo! The old withered almond tree has blossomed. I can see the flowers plainly in the moonlight."

"God has forgiven him," said Virginia gravely, as she rose to her feet, and a beautiful light seemed to illumine her face.

"What an angel you are!" cried the young Duke, and he put his arm round her neck and kissed her.

VII

Four days after these curious incidents a funeral started from Canterville Chase at about eleven o'clock at night. The hearse was drawn by eight black horses, each of which carried on its head a great tuft of nodding ostrich-plumes, and the leaden coffin was covered by a rich purple pall, on which was embroidered in gold the Canterville coat-of-arms. By the side of the hearse and the coaches walked the servants with lighted torches, and the whole procession was wonderfully impressive. Lord Canterville was the chief mourner, having come up specially from Wales to attend the funeral, and sat in the first carriage along with little Virginia. Then came the United States Minister and his wife, then Washington and the three boys, and in the last carriage was Mrs. Umney. It was generally felt that, as she had been frightened by the ghost for more than fifty years of her life, she had a right to see the last of him. A deep grave had been dug in the corner of the churchyard, just under the old yew-tree, and the service was read in the most impressive manner by the Rev. Augustus Dampier. When the ceremony was over, the servants, according to an old custom observed in the Canterville family, extinguished their torches, and, as the coffin was being lowered into the grave, Virginia stepped forward and laid on it a large cross made of white and pink almond-blossoms. As she did so, the moon came out from behind a cloud, and flooded with its silent silver the little churchyard, and from a distant copse a nightingale began to sing. She thought of the ghost's description of the Garden of Death, her eyes became dim with tears, and she hardly spoke a word during the drive home.

The next morning, before Lord Canterville went up to town, Mr. Otis had an interview with him on the subject of the jewels

copse (kops): dense growth of trees or shrubs.

the ghost had given to Virginia. They were perfectly magnificent, especially a certain ruby necklace with old Venetian setting, which was really a superb specimen of sixteenth-century work, and their value was so great that Mr. Otis felt considerable scruples about allowing his daughter to accept them.

"My lord," he said, "I know that in this country mortmain is held to apply to trinkets as well as to land, and it is quite clear to me that these jewels are, or should be, heirlooms in your family. I must beg you, accordingly, to take them to London with you, and to regard them simply as a portion of your property which has been restored to you under certain strange conditions. As for my daughter, she is merely a child, and has as yet, I am glad to say, but little interest in such appurtenances of idle luxury. I am also informed by Mrs. Otis, who, I may say, is no mean authority upon Art—having had the privilege of spending several winters in Boston when she was a girl—that these gems are of great monetary worth, and if offered for sale would fetch a tall price. Under these circumstances, Lord Canterville, I feel sure that you will recognize how impossible it would be for me to allow them to remain in the possession of any member of my family; and, indeed, all such vain gauds and toys, however suitable or necessary to the dignity of the British aristocracy, would be completely out of place among those who have been brought up on the severe, and I believe immortal, principles of republican simplicity. Perhaps I should mention that Virginia is very

mortmain: condition of holding property without the right to sell or give it away.

gauds: trivial ornaments.

99

anxious that you should allow her to retain the box as a memento of your unfortunate but misguided ancestor. As it is extremely old, and consequently a good deal out of repair, you may perhaps think fit to comply with her request. For my own part, I confess I am a good deal surprised to find a child of mine expressing sympathy with medievalism in any form, and can only account for it by the fact that Virginia was born in one of your London suburbs shortly after Mrs. Otis had returned from a trip to Athens."

Lord Canterville listened very gravely to the worthy Minister's speech, pulling his grey moustache now and then to hide an involuntary smile, and when Mr. Otis had ended, he shook him cordially by the hand, and said, "My dear sir, your charming little daughter rendered my unlucky ancestor, Sir Simon, a very important service, and I and my family are much indebted to her for her marvellous courage and pluck. The jewels are clearly hers, and, egad, I believe that if I were heartless enough to take them from her, the wicked old fellow would be out of his grave in a fortnight, leading me the devil of a life. As for their being heirlooms, nothing is an heirloom that is not mentioned in a will or legal document, and the existence of these jewels has been quite unknown. I assure you I have no more claim on them than your butler, and when Miss Virginia grows up I daresay she will be pleased to have pretty things to wear. Besides, you forget, Mr. Otis, that you took the furniture and the ghost at a valuation, and anything that belonged to the ghost passed at once into your possession, as, whatever activity Sir Simon may have shown in the corridor at night, in point of law he was really dead, and you acquired his property by purchase."

Mr. Otis was a good deal distressed at Lord Canterville's refusal, and begged him to reconsider his decision, but the good-natured peer was quite firm, and finally induced the Minister to allow his daughter to retain the present the ghost had given her; and when, in the spring of 1890, the young Duchess of Cheshire was presented at the Queen's first drawing-room on the occasion of her marriage, her jewels were the universal theme of admiration. For Virginia received the coronet, which is the reward of all good little American girls, and was married to her boy-lover as soon as he came of age. They were both so charming, and they loved each other so much, that everyone was delighted at the match, except the old Marchioness of Dumbleton, who had tried to catch the Duke for one of her seven unmarried daughters, and had given no less than three expensive dinner-parties for that purpose, and, strange to say, Mr. Otis himself. Mr. Otis was extremely fond of the young Duke personally; but, theoretically, he objected to titles, and, to use his own words, "was not without apprehension lest, amid the enervating influences of a pleasure-loving aristocracy, the true principles of republican simplicity should be forgotten." His objections, however, were completely overruled, and I believe that when he walked up the aisle of St. George's, Hanover

received the coronet: when Virginia married an English duke, she was entitled to wear the small crown of a duchess.

101

Square, with his daughter leaning on his arm, there was not a prouder man in the whole length and breadth of England.

The Duke and Duchess, after the honeymoon was over, went down to Canterville Chase, and on the day after their arrival they walked over in the afternoon to the lonely churchyard by the pinewoods. There had been a great deal of difficulty at first about the inscription on Sir Simon's tombstone, but finally it had been decided to engrave on it simply the initials of the old gentleman's name, and the verse from the library window. The Duchess had brought with her some lovely roses, which she strewed upon the grave, and after they had stood by it for some time they strolled into the ruined chancel of the old abbey. There the Duchess sat down on a fallen pillar, while her husband lay at her feet smoking a cigarette and looking up at her beautiful eyes. Suddenly he threw his cigarette away, took hold of her hand, and said to her, "Virginia, a wife should have no secrets from her husband."

"Dear Cecil! I have no secrets from you."

"Yes, you have," he answered, smiling, "you have never told me what happened to you when you were locked up with the ghost."

"I have never told anyone, Cecil," said Virginia gravely.

"I know that, but you might tell me."

"Please don't ask me, Cecil, I cannot tell you. Poor Sir Simon! I owe him a great deal. Yes, don't laugh, Cecil, I really do. He made me see what Life is, and what Death signifies, and why Love is stronger than both."

The Duke rose and kissed his wife loving-ly. "You can have your secret as long as I have your heart," he murmured.

"You have always had that, Cecil."

"And you will tell our children someday, won't you?"

Virginia blushed.

SYNTHESIS

What has Wilde done with the usual supernatural elements of a ghost story to make his situations and ghost seem amusing instead of tragic or terrifying?

Compare Wilde's use of satire with Fitzgerald's in "The Diamond as Big as the Ritz."

COMMENT

Oscar Fingal O'Flahertie Wills Wilde (as all those names signify) was born in Ireland. He was flamboyant and eccentric, and he used his sharp, aphoristic wit to satirize English society.

Many of Wilde's aphorisms are still quotable; these come from his play *Lady Windermere's Fan:*

"In this world there are only two tragedies. One is not getting what one wants, and the other is getting it."

"What is a cynic?—A man who knows the price of everything, and the value of nothing."

"Experience is the name everyone gives to their mistakes."

Portrait of Jennie

ROBERT NATHAN

Chapter I

There is such a thing as hunger for more than food, and that was the hunger I fed on. I was poor, my work unknown; often without meals; cold, too, in winter in my little studio on the West Side. But that was the least of it.

When I talk about trouble, I am not talking about cold and hunger. There is another kind of suffering for the artist which is worse than anything a winter, or poverty, can do; it is more like a winter of the mind, in which the life of his genius, the living sap of his work, seems frozen and motionless, caught—perhaps forever—in a season of death; and who knows if spring will ever come again to set it free?

Eben is trying to express his frustrations as an artist. Which disturb him the most?

It was not only that I could not sell my work—that has happened to good men, even to great men, before—but that I couldn't seem to get through, myself, to the things that were bottled up inside me. No matter what I did, figure, landscape, still-life, it all seemed different from what I meant—from what I knew, as surely as my name was Eben Adams, was the thing I really wanted to say in the world; to tell people about, somehow, through my painting.

I cannot tell you what that period was like; because the worst part of it was an anxiety it is very hard to describe. I suppose most artists go through something of the sort; sooner or later it is no longer enough for them just to live—to paint, and have enough, or nearly enough, to eat. Sooner or later God asks His question: are you for Me, or against Me? And the artist must have some answer, or feel his heart break for what he cannot say.

One evening in the winter of 1938 I was walking home through the Park. I was a good deal younger then; I carried a portfolio of drawings under my arm, and I walked slowly because I was tired. The damp mist of the winter evening drifted around me; it drifted down across the sheep meadow, and through the Mall which was empty and quiet at that hour. The children who usually played there had gone home, leaving the bare, dark trees and the long rows of benches wet and spidery with mist. I kept shifting the portfolio from one arm to the other; it was heavy and clumsy, but I had no money to ride.

I had been trying all day to sell some of my pictures. There is a sort of desperation which takes hold of a man after a while, a dreadful feeling of the world's indifference, not only to his hunger or his pain, but to the very life which is in him. Each day the courage with which I started out was a little less; by now it had all run out, like sand from a glass.

That night I was at the bottom, without money or friends, cold, hungry, and tired, without hope, not knowing where to turn. I think I was a little lightheaded, from

106

not having had enough to eat. I crossed the Drive, and started down the long, deserted corridor of the Mall.

In front of me, the spaced, even rows of lights shone yellow in the shadowy air; I heard the crisp sound of my own footsteps on the pavement; and behind me the hiss and whisper of traffic turned homeward at the end of day. The city sounds were muted and far away; they seemed to come from another time, from somewhere in the past, like the sound of summer, like bees in a meadow long ago. I walked on, as though through the quiet arches of a dream. My body seemed light, without weight, made up of evening air.

The little girl playing by herself in the middle of the Mall made no sound either. She was playing hopscotch; she went up in the air with her legs apart, and came down again as silent as dandelion seed.

I stopped and watched her, for I was surprised to see her there, all alone. No other little children were in sight, only the mist and the long, even rows of lights stretching away to the terrace and the lake. I looked around for her nurse, but the benches were empty. "It's getting pretty dark," I said. "Oughtn't you to go home?"

I don't believe it sounded unfriendly. The child marked her next jump, and got ready; but first she looked at me sideways over her shoulder. "Is it late?" she asked. "I don't know time very well."

"Yes," I said; "it's late."

"Well," she said, "I don't have to go home yet." And she added in a matter of fact tone,

"Nobody's ready for me."

I turned away; after all, I thought, what business is it of mine? She straightened up, and pushed the dark hair back from her face, under the brim of her bonnet. Her arms were thin, they made the sharp, bird-like motions of a child. "I'll walk a ways with you, if you don't mind," she said. "I guess it's a little lonesome here all by myself."

I said I didn't mind, and we went up the Mall together, between the empty benches. I kept looking around for

There is a muted quality in this scene. Think of it as the opening frames of a motion picture when the credits are being shown.

107

someone she might belong to, but there was nobody. "Are you all alone?" I asked after a while. "Isn't anybody with you?"

She came to some chalk marks left there by another child, and stopped to jump over them. "No," she said. "Who would there be?

"Anyway," she added a moment later, "you're with me."

And for some reason that seemed to her quite enough. She wanted to know what I had in the portfolio. When I told her, she nodded her head in a satisfied way. "I knew they were pictures," she said. I asked her how she knew.

"Oh, I just knew," she said.

The damp mist drifted along beside us, cold, with the smell of winter in it. It was my not having eaten all day that made everything seem so queer, I thought, walking up the Mall with a little girl no higher than my elbow. I wondered if I could be arrested for what I was doing; I don't even know her name, I thought, in case they ask me.

She said nothing for a while; she seemed to be counting the benches. But she must have known what I was thinking, for as we passed the fifth bench, she told me her name without my asking. "It's Jennie," she said; "just so's you'll know."

"Jennie," I repeated, a little stupidly. "Jennie what?"

"Jennie Appleton," she said. She went on to say that she lived with her parents in a hotel, but that she didn't see them very often. "Father and mother are actors and actresses," she declared. "They're at the Hammerstein Music Hall. They do juggling on a rope."

She gave a sort of skip; and then she came over to me, and put her hand in mine. "They're not home very much," she said; "on account of being in the profession."

But something had begun to worry me. Wait a minute, I said to myself, there's something wrong here. Wait, I thought . . . wait a minute . . . and then I remembered.

108

Of course—that was it: the Hammerstein Music Hall had been torn down years ago, when I was a boy.

"Well," I said; "well . . ."

Her hand in mine was real enough, firm and warm; she wasn't a ghost, and I wasn't dreaming. "I go to school," she said, "but only in the mornings. I'm too little to go all day yet."

I heard her give a child's sigh, full of a child's trouble, light as air. "I don't have very exciting lessons," she remarked. "They're mostly two and two is four, and things like that. When I'm bigger, I'm going to learn geography and history, and about the Kaiser. He's the King of Germany."

Try to determine the time period.

"He was," I said gravely. "But that was long ago."

"I think you're wrong," said Jennie. She walked a little away from me, smiling to herself about something. "Cecily Jones is in my class," she said. "I can fight her. I'm stronger than she is, and I can fight her good."

"She's just a little girl."

She gave a skip. "It's fun having somebody to play with," she said.

I looked down at her: a child dressed in old-fashioned clothes, a coat and gaiters and a bonnet. Who was it painted children like that? Henri? Brush? One of the old fellows. . . . There was a picture in the Museum, somebody's daughter, it hung over the stairs as you went up. But children always dressed the same. She didn't look to me as though she played with other children very often.

Eben always "sees" things from an artist's point of view.

I said yes, I supposed it was fun.

"Don't you have anyone to play with?" she asked.

"No," I said.

I had an idea that she was sorry for me, and at the same time glad that I had nobody else but her to play with. It made me smile; a child's games are so real, I thought, for children believe everything. We came to an interesting crack, and she hopped along on one foot until she got to the end of it. "I know a song," she said. "Would you like to hear it?"

Where on this page does the mystery really begin?

109

And without waiting for me to answer, looking up at me from under the brim of her bonnet, she sang in a clear, tuneless voice:

"Where I come from
Nobody knows;
And where I'm going
Everything goes.
The wind blows,
The sea flows—
And nobody knows."

Does the song extend—or alter—the mood built up so far?

The song caught me off my guard, it was so unlike what I had expected. I don't know what I had been waiting for—some nursery rhyme, perhaps, or a popular tune of the day; little girls whose parents were actors and actresses sometimes sang about love. "Who taught you that?" I asked in surprise.

But she only shook her head, and stood there looking at me. "Nobody taught me," she said. "It's just a song."

We had come to the great circle at the end of the Mall, and my path led away to the left, across the Drive again, and out the west gate. The winter evening wrapped us round in mist, in solitude and silence, the wet trees stood up dark and bare around us, and the distant city sounded its notes, falling and fading in the air. "Well, goodbye," I said; "I have to go now."

I held out my hand to her, and she took it gravely. "Do you know the game I like to play best?" she asked. "No," I said.

"It's a wishing game."

I asked her what she wished for most.

"I wish you'd wait for me to grow up," she said. "But you won't, I guess."

A moment later she had turned and was walking quietly back down the Mall. I stood there looking after her; after a while I couldn't see her any more.

When I got home I heated a can of soup on the gas

110

burner, and cut myself a slice of bread, and some cheese. It was heavy in my stomach, but it made me feel better. Then I took my paintings out of the portfolio, and set them up on the floor, against the wall, and looked at them. They were all New England scenes: Cape Cod, churches, boats, old houses . . . watercolors, mostly, with a few drawings among them. But none of the city . . . funny that I had never thought of that before. . . .

I went over to the window, and looked out. There wasn't much to see, a line of roofs and chimneys, dark and indistinct, a few lighted windows, and in the north some taller buildings dim against the sky. And over all, the damp, cold air of winter, the raw, heavy air of the coast. A tugboat hooted in the bay; the sad, mysterious sound passed over the roofs, and floated above the city's restless grumble like a sea bird over a river. I wondered why I had never wanted to do any pictures of the city. . . . I could do some pastels of the river, I thought, if I could get the cold tone of the sky. And that line of buildings south of the Park, in the evening—if I could get that dim blue mountain look they have. But all the time, in the back of my mind, I was thinking about the child I had met in the Mall. Where I am going, nobody knows; The wind blows, And nobody knows. It was a strange little song, its very tunelessness made it hard to forget, the tunelessness was so much a part of it.

I thought of the last thing she had said to me, before she turned and walked away. But people couldn't wait for other people to grow up; they grew up together, side by side, and pace by pace, one as much as the other; they were children together, and old folks together; and they went off together into that something that was waiting—sleep, or heaven, I didn't know which.

I shivered; the big gray dusty radiator in front of the window was only luke-warm. I should have to talk to Mrs. Jekes again, I thought. But I felt suddenly sad, as though someone had just told me an old story about grief. There

111

was no use trying to work any more that night; I went to bed, to keep my courage up.

Chapter II

I was behind in my rent again. I think Mrs. Jekes would have asked me to leave, if she could have found anyone to take my place; but nobody wanted a studio like mine, with the furniture falling to pieces, and the ceiling dusty with age. Just the same, she took what I had to say about the heat in very bad part. "This isn't a hotel," she said. "Not for what you pay, it isn't.

"That is," she added grimly, "when you pay it."

I used to dread my meetings with her. She would stand there in front of me, her mouth tight, her thin hands folded across her stomach, and a look in her eyes as though she were seeing through me into the future, and finding it as hopeless as the past. You may wonder that I didn't leave and go somewhere else; but the truth is, I had nowhere else to go. Cheap studios were hard to find; and besides, I was almost always in arrears, and so much without hope myself, those days, that I stayed on because I didn't believe that anything else would be any better.

It was a time of depression everywhere. Hatreds clashed and fought in the air above our heads, like the heavenly battles of angels and demons in the dawn of creation. What a world for a painter; a world for a Blake, or a Goya. But not for me. I was neither—neither mystic nor revolutionary; there was too much of my mid-western father in me for the one, and too much of my New England grandmother for the other. Yet their heaven had been bright with faith.

I believe that Mrs. Jekes admired my paintings, although she never said so. She used to stand and look at them, with her tight mouth and folded hands; and once she accepted a sketch of the town landing on the Pamet River in Truro, in place of a week's rent. It would fetch a

World War II is threatening.

William Blake and **Francisco Goya:** eighteenth-century artists famous for depicting death and the realities of war.

much bigger price today, I suppose, but I doubt if she knows it. Nor do I know what she saw in it—some memory, perhaps, of sunnier days. I had tried to put the stillness of summer into it, the peace of the ever-moving river, the quiet of old boats deserted in the grass. Perhaps she saw it there, too—or only guessed; I don't know.

She didn't care for my pictures of the city. Now that I look back at it, I can see that they were only an old story to her—only the city, in which she was caught like a fly in molasses. What did she care for the cold sky above the river, or the mountain blue of the windy, shadowy streets? She knew them only too well; she had to live her life with them.

But I was full of hope; it lasted for three days. By the end of that time, I had found out that I could not sell my city sketches, either.

It was late in the afternoon of the fourth day that the turn came. I didn't think of it then as a turn; it seemed to me just a piece of luck, and no more.

I was on my way home from tramping about the streets, my drawings under my arm, when I found myself in front of the Mathews Gallery. I had never been there before; it was a small gallery in those days, on one of the side streets off Sixth Avenue. There was a show going on, of some young painter's work—mostly figures and flower-pieces; and I went in more or less out of curiosity. I was looking around when Mr. Mathews came up to me, and asked me what I wanted.

I know Henry Mathews very well by now, I know all about him. In fact, it was he who sold my "Girl in a Black Dress" to the Metropolitan six years ago. I know him to be both timid and kind; he must have hated to see me come in, for he knew at once that I wasn't there to buy anything. But it was getting late, and he wanted to close up; and so he had to get rid of me. Miss Spinney ran the office for him in those days, too; she had gone home, otherwise he would have sent her out to talk to me. She

How is Mrs. Jekes described? Why is the comparison apt?

It is important to understand that Eben is telling the story in retrospect. Look for other evidence of this perspective.

113

knew how to deal with people who wanted to sell him something.

He came out of his little office at the rear of the gallery, and smiled at me uncertainly. "Yes, sir," he said; "what can I do for you?"

I looked at him, and I looked down at the portfolio under my arm. Oh well, I thought, what's the difference? "I don't know," I said; "you could buy one of my pictures, perhaps."

Mr. Mathews coughed gently behind his hand. "Landscapes?" he asked.

"Yes," I said; "mostly."

Mr. Mathews coughed again; I know that he wanted to say to me, My dear young man, there's not a chance. But he could not bring himself to say it; for he dreaded the look in people's eyes when he had to say no. If only Miss Spinney had not gone home—she would have sent me about my business in short order.

"Well," he said doubtfully, "I don't know. Of course, we buy very little . . . almost nothing . . . and the times being what they are . . . However, let me see what you have. Landscapes. Hmm . . . yes; too bad."

I undid the strings of my portfolio, and propped it up on a table. I had no hope of anything, but even to be allowed to show my work was something. It was warm in the gallery, and I was cold and tired. "Those are some studies from down on Cape Cod," I told him. "That one is the fisheries at North Truro. That's Cornhill. That's the church at Mashpee."

"Landscapes," said Mr. Mathews sadly.

All the tiredness, the hunger, the cold, the long waiting and disappointment, caught me by the throat, and for a moment I couldn't speak. I wanted to take my pictures, and go away. Instead, "Here are one or two sketches of the city," I said. "There's the bridge—"

"What bridge?"

"The new one," I said.

Mr. Mathews sighed. "I was afraid of it," he said.

114

"And here's a view from the Park, looking south. . . . "

"That's better," said Mr. Mathews wanly. He was trying not to look too discouraging; but I could see that he was unhappy. He seemed to be wondering what on earth to say to me. Well, go on, I thought to myself, why don't you say it? Tell me to get out. You don't want any of these. . . .

"There's the lake, with ducks feeding. . . . "

All of a sudden his eyes lighted up, and he reached out for the portfolio. "Here," he cried; "what's that?"

I looked, myself, with curiosity at the drawing he had in his hand. "Why," I said uncertainly, "that's not anything. That's only a sketch—it's just a little girl I met in the Park. I was trying to remember something. . . . I didn't know I'd brought it along with me."

"Ah," said Mr. Mathews happily; "but still—this is different. It's good; it's very good. Do you know why I like it? I can see the past in it. Yes, sir—I've seen that little girl before, somewhere; and yet I couldn't tell you where."

He held it out in front of him; then he put it down, walked away, and came back to it again. He seemed a lot more cheerful; I had an idea that he was glad because he wouldn't have to send me away without buying anything. My heart began to beat, and I felt my hands trembling.

"Yes," he said, "there is something about the child that reminds me of something. Could it be that child of Brush's up at the Museum?"

I drew in my breath sharply; for a moment I felt again the dream-like quality of that misty walk through the Mall with Jennie. "Not that it's a copy," he said hastily, "or even the same child; and the style is very much your own. There's just something in each that reminds me of the other."

He straightened up briskly. "I'll buy it," he said. But all at once his face fell, and I could see that he was wondering what to pay me for it. I knew that it wasn't worth much, just a sketch done with a little wash . . . if he paid me what it was worth, I should hardly have enough for one decent meal. I am sure now, as I look back on it, that he was thinking so too.

"Look here, young man," he said. . . . "What's your name?"

I told him.

"Well, then, Mr. Adams, I tell you what I'll do. I'll take the girl—and that park scene—and give you twenty-five dollars for the pair."

My hands were trembling in good earnest now. Twenty-five dollars . . . that was a lot of money to me then. But I didn't want to seem too eager. What trouble we go to, trying to fool people who see right through us anyhow.

"All right," I said; "it's a deal."

Before he went back to his office to get me the money, he took a little pad out of his pocket, and wrote something down on it. I happened to glance at it where he had left it lying open on the table. It must have been the gallery expense account, for there were two columns of figures, marked Sales and Expenses. Under Sales he had written: 1 small etching, water scene, Marin, 2nd impression, $35; 1 colored print, blue flower-piece, Cézanne, $7.50; 1 litho, Le Parc, Sawyer, pear wood frame, $45.

Under Expenses he had written:

lunch, with beer	$.80
cigar	.10
hat check	.10
bus (both ways)	.20
stamps	.39
Spinney	5.00
flag from man in veteran's hat	.10
2 watercolors, Adams	15.00

For a moment my heart sank, for I had thought he had said twenty-five. But before I had time to feel too badly about it, he came out again with the full amount, two tens and a five. I tried to thank him, but he stopped me. "No," he said, "don't thank me; who knows, in the end I may have to thank you."

He gave me a timid smile. "The trouble is," he said,

Eben is saying that pretense is a considerable factor in the make-up of human beings. Do you agree?

116

"that nobody paints our times. Nobody paints the age we live in."

This is a very significant statement.

I murmured something about Benton, and John Steuart Curry. "No," he said, "we'll never find out what the age is like, by peering in a landscape."

I must have looked startled, for he coughed in a deprecating way. "Let me tell you something, Mr. Adams," he said. "Let me give you some advice. The world is full of landscapes; they come in every day by the dozens. Do me a portrait of the little girl in the Park. I'll buy it; I'll buy them all. Never mind bridges; the world is full of bridges. Do a great portrait, and I'll make you famous."

Clapping me timidly on the shoulder, he ushered me out into the cold winter air, blue with twilight. But I no longer knew whether it was winter or not. Twenty-five dollars . . .

It was not until long after that I found out the truth about that fifteen dollars in the expense account. It was all he thought they were worth, and he was afraid of what Miss Spinney would say in the morning. He meant to make up the difference out of his own pocket.

Chapter III

So swift is the hot heart of youth, that I thought I had already made a success, and wanted all the world to share it with me. That night I had supper at Moore's Alhambra, on Amsterdam Avenue; for all my glory, that was the best I could do for myself. As I came in, Gus Meyer, who owned the taxicab that used to stand at the corner of our street, waved to me from a table. "Hi, Mack," he exclaimed; "park yourself." He called everybody Mack; it was his way of telling people that they meant nothing to him personally; or else that he liked them.

"Well," he said, after I was seated, "how are you doing?" He had a big plate of pigsknuckles in front of

117

him, and a glass of beer. "The specialty today," he said; "you'd ought to have some."

Fred, the smaller of the two waiters, came over and I gave him my order. "I'm doing all right," I said to Gus. "I just sold two pictures to an art gallery."

His fork stopped halfway to his mouth; and he gaped at me. "You mean you got money?" he asked.

How does the author suggest different social classes?

He put his fork down, and shook his head in wonder. "I guess you probably had it coming to you," he said. "But don't lose it, now. Put it in a bank, like you read about in the advertisements."

I told him that most of it would have to go to my landlady, and he looked sorry for me. "An artist don't make so much," he remarked, to comfort me. "It's the same as me. You don't get a chance to lay nothing aside."

For a moment or two he gazed with a peaceful look at his plate. "I had six hundred dollars once," he remarked. "But I spent it."

Almost as an afterthought, he added, "I gave some of it to my mother."

And he returned to his eating, with an air of having finished off the matter.

"This is elegant pigsknuckles," he declared.

For a while we ate in silence. When he was finished, he pushed his empty plate away, and taking a wooden toothpick from a glass on the table, leaned back to remember, and to reflect.

"Some day," he said thoughtfully, "there'll be no more pigsknuckles, and no more beer. When that time comes, I don't want to be here, neither."

"I don't want to be here now," I said; "but I am."

"Well," he said, "you can't do nothing about that. Here you are, and here you stay. So what's it all about? I ask myself."

He gave his toothpick a long, careful look. "But I don't answer," he declared. "You're born poor, and you die poor; and if you got anything, they try to take it off you."

I made the obvious answer, that some men though

118

born poor died rich. "Then they got other troubles," said Gus. "I don't envy them. All I want is a new coil for the cab. She stalls on me."

"I want more than that," I said.

"You got the wrong idea," he said. "I had six hundred dollars once, and I spent it."

I reminded him that he had given some of it away to his mother.

"So what?" he said. "A feller's got a mother, he's got to look after her, don't he?"

"I don't know," I said. "I haven't got one."

"I'm sorry, Mack," said Gus. He remained downcast, and silent. "Maybe you're married," he said presently. I told him no.

"Well, you're young yet," he said. "Some day you'll meet up with the right one, and you'll be all set." He leaned forward, and looked at me earnestly. "You're a nice kid, Mack," he said. "Put your money in a bank, so when you meet up with the right one, you'll be all set."

I didn't want to talk about things like that. "Listen," I said; "I haven't any money. I never have had any. I just go along, and trust to God."

"Sure," he agreed; "sure. But that don't signify. What you want to ask yourself is, what does God think about it?"

It brought me up short, and made me feel a little uncomfortable. "I don't know, Gus," I said. "What do you think He thinks?"

The toothpick was well chewed out by now; he wrapped his legs around the rungs of his chair, and leaned back. "I wish I could tell you, Mack," he said; "I do indeed. Sometimes you'd almost think He don't know we're here at all. And then when it looks worst, you get a break; along comes a fare for Jersey City, or some drunk tips you what's left of a five dollar bill. That don't make you believe in God, but it shows which way the land lies."

"The pillar of fire," I said, "which went before the chosen people."

pillar of fire: *Exodus,* the second book of the Old Testament, tells how the Israelites—the chosen people—were led out of Egypt. God took the form of a pillar of smoke by day and of fire at night.

119

But Gus shook his head gloomily. "That was the toughest break we ever got," he said. He brought his chair down, and leaned forward across the table. "Listen, Mack," he said, "did you ever ask yourself what for were we chosen? How I see it is, we weren't chosen for no favors. We were chosen because we were tough; and He needed us like that, so we could tell the world about Him. Well, the world don't want to listen; they want it their way. So they kick us around. God don't care; He says, just keep on telling them."

"And Jesus?" I asked.

"He was a Jew, wasn't He?" said Gus. "He told them; and what did it get Him? If you did what Jesus said today, you'd be kicked around so fast you wouldn't know your tail from a hole in the ground."

He sat up and looked at me, a dark look, like one of the old prophets. "That's where we got a tough break," he said; "being chosen."

old prophets:
prophets in the Old
Testament.

"Have another beer," I said; "on me."

"Okay," he said. "I don't mind if I do."

Mr. Moore brought over our beer himself. He was a big man, stout and anxious. "How are you, Gus?" he said. "You look fine. Was everything all right?"

"Elegant," said Gus. "Meet my friend. What's your name, Mack?"

Mr. Moore and I shook hands, and he sat down at our table. "Mind if I sit with you for a minute?" he asked.

"Not at all," I said.

"Mack here is a artist," said Gus. "A painter. He just made a lot of money."

The proprietor of the Alhambra beamed at me. "Well, now," he said, "that's fine. You satisfied with everything?"

I said yes, that everything was fine.

"We got a nice little place here," said Mr. Moore, looking around slowly, as if he were seeing it all for the first time. "We try to have everybody satisified."

I felt warm and happy; it was good to be with people, to

120

talk about things without thinking all the time, What am I going to do now?

"You're in a good business, Mr. Moore," I said. "But I guess you know it."

He looked at me, suddenly cautious. "Well, now," he declared, "I don't know. We have a lot of trouble in this business, what with the unions and all. And food costs a lot. We don't make out any too good in this business. At night we don't fill half our tables. It's a lunch business mostly."

"You'd ought to brighten up the place," said Gus. "You take my cab; I give the old bus a going over once a week. Make it shine. That attracts the customers; they like things to look good."

"Sure," said Mr. Moore. "Only I can't afford it."

Gus broke his toothpick in half, and reached for another. "Mack here is a painter," he said. "Leave him paint you something."

Mr. Moore looked from Gus to me; he took up a bowl of sugar, and set it down again. "Well, now," he said, "that's an idea." But I could see that he was waiting to hear what I might have to say.

I thought it was a good idea, too, although it surprised me; it wasn't the sort of thing I would have thought of myself. "Of course," said Mr. Moore. "I couldn't pay much."

"All right," said Gus; "you can feed him, can't you?"

"Yes," said Mr. Moore thoughtfully; "I can feed him."

"Well, Mack," said Gus; "there's your meal ticket."

"It's a good idea," I said.

Mr. Moore gave me a sideways look. "Maybe you could paint me a little something over the bar," he said. "Something tasty, like you'd enjoy standing and looking at."

"He means something with dames in it," explained Gus. "You know—sitting in the grass without nothing on."

The restaurant owner moved uncomfortably; and his

fat face grew pink. "It ought to be ladies," he said, "on account of people being a little particular."

"A sort of modern 'Picnic in the Park,'" I said, nodding my head. "Yes."

He looked more uncomfortable than ever. "It has to be clean," he said. "Something that wouldn't get me into trouble."

I told him that I thought I knew what he wanted, and he looked grateful. "All right," he said; "go ahead. You can eat here while you're doing it, and afterwards, if it's all right, we can come to an agreement."

It was not a very business-like arrangement, but we shook hands, and he beckoned to the waiter. "Your little dinner was on me," he said, taking our bill and scribbling across it.

Characterize Gus.

When we got outside, Gus patted me on the shoulder. "You're in the money now, Mack," he said. I tried to thank him, but he waved it aside. "Listen," he said; "I got my own dinner out of it, didn't I?"

And as he climbed into his cab, he added with a chuckle, "Keep it clean, Mack."

What does this business arrangement tell you about Eben? Does it diminish him as an artist? Why or why not?

I went home thinking what a good world it was. That night I gave Mrs. Jekes the money for two weeks' rent I owed her, and a week's rent in advance. "What's the matter," she inquired; "you been robbing a bank?"

It didn't even spoil things any, to have her say that. "No," I said. "I'm doing some murals."

Chapter IV

It was on a Sunday morning that I saw Jennie again. There had been two or three weeks of clear, cold weather, and the big lake in the Park at Seventy-second Street was frozen, and good for skating. I took out my old pair of Lunns, and went over. The ice was crowded with skaters; I sat down on a bench by the shore to put on my skates, and strapped my shoes to my belt. I stepped off the edge in a wide glide, drew up in a turn that made the snow fly, and set off with the sun in my face.

It was one of those days of beautiful weather such as we get in New York in winter, with a blue-white sky, and light, high, white-gray clouds going slowly over from west to east. The city shone in the sun, roof-tops gleamed, and the buildings looked as though they were made of water and air. I struck out in a long stride, taking deep breaths, feeling young and strong, feeling the blood run warm in my veins, and the air cold and fresh on my face. Couples crossed me, going by with linked hands and red cheeks; schoolboys fled past, like schools of minnows, bent over, on racing skates, cutting ice and wind. An old gentleman was doing fancy figures by himself; dressed in brown, with a red woolen scarf, he swung forward, turned, jumped, and circled backward, his skates together in a straight line, knees bent, and arms akimbo, intent and proud. I stopped and watched him for a moment, and then went on again, into the sun. All around me was the quiet flow of skaters moving and gliding, the creaking sound of steel on ice, the cold air, the bright colors.

I found Jennie near the bridge between the two ponds. She was all in black velvet, with a short, wide skirt, and white boots attached to her round, old-fashioned skates. She was doing a figure eight; and none too well, I thought. But she seemed to me to be taller than I had remembered her—older, too; I wasn't even sure that it was she, until she looked up and saw me. "Hello, Mr. Adams," she said.

She coasted over to me, and put out her hands to stop herself. "I didn't know it was you," I told her. "You look older than last time." She smiled, and pressed the toe of one skate down into the ice to hold herself. "Oh well," she said; "maybe you didn't see me very good."

I don't know how long we stood there, smiling at each other. In a little while, Jennie put her arm in mine. "Come along," she said. "Let's skate."

We started off together arm in arm; and once again the

world around me grew misty and unreal. Skaters flowing like a river around us, the little flash of steel in the sun, the sound of that river moving, forms seen for a moment and then gone—our own quiet and gentle motion—all served to bring back to me a feeling I had had once before . . . that feeling of being in a dream, and yet awake. How strange, I thought. I looked down at the slender figure at my side; there was no question about it, she was taller than I had remembered.

Eben seems uneasy as he tries to reconcile what he remembers about Jennie with what he sees now.

"It seems to me," I said, "that you've grown a lot since I saw you."

"I know," she answered.

And as I said nothing, but only smiled uncertainly, she added seriously, "I'm hurrying."

She seemed as light as a feather beside me, but I could feel her arm in mine as we skated. I could see the wide black ripple of her skirt flare out as we swung along; and I wondered if we looked like something in an old print. "How are your parents?" I asked her. "Are they having a good season?"

"Yes," she answered. "They're in Boston now."

I thought: and they left you here all alone. But I suppose that's better than taking you everywhere with them. . . .

"I did a little sketch of you," I told her, "and I sold it. It brought me luck."

"I'm glad," she said. "I wish I could see it."

"I'll do one some day just for you," I said.

She wanted to know more about the sketch I had made. I told her about Mr. Mathews, and the portrait he had asked me to do; and about Gus, and the picture I was painting over Mr. Moore's bar. She wanted to see that, too; but it was the portrait for Mr. Mathews that interested her most. "Who will it be of?" she asked; I thought that her voice sounded almost too casual. "I don't know," I answered. "I haven't found out yet."

She skated along a moment or two without saying anything. Then, "Perhaps . . . " she said. And all at once,

124

in a breathless rush—"Will you let it be me?"

Of course, I thought . . . who else? I realized suddenly that there was no one else, that there never could be anyone else for the picture that Mr. Mathews wanted. If only she were a little older. . . .

"I don't know," I said. "Perhaps."

She gave my arm another squeeze, and made a wild swoop to the right. "Hooray," she cried; "I'm going to have my picture painted.

"Won't Emily be mad."

"Emily?" I asked.

"Emily is my best friend," she explained. "She had her picture painted by Mr. Fromkes, and I said you were going to do mine, and she said she'd never heard of you, and so I slapped her, and we quarreled."

"Well," I said. "But I thought it was Cecily you always fought with."

She looked away suddenly, and I felt her hand tremble on my arm. "Cecily died," she said in a whisper. "She had scarlet fever. Now my best friend is Emily. I thought you'd know."

"How would I know?" I asked.

She stumbled suddenly. "My shoe is untied," she said. "I've got to stop."

We coasted to the bank, and I knelt down to tie her shoelace. Kneeling there, I looked up at her, the flushed face of the child, framed in its dark hair, the brown eyes tenderly dreaming, lost in some other time, some other where and when. . . . I thought: she is playing at being Cinderella, or perhaps Snow White, so proud to have me kneeling in front of her, tying her shoelace.

We had come to shore near the little refreshment booth which they build each year for the skaters, and I asked Jennie if she would care to go in and rest, and if she would like a cup of hot chocolate. She came out of her dream with a long sigh; then her whole body began to quiver, and she clapped her hands gleefully. "Oh yes," she cried. "I love hot chocolate."

125

Which war do you think she has in mind? See the note on page 109.

Sitting at the counter together, while the hot, watery brew steamed under our noses, we talked about the weather and the world. She wanted to hear, all over again, about how I had sold the sketch of her to Mr. Mathews; and I for my part wanted to know how she was getting along in school. "It's all right," she said, but without much enthusiasm. "I'm having French."

"French?" I asked; startled, because the last time she had been just beginning her sums. "Yes," she said. "I can say colors, and I can count to ten. *Un, deux, trois, quatre . . .* I can say the war, in French. *C'est la guerre.*"

I couldn't make out what she was talking about. "The war?" I asked. "What war?"

But she only shook her head. "I don't know," she said. "It's just the war."

But then her eyes grew wide, and she looked at me in fright. "They won't hurt children like me," she asked; "will they?"

"No," I said. "No."

She took a deep breath. "That's good," she said. "I don't like being hurt."

And she dipped her little nose happily into the chocolate again.

I was happy, too, sitting there, with the air smelling of ice and damp wool, peppermint, and wet wood and leather; and Jennie next to me, drinking her chocolate. Perhaps there was something strange about it; but just the same, it felt altogether right, as though we belonged just there, where we were, together. Our eyes met in a glance of understanding; we looked at each other and smiled, as though we had both had the same thought.

"This is lots of fun," she said.

The chocolate was finished at last; we climbed down from our stools, and clumped our way to the door. "Come along," I said; "we've time for one more round." She took my arm, going down the steps to the ice. "I hate it to stop," she said, "because when will we ever have it again?"

126

We set off together, hand in hand, and made a grand tour of the lake; after that it was time for me to be getting back to work at the Alhambra. I said goodbye to her at the bridge between the two ponds, where we had met. But before I left, I wanted to get one thing straight in my mind.

"Jennie," I said, "tell me—when did Cecily die?"

She looked away; it seemed to me that her eyes grew clouded, and that her small face grew dim.

"Two years ago," she said.

Chapter V

"She has a look," I said, "of not altogether belonging to today."

I was showing Mr. Mathews some sketches I had made of Jennie in her skating costume, little pictures of the child in motion, doing an inner edge, or poised on her toes as though to run—the same sketches, as a matter of fact, which were shown last year at the Corcoran, as part of the Blumenthal collection. Miss Spinney was there, too, looking over his shoulder; it was my first meeting with her. I liked her dry voice, her sharp, frosty eyes, and her rough way of talking; for her part, she liked my sketches. When it came to painting and painters, there was no getting around Miss Spinney; she judged a man by his work, and nothing else; she wanted it, or she didn't want it.

Mr. Mathews held the sketches out at arm's length, with his head tilted back, looking at them down his nose. "This girl looks older to me than the first one," he said. "But I rather like it, on the whole. She was, perhaps, a little young, before . . .

"Yes," he said; "they aren't bad—are they, Spinney?"

"Is that all you can say?" remarked Miss Spinney. "That they aren't bad?"

Mr. Mathews tilted his head a little to one side, like a

This statement has more than one level of meaning.

127

bird. "The thing I like about them," he said, "is the way you've managed to catch that look of not belonging—how was it you said?—not altogether belonging to today. There ought to be something timeless about a woman. Not about a man—we've always been more present-minded."

"You can have the present," said Miss Spinney. "And you know what you can do with it."

Mr. Mathews, who was used to Miss Spinney, went right on. "I don't know what the matter is with women today," he said, sighing. "In my opinion, they lack some quality which they used to have—some quality of timelessness which made them seem to belong to all ages at once. Something eternal—you can see it in all the great paintings from Leonardo to Sargent. Did you ever stop to think how much more real and alive those long-dead women seem to us than the men? The men are done for—finished; there's not a one of them, except perhaps some of the Holbeins, that you'd ever expect to see in the world again. But the women—why, you could meet them anywhere. Mona Lisa, or Madame X . . . on the street, anywhere."

He looked at me accusingly. "The portrait of today," he said, as though it were all my fault, "is planted in the present as firmly as a potato."

"Have you seen Tasker's new portrait of Mrs. Potterly?" asked Miss Spinney.

Mr. Mathews coughed grimly behind his hand. "I understand he received three thousand dollars for it," he remarked.

"One thousand five hundred," said Miss Spinney, "and his trip to Florida."

"One cannot make a living at that rate," said Mr. Mathews.

At my hoarse croak, half-envy and half-derision, Miss Spinney turned to me and laid a warning hand on my arm. "Now, now, Adams," she said; "control yourself.

"You'll be getting that, too, some day."

128

It seemed fantastic to me then, fifteen hundred dollars for a portrait; I thought that Tasker must be either a genius or a scoundrel. A man changes his mind about such things as he grows older; but it made me feel bold, and—as I look back at it now—probably a little reckless, too.

"All right," I said; "in that case, what do I get for my sketches?"

"Spinney," murmured Mr. Mathews, "you talk too much."

And Miss Spinney replied almost at the same moment, "They are hardly worth anything at all."

It was a cruel way to take me down, though I dare say I deserved it. I picked up my sketches, and started to put them away.

"My dear young man," began Mr. Mathews unhappily. "Look here. . . . "

But I meant to carry it off with a high hand. "Goodbye," I said; and to Miss Spinney, "I'm very glad to have met you."

She looked at me for a moment with eyes like black frost. I thought she was going to help me to the door, but all at once, to my surprise, her face grew warm and rosy, and she burst out laughing. "I like you, Adams," she said, and fetched me a terrific clip on the back. "You're proud, aren't you?

"Come along—take them out again, and let's have a look at them."

She went over them a lot more carefully than Mr. Mathews had done; for one thing, she seemed less interested in Jennie, and more interested in my drawing. Mr. Mathews watched her in a timid sort of way; he wanted her to like them, because that would help him to feel right about me. He kept drumming with his fingers on the table, and clearing his throat.

Why is she less interested in Jennie than the other two are?

"I suppose it could be the clothes," he said, "that make her look a little older."

I didn't think so, but I didn't know how to say what I

thought; I stood there feeling uneasy, feeling my heart beating a little fast, and wondering what Miss Spinney would say. She put the sketches down at last, and gave me a clear, hard look. "All right, Adams," she said; "we'll give you twenty-five dollars for the lot."

I suppose I might have taken it, if I had been able to forget her remark about the sketches not being worth anything. I was still a little angry, and I wanted to stand up to her. I was young; and I didn't know very much about art dealers. "It isn't enough," I said; and I got ready to go.

I thought to myself that I didn't care, that I'd sell them to somebody else. But I did care, and I had no way of hiding it. "Look, Adams," she said; "you're a nice boy, but you don't know the art business. I know you can paint; but we aren't collectors, we don't buy things we like just for the fun of sitting around and looking at them the rest of our lives. If we buy these sketches, we've got to sell them, too. We can give you thirty dollars. What do you say?"

"Yes," said Mr. Mathews eagerly; "what do you say, young man?"

I took a deep breath, and said "Fifty dollars."

Miss Spinney turned slowly away; I thought that she was angry, and I thought what a fool I was being. I was stubborn, but I was unhappy; I looked at Mr. Mathews, but he was looking at Miss Spinney, and drumming on the table. I started to say, "All right, take them," but she didn't wait for me. "The hell with it," she said. "Give him the fifty."

Mr. Mathews jumped with relief. "That's right, Spinney," he exclaimed. "That's right; I'm glad you see it my way."

She shrugged her shoulders. "I'm just a potato, Henry," she said, "with nothing eternal about me. You'll have to sell them yourself."

"Yes," he said. He took up the sketches, looked at them, put them down, and then picked them up again. "Yes," he said; "yes, of course. I'll sell them—never

130

fret; I'll find a customer for them. Not right away, per-haps . . . "

They gave me fifty. It doesn't seem important now, but it did then. I was getting my meals at Moore's Alhambra, and so it seemed like a fortune to me, almost as much as Tasker's fifteen hundred. I suppose it seemed like such a lot because it was my own. It was real, and I could spend it.

Before I left, Mr. Mathews spoke to me again about doing a portrait for him, but this time he said in so many words that he wanted it to be of Jennie. "There's some-thing in the girl," he declared, "reminds me of some-thing. . . . I haven't placed it yet, but I can tell you what it feels like. It feels like when I was young."

He looked up at me apologetically. "I don't know if I can express it any other way," he said. "I shouldn't think you'd understand."

But I thought I understood. "Do you mean that she's old-fashioned?" I asked.

"No," he said, "that isn't what I mean. Not altogether."

"Well, I do," I replied. "I think she's old-fashioned."

Miss Spinney saw me to the door. "Goodbye," she said; "come in again. And if you have any nice flower-pieces, about two or two-and-a-half by four . . . " She looked around for Mr. Mathews, and seeing him behind her with his back turned, lowered her voice to a whisper. "I like flower-pieces," she said.

What are Miss Spinney's personal strengths? Mr. Mathews'?

I went over to Fifth Avenue, because that was the avenue I wanted to walk on. For the first time I felt that it was my world, my city, that it belonged to me, to my youth and to my hopes; there was a taste of exultation in my mouth, and my heart, filled with joy, lifted like a sail and carried me along with it. The windy, high walls over my head, the wide and gleaming shop windows strung out before me with their mingled colors, the women's bright, hard faces, and the sun over everything—the sun and the wind—

I thought of Jennie's song. And then I thought to

myself that I didn't know where she lived, or even how to find her; and the light went out of everything.

Chapter VI

"So what you want," said Gus, "is I should find a girl whose name is Jennie. You don't know where she lives, nor nothing about her. So you've got what I would call a good start."

"Her parents are jugglers," I told him. "On a tight-rope."

"That makes it easier," he said. "Are they on the circuit?"

I didn't know. I told him that their name was Appleton.

"Appleton," he grumbled; "Appleton." He set himself to think for a moment. "There used to be an act called by that name," he declared. "Down at the old Hammerstein."

"That's right," I said eagerly. "That's where they were."

Gus looked at me strangely. "Well, then, Mack," he said, "they'd be in the old folks' home by now. This must be some other people.

"You sure you seen this girl?"

"Yes," I said. "I made some sketches of her."

He shook his head uncertainly. "That don't signify," he remarked. "I was thinking maybe you made her up."

"No," I said. "I didn't make her up."

We were standing in front of his cab, on the corner, in the gray, raw, morning air. There was snow coming. I could smell it back of the wind, and I shivered a little. But Gus, in his two tattered sweaters, one over the other, didn't seem to feel it; he was used to cold, as he was to heat; he made me think of some old fisherman at Truro, whipped by years of weather, blackened and toughened by the sea. But there was no clear salt for Gus; his tides and channels were the streets, and his face was a city face pale, quick to anger, quick to rejoice, alert, sly, and

132

confident. None of the slow brooding of the ocean there, the patient, sea-way thought . . .

"I'll take a look around if you want," he said, "and ask some people I know. But listen, Mack—" his voice sank to a low and urgent level—"don't go getting into any trouble with the police. A girl as young as that—

"I don't want no trouble myself, neither," he added as an afterthought.

"All I want to do," I said, "is to paint her picture."

And I thought that was all; I would have sworn that was all I wanted.

Back in my studio again, I tried to work. I was doing a fair-sized canvas of the lake with the skaters on it, from memory and from some sketches, but it was hard to get on with. My heart wasn't in it; my mind flew off in a dozen directions at once. I kept wondering whether I oughtn't to start a flower-piece for Miss Spinney, and whether Gus would be able to find out anything about the Appletons; and I kept thinking about the Alhambra, about my picture over the bar; there was still a lot of work to be done on it. I was restless and uneasy, my brush was uncertain, and the light was poor. I was glad when it was lunch time, and I could put my things away, and go out.

Gus wasn't at the restaurant when I got there. I ate by myself, and then put up my step-ladder back of the bar, and went to work. He came in after I had been working about an hour, and sat down at a table where he could watch me. I looked down at him anxiously, but he shook his head.

"No luck, Mack," he said. "I'm sorry."

"Didn't you find out anything at all?" I asked. He looked back at me with a strange expression on his face. "There were some Appletons did a tight wire act, like I thought," he said, "back in 1914. They had a sort of accident; it seems the wire broke on them one day, back in '22."

We stared at each other for a moment, and then the waiter came with his beer. Gus took a long drink, and,

Can you explain this reaction?

133

leaning back, gazed solemnly up at my picture. "It's coming along fine," he said.

I had painted a picnic by the shore of a lake not unlike the lake in the Park; and there, by the side of the water, under the trees, my women were gathered to tease and gossip on the grass. They were innocent figures, and I knew that Gus thought that they could do with some men. To that extent he was a realist; but he did not go to extremes. What he asked of a picture was simply this: that it should remind him with the clearest force of what he already knew, along with some further suggestion of a better and a happier world.

"Yes, sir," he declared; "when I see things like that, I think I've been wasting my time."

All at once he sat up in his chair, and pointed to the figure of a young woman lying on her side, her face half turned away, at the edge of the water. "What's the matter with that one?" he demanded. "She don't look so good to me."

"Why?" I asked carelessly, without looking up. "What's the matter with her?"

"She looks drowned," said Gus.

I turned quickly back to the picture. "What do you mean?" I said. But even as I spoke, I saw what he meant; there was something about the way I had placed her under the trees which made her face seem dim, and green with leaf-shadow; her dark hair gave the impression of being wet, and her whole body seemed shadowy with water. . . . I felt an indefinable anguish as I looked at it, which I attributed to anger at my own lack of skill; and reached hurriedly for my tube of raw umber.

Why is Eben disturbed by Gus' criticism? How would you account for the drowned effect?

But even after I had brought her out into the sun again, I felt a depression which I could not account for. It was that figure, half-seen, half-hidden, which I had imagined secretly in my heart to be Jennie—as she would some day be—and I could not bear to think that brush and heart had so failed each other.

However, Mr. Moore was well satisfied with the picture.

"Well, now," he said, coming over and looking up at me where I sat on my step-ladder, "that's just about what I wanted. Yes, sir, that's what I had in mind. I'd call it entertaining, but it don't offend. I've got a spot over the service door I've been thinking about; we could maybe do a little something there."

"What's the matter," said Gus; "you want a museum?"

"I like to have it nice here," said Mr. Moore. "A picture brightens things up for the customers."

"All right," said Gus; "tell him to do one of me and my cab. That'll be nice for you, and nice for me, too.

"Only make it look good," he added. "Don't drown me."

The first snow was falling as I went home, small flakes coming down slowly, twisting down through the gray levels of air, on the northeast wind. The whole city was gray under the heavy sky which seemed to press against me as I walked. I thought of the Cape, of how this storm must be already singing across the dunes, driving its wet snow in from the sea over the little houses huddled in their hollows, the foam breaking below the cliff at High Land, the thunder of surf filling the long nooks and valleys like the sound of trains rolling and rumbling behind the hills—the storm and the snow driving south, out of the black, empty, wrinkled ocean, out of Labrador, out of Greenland, waters dark with winter and night. How little we have, I thought, between us and the waiting cold, the mystery, death—a strip of beach, a hill, a few walls of wood or stone, a little fire—and tomorrow's sun, rising and warming us, tomorrow's hope of peace and better weather. . . . What if tomorrow vanished in the storm? What if time stood still? And yesterday—if once we lost our way, blundered in the storm—would we find yesterday again ahead of us, where we had thought tomorrow's sun would rise?

I let myself into the house, shaking the snow from my shoulders on the door sill. As I stood there in the hall, which was as cold and somber as myself, Mrs. Jekes came out of her parlor and looked at me with eyes in which there was suspicion, resentment, and a curious excitement. It was apparent that she had been waiting for me. "Well," she said; "there you are. Hah."

And she folded her hands virtuously in front of her.

I looked back at her without speaking. My rent was paid, and I couldn't think of any reason to be anxious. I had an idea that she disliked me, and that she was glad to have some bad news for me; but what she said next wasn't what I expected at all.

"You have a visitor," she said. "A young lady."

And as I only stared at her with my mouth open, she added harshly,

"Fine doings, I must say."

With a sniff of disdain, she turned to go back into her parlor again. "The young lady is waiting for you upstairs," she said, and closed the door, as though to say, "I wash my hands of all of it."

I went up slowly, puzzled and concerned, my heart beating fast. I had no friends, there was no one it could be. It seemed impossible that anyone should be waiting for me.

But I was wrong. I knew it even before I opened my door; some inner sense told me.

It was Jennie. She was sitting in the old chair near the easel, prim and upright, her hands tucked away in a little muff in her lap, her toes just touching the floor, a round fur bonnet like a little cake on the top of her head. I came in slowly, and leaned for a moment against the side of the door, looking at her. I felt almost weak with happiness.

"I thought maybe you wanted me to come, Eben," she said.

Chapter VII

She sat quietly in the big chair while I put away my brushes and went to look for something with which to make tea. Her gaze, moving slowly about, lingered on everything, the shabby furniture, the dusty walls, the

136

stacked canvases on the floor, the closet bursting with odds and ends of clothing, sketches, paints, cans, and broken boxes, the tumbled cot with its dilapidated blankets—all that I myself had never thought to look at very carefully, or even notice, before she came. But now I saw it all, and for the first time, as she did. Her eyes widened, and she took a long breath.

"I've never been in a studio before," she said. "It's lovely."

The tin kettle still had some water in it left over from the morning, so I lit the gas ring under it, and went to search in the closet for a box of crackers. "It's an awful place, Jennie," I said. "It's pretty dirty."

"Yes," she agreed, "it is. I didn't want to say it . . . but I guess as long as you said it first . . . "

She got up, and took off her bonnet and laid it with her coat and her muff very neatly on the chair. "I don't suppose you have an apron?" she asked. "And something to dust with?"

I looked at her in consternation. "You're not going to try to clean it?" I cried.

"Yes," she said. "While the water's boiling . . . "

All I could find was a towel and a clean handkerchief. She tied the handkerchief over her hair and under her chin, the way they do on the Cape, and took up the towel with an air of determination. Then, with her slender legs planted wide apart, she looked around once more like a general before a battle, and her face fell. "Oh goodness," she cried; "I don't know where to begin."

I found the crackers, and some lumps of sugar for the tea, and I went down the hall to rinse the cups in the basin. I peered over the bannisters as I went by, to see what I could see; sure enough, there was Mrs. Jekes standing very still in the hall below, listening with all her might. I wondered what she expected to hear, and let out a shrill whistle to show her what I was doing. She looked up, startled, and then scuttled back into her room again.

When I returned to the studio, Jennie was seated on

the floor, the dust-rag towel beside her, and my sketches of the city spread out around her. Smiling, she looked up at me as I entered, a dark smudge across her chin, and another along her arm between her wrist and elbow. "I was looking at these," she said. "Do you mind?"

I told her no, of course I didn't mind.

"They're beautiful," she said. "I think you're a very good artist. Only, some of them . . . " she held a small canvas up to the light . . . "I don't know where they are. I've never seen those places."

I glanced over her shoulder as she sat there on the floor. She was looking at a little picture I had done in tempera of the skyscrapers at Radio City. "Yes," I said; "well . . . they're new, I guess. They haven't been built very long."

"I guess that's it," she agreed.

She looked for a long time at the picture, holding it out toward the window, toward the last gray light of afternoon. "It's funny," she said at last, "how sometimes you've never seen things, and still, you know them. As though you were going to see them some time, and because you were going to see them you could remember what they looked like. That doesn't sound right, does it?"

"I don't know," I replied. "It sounds pretty mixed up."

"I guess so," she said. "I guess it does. You couldn't remember what you hadn't ever seen."

She sat with the picture on her lap, staring in front of her. It was almost dark by now in the room, the snow outside, falling more heavily, making a **gray** light in the window, and everything in shadow. She seemed to be gazing through the shadows themselves into some other where, somewhere far off and strange, for her bosom rose and fell, her lips parted, and a long sigh escaped her. The snow, caught in a sudden rift of wind, made a soft, spitting sound on the windowpane, and in the river somewhere a boat sounded its lonely hoot. She stirred uneasily; her hand crept up and touched mine. "No," she said in a whisper; "you couldn't possibly."

I went over and snapped on the lights, and the bare, untidy room sprang out of the gloom at us, harsh and real, its four stained walls holding the present in a cube of unmoving light. Jennie gave a sort of cry, and rose to her feet. "What a silly," she said; "here I haven't dusted hardly at all."

"Never mind," I told her; "the water's boiling. Let's have our tea."

She was all gayety after that, sitting up in the chair again, with her toes barely touching the floor, pouring water out of the rusty kettle, passing the crackers, and talking happily about a thousand things. I had to tell her all about Miss Spinney, who had such a hard heart and liked flower-pieces, and how we had fought over the sketches, and I had won; and she clapped her hands with excitement. "Oh, Eben," she cried, "you are a good one." She wanted to hear about Gus and his taxicab; she thought he must be very rich to have a cab of his own. "Do you think some time he'd let me ride in it?" she asked. "I've never ridden in a taxicab.

"But I've been in a hansom, once, with mother in the Park; the driver sat up on top, and had a high hat."

She told me that her friend Emily was going away to boarding school. "I think perhaps I'll go with her," she said. "It's a convent, really, called St. Mary's, but it isn't Catholic. It's on a hill, and you see the river; and Emily says they go out every Easter and bless the pigs. I don't want to go very much, but mother says I have to, and anyway, Emily's going. . . . I'll miss you, Eben."

"I'll miss you, too, Jennie," I said. "Will you pose for me, before you go?"

"I was hoping you'd say that," she answered. "Yes, I will."

"Will you come tomorrow, then?"

But she looked away, and her face took on a puzzled expression. "I don't know," she said. "I don't know if I can."

"The day after?"

She shook her head. "I'll come as soon as I can," she answered; and that was all she would say.

I told her about Tasker's portrait of Mrs. Potterly, and the great price—as it seemed to me—he had got for it. Her face lit up, and she gave a little laugh. "Will you be glad to be so rich?" she asked. "You mustn't forget me."

"Forget you?" I cried incredulously.

"Oh well," she said; "when you're rich and famous.

"But I guess you won't," she added contentedly. "Because maybe I'll be rich and famous, too, and we can be it together."

I said, "I don't think I care very much about being rich, Jennie. I just want to paint—and to know what I'm painting. That's what's so hard—to know what you're painting; to reach to something beyond these little, bitter times. . . . "

"Are these bitter times, Eben?" she asked in surprise.

I stared at her, thinking: of course, how would she know about bitterness, how would she know about the artist at all? caught in a mystery for which he must find some answer, both for himself and for his fellow men, a mystery of good and evil, of blossom and rot—the mystery of a world which learns too late, always too late, which is the mold, and which the bloom . . .

She had been watching my face, and now she held out the box of crackers to me. "Here," she said, "take one. Then you won't feel so bad." I burst out laughing at myself, at both of us; and she laughed, too.

But presently she grew serious again. "You're not sad any more, are you, Eben?" she asked. "I mean—you were so sad the first time I saw you."

"No," I said, "I'm fine now. I was scared that night I met you. I felt as though I were lost. . . . "

She cowered down in her chair, and put her hands up as though I were about to strike her. "No," she cried out. "Oh no—don't ever say that, not ever again. And besides, you weren't lost—you were here, and here isn't lost. It can't be; it mustn't be. I couldn't bear it."

Can you explain Jennie's reaction?

140

And turning to me almost piteously, she added, "We can't both of us be lost."

It lasted only a moment, and then it was gone—and we were back again, in my room, with the yellow-lighted walls, and the gray snow outside, and my pictures spread out on the floor about me, the world I knew, the world I saw every day real and around me. "No," I said, "I'm not lost. Why should I be?

"What a foolish way to talk."

She smiled up at me in a forlorn sort of way. "Yes," she said; "it's foolish. Don't let's talk like that any more."

"Because," I said, "with little girls like you . . . "

"Yes," she agreed gravely; "little girls like me." She got up, and gave me her cup, and the tea pot. "Here," she said. "You go and wash them out, before you forget."

"All right," I said. "Wait for me; I'll be right back."

"Yes," she said. "I'll wait for you."

I went down the hall; it was dark on the stairs; the door of Mrs. Jekes' parlor was tight shut. I could hear the snow pitting down on the skylight in the roof. I rinsed the cups out, and hurried back. "Jennie," I said.

But she was gone; and the room was empty. I hadn't heard her go; I hadn't heard the hall door close. But she was gone.

It wasn't until later that I remembered that I hadn't even asked her where she lived.

In what sense does Jennie feel lost? Eben? How is each helping the other?

Chapter VIII

Review the situation at this point. What people have been introduced? What is their relationship to each other?

After the storm, the city sparkled for a little while; then the snow was gone, upgathered in hard white hills and carted off in trucks to the river. For a day the air was full of winter sounds, the sounds a child remembers from his youth—the wooden tock of shovels on the ice, the clink of picks, the whine and whirr of motors, and the little musical note of chains over the snow. I did a sketch of the river, with its swift and leaden current, and a little

141

oil painting of the Park, with children coasting. But mostly I was content to do nothing, to wander in the city, and to let my mind drift where it pleased. I kept thinking about the portrait I wanted to do of Jennie, and wondering when I would see her again. I no longer thought of her as a child. She seemed to me at that time to be of no particular age, or at that age between ages when it is impossible to say that the child is a young lady, or that the young lady is still a child. From the mystery which surrounded her, my mind hung back, my thoughts turned themselves away. It was enough for me to believe that wherever in this world she actually belonged, in some way, for some reason, she belonged with me.

Even if I had known, it could have made no difference; I can see that now. It was not in my hands, nothing was in my hands; I could not bring the spring nearer before its time, I could not keep the winter from vanishing behind me.

Sometimes in late summer or in early fall there is a day lovelier than all the others, a day of such pure weather that the heart is entranced, lost in a sort of dream, caught in an enchantment beyond time and change. Earth, sky, and sea are in their deepest colors, still, windless, and shining; the eye travels like a bird out across the distance, over the motionless air. All is fixed and clear, never to end, never to change. But in the evening the mist rises; and from the sea comes the gray warning.

In Truro they call it a weather breeder. So it was with me; it seemed to me that the entire world was bathed in a pure and peaceful light. Death had been arrested, and evil was far away; man's cries, the madness, the anguish, were stilled, and in the stillness, like far-off surf, I heard the sound of yet more distant things. Far beyond the close horizon of death, there is something else; beyond evil, some spirit untouched, untroubled, and remote.

Once upon a time, not so very long ago, men thought that the earth was flat, and that where earth and heaven

142

met, the world ended. Yet when they finally set sail for that tremendous place, they sailed right through it, and found themselves back again where they had started from. It taught them only that the earth was round.

It might have taught them more.

This short and happy season was made even happier for me by the visit of my friend Arne Kunstler, from Provincetown. He arrived one morning in his sheepskin jacket, big, red-faced, and bearded like an artist of the 'eighties. But the resemblance stopped with his beard; there was nothing else of the 'eighties about him. He brought a bundle of canvases down with him from the Cape, and set them up on stretchers in my room. The wild and violent pictures flamed at me from the walls and from the floor, like scenes from an inferno. Next to them, my own paintings seemed restrained and mild, colorless and discreet.

He was not pleased with me. "What is this work you are doing, Eben?" he cried. "Portraits—flower-pieces—what has come over you? Not," he added, "that you ever were on the way to being an important painter; but I always thought there was hope for you, at least."

His voice, like that of an old sea-captain, was always pitched at half a gale. Poor Arne, I never took him very seriously, for all his roaring; and as for his painting, I had long ago given up trying to understand it. But I was fond of him, for we had been students together; and I was delighted to see him. His mind was a cave of winds, blowing from all corners at once, a tempest of ideas; he was in love with color, he was like a Viking gone berserk in a rainbow. He lived on next to nothing: I doubt if he sold more than a canvas a year. But he was a happy man, for he never doubted his own genius. His wants were few; and his sorrows were vast, and without pain.

His favorite remark was this: "Art should belong to the masses." But when I declared that the masses would never understand his paintings, he stared at me in astonishment. "Understand?" he thundered; "under-

What is there about the personality of Arne that makes this statement from him seem appropriate? Do you agree with Arne or with Eben?

143

stand? Who asked them to understand?

"Art can have meaning only to the creative spirit itself.

"Besides," he added, "the masses aren't as stupid as you think. Look how they took to Homer."

"Not to his watercolors," I replied. "And anyhow, what in the name of heaven have you and Homer in common?"

Winslow Homer:
American painter
(1836–1910).

He couldn't answer that, of course. "Oh well," he mumbled, half in his beard, "I was only trying to show you. . . . But you'll see," he bellowed, "just the same."

He brought the past back with him, the old, free, careless days in the wind and sun of New England, the winter at the Atelier Dufoix in the Rue St. Jacques—the great cold shadowy room with its charcoal stove, and the shivering students, the evenings in the little bistro on the Boule Miche'—the early lessons here at the Academy, under Hawthorne and Olinsky—days of work, and nights of argument, when it was enough to settle forever such things as the eternal verities, and never stop to think of what was to become of the artist and his pictures. I took him to the Modern, to see the Modiglianis, and to the Ferargil, to see the single Brockhurst, my own favorite; but he was as contemptuous of the one as of the other, he had no use for any work except his own.

It was the city he admired most, and coming from the flat, windy winter on the Cape, he helped me to see with fresh eyes the soaring stone, the sun-drenched skylines, the brawling shadows all around me. And my heart, in which the old brew of doubt and anxiety had already begun to clear, stirred by hope, by the bright weather, and by something else which I did not know how to name, opened itself in a thrust of joy to the future.

Needless to say, Mrs. Jekes took an instant dislike to him. The very first night, she came hurrying up the stairs, pale and grim, to ask us to make less noise—though she did not so much ask us, as tell us, standing there in the doorway with her hands folded across her stomach, and her eyes steeped in bitterness. "I don't know what sort of a house you think this is," she said, "or what you think you're doing in it; but there's others want to sleep if you don't, and I can always call the police if I have to."

I can hardly blame her, for we were young, and happy, and we must have been making a lot of noise. I was afraid that Arne would throw something at her, but after one long, startled look, he only mumbled, "Yes, ma'am," and went off into a corner. After she had left, marching down the stairs with a tread like an army, I saw that he was pale, and actually uneasy. I started to laugh at him, but he stopped me. "No, Eben," he said, "you're wrong to laugh. That's a dreadful woman. She comes in here like black ice, and my pictures freeze over. Oh no, oh no, I am going to whisper from now on."

But although I laughed at him, I remembered what he said.

For a week or so, I roamed about the city with Arne, delighting in the fine weather, and in the companionship of my friend. I took him to the Alhambra where, I need hardly add, he thundered at my mural like Dufoix himself in the old days in Paris. In his opinion, I had painted a stupid and vulgar scene; nevertheless, with a plate of sauerbraten in front of him, he went so far as to consider the possibility of doing a panel himself, perhaps the one over the service door, in return for a week's good eating. Mr. Moore thought it over for a while, but after he had seen an example of Arne's work, he shook his head regretfully. "It's not that I don't think Mr. Kunstler is a fine artist," he said, "but I've got to think of the customers. I want everybody to be satisfied around here."

"Never mind," said Arne. "Forget it."

"Yes," said Mr. Moore. "Well, thanks for the offer."

It was Gus who did his best to console him. "Never mind, Mack," he said; "some people don't have no eye for anything but their food. Now you take me; I like to look at something pretty when I got the time. But you take most people, they don't feel that way. What they say is, bring in the soup, and get on with it."

"Forget it," said Arne. He waved his arm in a dignified

What insight into Mrs. Jekes' character provokes this response from Arne?

What light does this shed on Arne and his "Art should belong to the masses" theme?

145

way. "The artist ought not to have to paint for a living," he declared. "Eben, let us all have another glass of beer, and I will repay you some day when I am able."

"Ho," said Gus; "there's a man for you."

His big, red-knuckled hand wrapped around his glass, Arne beamed at us all. "Here's to art," he said.

"And to friends," I added.

"Any friend of Mack's here is a friend of mine," said Gus.

We dipped our noses into the yellow foam. "Just the same," said Arne in a mild bellow, coming up for air, "art can only mean something to the artist who creates it."

Chapter IX

Arne went back to Provincetown by boat and bus, leaving behind him by way of a gift, or to repay me for his bed and board, a picture of what he said was a sunset, all in such tones of light as had never been seen on earth before, at least not since the age of reptiles—and which, once his back was turned, I lost no time in hiding under the bed.

During the fortnight which followed, I was busy both at home and at the Alhambra. Among other things, I finished a flower-piece for Miss Spinney, and took it down to the gallery to give to her. As I had feared, Mr. Mathews groaned when he saw it. "Look here," he exclaimed; "whatever put that into your head? A flower-piece . . . and gladiolas, of all things. What do you expect me to do with it, young man?"

I replied that Miss Spinney had asked for it, and that gladiolas were all that I could get at the florist. "It's winter now," I reminded him. "There aren't any summer flowers."

"Spinney," said Mr. Mathews, "you will be my death." And he gave a cry of indignation.

"Never mind," said Miss Spinney calmly; "I like it. Give

Adams thirty dollars, and I'll sell it myself before the week is up."

But for once Mr. Mathews refused to be bullied. Faced with a flower-piece, he put his foot down. "Twenty-five," he said, like a mouse at bay, "and not a penny more."

Miss Spinney looked at him carefully; she knew when to insist, and when to give in. "All right," she said; "twenty-five, then. Is that enough, Adams?"

As a matter of fact, I would have let her have it for less than that, or for nothing. "It isn't enough," I said, "but I'll take it."

"You're hard as nails, aren't you?" she said with her wintry smile. "So am I. That's why I like you.

"Just the same," she added grimly, "we've lost money on you so far. So don't go getting ideas."

Mr. Mathews scratched his chin in an unhappy way. "Well, now," he said uncomfortably, "that isn't strictly true, Mr. Adams. I mean to say, we've only sold one sketch, but of course we still have the others."

"Forget it," said Miss Spinney. "Adams here is all right. He understands me."

Nevertheless, as I went out, she drew me aside and pressed a five dollar bill into my hand. "When I say thirty," she declared, "I mean thirty." I tried to give it back to her, but she pushed me out of the door. "On your way, Adams," she said; "on your way. Don't irritate me."

The next day I prepared a five-foot canvas; I stretched and mounted it, wet one side of it with water, and worked in a light surface of white lead with my palette knife. Then I set it out to dry. It was a trick Jerry Farnsworth had taught me up on the Cape.

After that there was nothing to do but wait.

Jennie came at the end of the week. I heard her light step on the stairs, and ran to open the door. She looked pale, I thought, and she was dressed in some kind of mourning. She stood in the doorway, and looked at me in a pitiable way.

"It's father and mother," she said. "They had an

accident." She tried to smile, but her eyes filled, and she had to wink hard to keep the tears back. "They're dead," she said, almost in surprise.

"I know," I answered, without thinking; and then bit my lip. I took her hand, and led her into the room. I thought that I ought to say something, that I ought to explain how I knew. . . . "I read about it," I told her. "In the paper."

"Oh," she said vaguely. "Yes." But she wasn't thinking about me.

I made her sit down, and took her hat and coat and laid them on the bed. "I'm sorry, Jennie," I said.

She drew a deep breath. "They were sweet to me," she said in a voice which trembled a little. "I didn't use to see them very much. But . . . the way they died . . . "

"I know," I said.

"Oh, Eben," she cried; and hid her face, and wept.

I wanted to comfort her; but I thought it would be better if I let her cry herself out. Turning my back, I walked over to the window, and stared at the deep blue sky. "Look," I said after a while; "you don't want to pose, do you? I mean—after this?"

I wasn't looking at her, but I could hear her sit up, and blow her nose. "I wanted to come," she said unevenly. "I wanted to see you. Just to be here." She gave a little hiccup, after crying; and then a shaky sigh. "I might as well pose," she concluded. "I don't look very pretty, though."

I thought that if anything, she looked prettier than before. The tears had left no mark on her young face, but they had washed her eyes and left them dark and dreaming. I placed her in the chair, and put a piece of old, yellow silk behind her, something I had bought years before in Paris. It took a long while to get the light to fall just as I wanted it, and to set my easel at the right angle; and all that time she just sat there quietly, staring in front of her, without saying anything. When I was satisfied that I had everything the way I wanted it, I set my canvas up, and began to work.

148

The picture I started that day needs no description, for most of you have seen it in the Metropolitan Museum, in New York. It is the picture of a girl somewhere in her early 'teens, seated in front of a golden screen. The Museum calls it "Girl in a Black Dress," but to me it has always been simply Jennie.

I worked in silence, almost in a dream, filled with a strange excitement. So lost was I in what I was doing, that I failed to keep track of the time; I must have been painting well over two hours, when I suddenly saw Jennie droop forward in her chair, and start to slip to the floor. I dropped my brush and ran to her, with my heart in my mouth. But when I lifted her in my arms, she opened her eyes, and smiled timidly up at me. "I'm tired, Eben," was all she said.

She seemed to me to weigh almost nothing. I laid her down on the bed, with her coat over her; and put some water on the stove to heat for tea. When it was ready I made her drink it, and a little color came back into her cheeks. "I'm better now," she said. "I'm not so cold. I can sit there again, if you want me to."

But of course I didn't want her to. "No," I declared, "it's time for you to rest. You've been the best kind of model; we've done very well, we've got a good start. There's lots of time."

She gave another little sigh, almost like a whisper. "No," she said, "there isn't. But I'll do as you say; I'll rest, if you say so."

Shivering a little, she lay back beneath her coat, with closed eyes, her night-dark hair spread out on my pillow, her hand cold as earth in mine. I stood looking down at her, the narrow curve of the young brow, the long lashes which rested so gently on the cheek beneath them; and I felt my heart contract with a sort of fear, and yet at the same time with delight. Who are you? I thought; and what has brought you here to me? . . . child and stranger, lost and lonely, out of some story in the past? . . .

My hands must have trembled a little, for she opened

How is Eben changing in the way he feels about Jennie?

149

Eben feels dismay at Jennie's dependence on him. Is this understandable? Why or why not?

her eyes and looked gravely up at me. "You're all I have now, Eben," she said.

At my start, half-surprise and half-dismay, she let go of my hand, and sat up, huddled under her coat, her thin arms wrapped around her knees. "Except for my aunt," she said, to reassure me. "Only I don't know her very well. She's going to take care of me from now on."

"Well," I said uncomfortably, "that's all right, then, isn't it?"

She looked at me beseechingly; it was her turn to ask for reassurance. "You do want me to come," she asked uncertainly, "don't you? To pose, I mean?

"You don't want me never to come again?"

I couldn't speak, but she must have seen in my face the answer to her doubts, for she smiled, and brushed the hair back from her face with the same gesture I had seen her use that first evening—how many years ago? —in the Mall.

"I'll come as soon as I can," she said.

"Jennie—" I began hoarsely.

"Yes, Eben?"

I looked away; after all, what was there to say? Nothing; I did not even know what I had been thinking. "Where does your aunt live?" I asked. At least, I thought, I shall know where she is, and then if I must, I can find her. But she shook her head. "What does it matter where I live?" she said. "You can't come to me.

"I can only come to you."

She spoke sadly, with exquisite gentleness, but with infinite finality. For a moment we looked at each other across a gulf of more than air—a gulf over which no soul had ever passed before, either to go or to return. . . . She made a little, helpless gesture, as though to reach out to me. And then the moment was gone, and she withdrew once more into herself, a stranger, dreaming of something I could not see.

But I knew then that we both knew.

After a while she got up and put on her hat and coat.

150

"Goodbye, Eben," she said. "I'll come back as soon as I can. I'll hurry—truly."

She looked up at me with eyes wide and dark and earnest. "I didn't want you to know," she said.

She turned once, in the doorway. "Try to wait," she whispered.

"Try to wait for me."

Chapter X

One must sometimes believe what one cannot understand. That is the method of the scientist as well as the mystic: faced with a universe which must be endless and infinite, he accepts it, although he cannot really imagine it. For there is no picture in our minds of infinity; somewhere, at the furthermost limits of thought, we never fail to plot its end. Yet—if there is no end? Or if, at the end, we are only back at the beginning again? . . .

Do you agree or disagree?

When Jennie returned, a fortnight later, I realized how much taller she had grown in the last few meetings. She was dressed in a uniform such as young ladies wear at a convent boarding school—a middy blouse, and a skirt which hung almost to her ankles. She came bounding up the stairs, and threw her hat on the bed. "Eben," she cried, "what fun."

For a moment I was thoroughly taken aback, for if I had expected anything at all, it was certainly not that. There was nothing to remind me of the last time I had seen her; in fact, there was nothing of the child about her at all, as far as I could see. On the contrary, she seemed to stand almost within the shadow of vigorous young womanhood. I thought: I must finish my portrait quickly, before it's too late. . . .

I couldn't avoid saying, "You've grown, Jennie. And those clothes . . . "

She looked down at herself, and laughed ruefully. "I know," she said. "Aren't they awful? They make us wear them at the convent."

Breaking off suddenly, she looked at me in a startled way. "Oh," she cried; "of course . . . you didn't know . . .

"I'm at St. Mary's now, with Emily. My aunt sent me."

"I suppose I guessed as much," I answered. "Well—I've been waiting for you. We'd better begin."

She took her place in the chair, and I brought out an old black coat of my own to put over the middy blouse. "I can do the dress some other time," I told her. "I won't need you for that."

She sat up very stiff and straight in the chair. "Well," she said with a pout, "aren't you glad to see me?"

It was a very different sitting from the one before, and harder, too. Jennie was restless, and in high spirits; she wanted to stop every few minutes, to talk or to walk around. She was full of her life at school, enchanted with the friendships, the comings and goings, the daily incidents of the convent society—happy at having friends, at having secrets—at being, for the first time in her life, part of a little community. There was the plain-song she had to tell me about; the daily walks to the little green-house, where the girls were allowed to buy fruit from one of the sisters; the little bunches of flowers they gave one another, which they called "bunching"; the convent-school itself, high on its hill above the shining river; and Sister Therese, who taught her mathematics and history, and whose calm, untroubled face had already roused in Jennie's breast the first sharp, sweet experience of love. And then there was Emily, of course, whose secrets and whose room she shared, who exchanged stockings and blouses with her, and on whose dresser there was a picture—but only when nobody would be likely to come in—of a young man in a high collar, with dark eyes and wavy hair, and the printed name beneath it, Mr. John Gilbert.

Yes—Jennie had changed; I even noticed that she had filled out a little. On the whole, I thought it a change for the better. I let her talk on and on, barely listening, my fingers racing in tiny spurts over the canvas, trying at

152

their best speed to follow my eyes; and my eyes, in turn, searching for what they could not see—not only what was there, but what had been, and what would some day be. I felt that I was truly working against time, and felt myself carried forward on a wave of exultation as the picture bloomed under the brush, as I saw, each time I stepped away from it, its growing strength, its gathering beauty.

We stopped at noon for a bite of lunch, although I would gladly have gone on without any. But that would never do for Jennie. It turned out that she had been planning all along to cook lunch for me, on my little gas stove; and that she had even taken lessons in cooking in school. Unfortunately, there was nothing in the studio, as far as I could see, for her to cook.

"I have some sardines," I said, "and some cheese, and crackers, and milk. I'm sorry, Jennie. You see, I didn't know you were coming."

She laughed happily. "That's all I can cook, anyhow," she said. "I could cook an egg, but it doesn't matter. I'll cook the cheese."

And she did, actually, get the cheese to melt, though not without some scorching, and a smell of burning that I was afraid would bring up Mrs. Jekes. After it was melted, she dropped it on the crackers, and there it lay, altogether inedible, and more and more like rubber. I ate a few sardines, and after a while, she did, too. "Isn't this fun?" she said.

And of course, to her, it was. For if Emily had Mr. Gilbert, Jennie had me—her own exciting secret, to be shared in whispers if she felt like it, or held close and inviolable to her breast. Everyone has a secret at that age; a special secret, a private secret—for everything between earth and sky is part of the one great, general secret which young hearts whisper to one another. New sights—new sounds—new meanings—new joys and fears—her heart, which through her childhood was all one color, has turned into a kaleidoscope, made up of shining fragments which fall at each turn of the glass

into ever newer, more breath-taking patterns. Emily . . .
Sister Therese . . . plain-song and flowers . . . and finally, myself—all her own, her own private secret, which no one else can know, until she tells.

"The girls keep asking me about you," she confessed. "But I won't tell them anything. Except . . . " she considered a moment . . . "that you're very handsome . . . " And she began to count off on her fingers.

"Jennie," I said; "don't be silly."

" . . . and that you're a great artist; and that you nearly starved to death. . . . "

She smiled at me shyly. "They loved that part of it," she declared. "They thought it was very romantic."

"Good God," I said.

"Well, they did," she insisted. "And they think it's romantic my coming to see you like this, too."

Her voice was still full of laughter, but her cheeks were pink, and she kept her head bent. "Perhaps it is," I replied a little grimly. "But we've got work to do, and if you've finished with that last bit of milk, we might begin."

Her eyes flew to my face in dismay. "You're not angry, are you, Eben?" she faltered. "I was only joking."

"Of course I'm not angry," I said a little too gruffly, and stood up. "Let's get back to work—shall we?"

She took her place again in a somewhat chastened mood; but she couldn't stay quiet for long. "Eben," she said.

"Mmm?"

"I didn't really say you were handsome."

But that didn't comfort me much.

guimpe (gimp): blouse worn under a dress or jumper.

"I wish I had nicer clothes to wear," she said after a while. "We have a blue dress with a guimpe, for Sundays, and we have to wear long white veils in church. Emily's fell off the last time; she didn't pin it on right, she was in such a hurry, and she got a whole day's silence."

Receiving no reply to this bit of information, she went on to other things. "I like some of my lessons," she said.

154

"I like things like science, and math. But I don't like history. It makes me feel too sad.

"I have a funny mind, I guess."

I was holding one brush in my teeth while I worked with another, and I mumbled something in reply.

"You have a funny mind, too," she said.

"Perhaps I have," I agreed absently. "Perhaps I have. Just turn your head a little to the right—"

"Eben," she began presently in a queer, breathless voice, "do you think sometimes people can know what lies ahead? I mean—what's going to happen to them?"

But I was working, and thinking only of what I was doing. Otherwise, I would have stopped—and thought —and perhaps have been too much troubled by the question to make any answer at all. As it was, I only half heard it; and I answered without thinking.

"Nonsense," I said.

Jennie was silent for a moment; then, "I don't know," she said slowly. "I'm not so sure. You know how you feel sad about things sometimes—things that haven't happened. Perhaps they're things that are going to happen. Perhaps we know it, and are just afraid to admit it to ourselves. Why couldn't you, Eben—if you could see ahead—feel sorry for what was coming? Only you wouldn't know it was coming, you'd call it worry, or something."

I heard it, but I wasn't really paying attention. "You sound like the White Queen," I said.

"The White Queen?"

"The one in Alice," I told her. "She hollered first, and stuck herself afterwards."

"Oh," said Jennie in a small voice. Even with the little mind I had to attend to anything but my painting, I could tell that I had hurt her.

"All right," she said. "I won't talk any more."

And for the remainder of the sitting, she sat there silent and unsmiling, drawn back once more into herself, dreaming and distant. But I was too busy to try to

Why should history make Jennie feel sad?

How does Eben treat the "new" Jennie?

155

explain; and besides, it did the picture good. When the light began to fail, I put down my brush, and took a deep breath.

"I think I've got it, Jennie," I said.

There was no answer; she seemed to be half-asleep. I went quietly down the hall to the wash room, to freshen up; I doubt if I was away for more than a minute or so. But when I got back, Jennie was gone.

She left a note for me, on the bed. "Eben dear," it said; "I'll be back again some day. But not soon. In the spring, I think.

Jennie."

Chapter XI

Eben is checking Jennie's statements. What does this reveal about his state of mind?

Even before I telephoned out to the school, I knew what the answer would be. "I'm sorry; there is no one here by that name." I didn't ask them to go back over their files; I knew what the answer would be to that, too.

So there it was.

I must try to describe, if I can, my state of mind in the weeks which followed. I knew that what I had been asked to believe, was impossible; yet I believed it. And at the same time, I was afraid. The fact that my fears were formless, that I did not know what I feared, made it all the worse; for waking or sleeping, nothing frightens us more than the unknown.

I do not know which was harder to bear—the feeling of being afraid, or the sudden sense of desolation which swept down upon me after Jennie had left. She was gone beyond the farthest sea; and there was nowhere I could even look for her.

It made the world around me seem curiously empty—silent, and empty, like the wooden belly of a violin on which nothing is being played. One note would bring it all to life; one note would make an instrument of it. But the note is not played; no one touches it. It remains an empty box.

156

At first, I was absorbed in my own helplessness; and at the same time, baffled by it. Never before had it occurred to me to ask myself why the sun should rise each morning on a new day instead of upon the old day over again; or to wonder how much of what I did was really my own to do. It may be that here on this earth we are not grateful enough for our ignorance, and our innocence. We think that there is only one road, one direction—forward; and we accept it, and press on. We think of God, we think of the mystery of the universe, but we do not think about it very much, and we do not really believe that it is a mystery, or that we could not understand it if it were explained to us. Perhaps that is because when all is said and done, we do not really believe in God. In our hearts, we are convinced that it is our world, not His.

How stupid of us. Yet we are created stupid—innocent and ignorant; and it is this ignorance alone which makes it possible for us to live on this earth, in comfort, among the mysteries. Since we do not know, and cannot guess, we need not bother our heads too much to understand. It is innocence which wakes us each morning to a new day, a fresh day, another day in a long chain of days; it is ignorance which makes each of our acts appear to be a new one, and the result of an exercise of will. Without such ignorance, we should perish of terror, frozen and immobile; or, like the old saints who learned the true name of God, go up in a blaze of unbearable vision.

I went back to work; and there, before my easel again, I got back a little of my peace of mind. I realized that I was still anchored to earth, and that no matter what God was about, if I was to live, it would have to be by my own efforts. Little by little the sense of being helpless, the fog of fear, burned itself out of my heart, and left me clear, and grateful—and lonely.

It was this loneliness, which I had not expected, and to which I was unused, which kept me from taking the finished portrait to Mr. Mathews at once. It was all I had of Jennie, all I had to remind me that she was really there in the world; and I could not bring myself to part with it. I found that I kept waiting for her to come back; some part of me which had always been whole and satisfied, was suddenly so no longer; something was missing.

Mrs. Jekes found me talking to the portrait one day. I don't know what I was saying—probably something I had said before, to the real Jennie. She came quietly up behind me, with a duster in her hand, and stood looking over my shoulder. "Well," she said; "well."

It startled me; and disturbed me, too. I moved away, trying to look as though I hadn't been talking out loud to myself, as though it were all a mistake, as though it were something quite natural. But Mrs. Jekes wasn't fooled. "That's the girl who's been visiting you," she said, and her voice was full of malice.

"That's your sweetheart."

I whirled on her in a rage. "You're a fool," I shouted. I wanted to strike her, to push her out of the room. But she stood her ground, and gave me back look for look. "It isn't me is the fool," she said bitterly.

She moved to the door with a sort of bleak dignity. "You can always leave this house if you've a mind to," she said. "There's others will be glad to take your place."

And she added, as she went out,

"You're not a gentleman."

I wanted to run after her and tell her that I was leaving, that I was leaving at once . . . but before I had taken two steps, I halted in dismay. For I realized that I couldn't leave. This was Jennie's room: this was where she had sat, where we had had lunch together, this was what she loved to come back to—how could I leave it? It was full of memories of her.

And besides—if I moved—how would she ever find me again?

I closed the door gently, and turned slowly back into the room again. I'd have to stay; I'd have to tell Mrs. Jekes that I was sorry for what I had said. It put a bitter taste in my mouth. I took Jennie's picture, and turned it

Why does Mrs. Jekes imply that it is Eben who is the fool?

158

to the wall. I didn't want to think about her for a while.

Just the same, I thought about very little else. That was early in March; it was early in April before I saw her again. At least, I know now that I saw her; though I wasn't sure at the time. It was only for a moment; and I had no chance to talk to her.

It was at the gallery, at an exhibition of some of Jerry Farnsworth's things, with one or two of Helen Sawyer's landscapes hanging with them—scenes of the Cape, the crossing at North Truro, an old house, and a painting of the Pamet where it flows past the town landing at Truro. There had been a good crowd in to see them, quite a lot of people; and I had gone back into Mr. Mathews' little office in the rear of the gallery, to talk to Miss Spinney. She had sold the flower-piece at a profit; and she was feeling friendly, and pleased with herself.

"Adams," she said, after she had greeted me, "tell me something: what is it makes a painter? A man will starve all his life, go around with holes in his pants and his toes sticking out of his boots, and still all he wants to do is slap some paint on a yard of canvas. Who's crazy—him or us? What did you do with the twenty-five dollars you got off us the last time?"

"I spent it," I said.

"Sure," she agreed; "I didn't think you'd bought a bond with it. Only, why not a new coat, or a pair of shoes?"

I looked down at my scuffed and broken shoes, and shrugged my shoulders. I didn't see what business it was of hers. "Oh well," I said, "I could get them shined, and they'd look all right. That is, if I ever thought about it."

"Have they got any soles left on them at all?" she asked.

I grinned at her, but I kept my feet planted firmly on the floor, for I knew it would be like her to pick one of them up the way a blacksmith does when he wants to shoe a horse. "I didn't know you cared," I murmured.

"Don't be an ass," she said. But a slow blush ran up her

159

neck, up over the clean, strong lines of her jaw.

"All right," I said, feeling a little silly, "next time throw in a pair of shoes with the price."

She swore at me like a truck driver; and I went out to look for Mr. Mathews.

I didn't see him at first, for he was at the door saying goodbye to one of the customers. The gallery was nearly empty by this time; a few people were still standing in front of Farnsworth's "Rest After Work," but otherwise the big room was deserted. The Sawyers were over in a far corner, near the door; and I started toward them.

Like all galleries, the room itself was only dimly lighted; the pictures on the wall seemed to have their own light, to give out reflections of sun and sea, or morning sky and noonday earth, which made the air of the room itself seem shadowy and vague. I thought I heard Miss Spinney come out of the office behind me, and turned back for a moment. But there was no one there. When I turned around again, it seemed to me that my heart stopped beating.

There was somebody in front of the Sawyers—a young girl, dressed in a middy blouse, and a skirt which hung almost to her ankles. She was standing directly in front of the picture of the Pamet; that much I could see across the room, in the shadowy light; but no more. She had her hands to her face; and I thought that she was weeping.

"Jennie," I said; or perhaps I only thought I said it. I tried to move, to get across to her, but my legs were like lead. It was all I could do to put one foot before the other. I could feel the slow, heavy surge of my heart, as I kept trying to breathe, catching at my breath, the way you do in a gale.

She lifted her head, and for a moment I had a glimpse of her face, wet and shiny with tears. And then—she was gone. It was just as simple as that. Perhaps she went out through the door—I don't know. Mr. Mathews, coming in at that moment, bent aside as though to let someone pass. Perhaps it was Jennie.

Consider the shadowy atmosphere of this scene. What does it add to the reality or unreality of the relationship between Jennie and Eben?

He came across the floor to me, smiling; but when he saw my face, his expression changed. "Good heavens, Mr. Adams," he cried, "is anything the matter? You look sick, man."

I shook my head; I couldn't say anything. I passed him without speaking, and stumbled out of the door. He looked after me in bewilderment. I left him there wondering what had happened to me.

There were only the usual passers-by in the street. I hadn't expected there would be anyone else.

Chapter XII

Spring was early that year; the rainy winds blew themselves out before the end of April. One day the grass in the Park smelt sweet and fresh, and a robin sang on the lawn below the Mall. From then on, the sky seemed made of another blue, and the clouds, too, were a different white, with tones of yellow in them. Yellow is the true color of spring, not green; the new grass, the clouds, the misty, sunny air, the sticky buds like little feathers on the trees, all are mixed with yellow tone, with the haze of sun and earth and water. Green is for summer; blue, for fall.

The city comes up dreaming from the winter, its high roofs seem to melt in the air. The wind blows from the south, across Jersey; it smells sweet, it brings the smell of earth with it. People move more slowly, there is a gentleness about them, the cold is not yet out of their bones, they warm themselves in the sun. The days are longer, and the shadows are not as deep; evenings come down almost imperceptibly, there are long twilights, the dusk is peaceful, and the sounds of evening are tranquil and comforting. Summer lies ahead, the summer of the heart; it is coming, it has been caught sight of, it is on the way, bringing flowers and sea-bathing.

Summer is the worst time of all to be alone. Then earth is warm and lovely, free to go about in; and always somewhere in the distance there is a place where two people might be happy if only they were together. It is in the spring that one dreams of such places; one thinks of the summer which is coming, and the heart dreams of its friend.

Now in the Park I began to see people walking together, slowly, arm in arm, not hurrying as they did in winter, but taking time to talk to each other, stopping a moment to laugh at the children, or to watch the swans on the lake. When summer came, they would be together still; they could enjoy the spring. But for me, it was different. I had no way of knowing when I should see Jennie again. And as the days passed, I missed her more and more.

There is one thing about distance: that no matter how far away it is, it can be reached. It is over there, beyond the Jersey hills—one can drive to it—it is north, among the pines, or eastward to the sea. It is never yesterday, or tomorrow. That is another, and a crueler distance; there is no way to get there.

Yet, though I missed her, though I could not reach her, I was not altogether without her. For I found that my memory had grown sharper; or else it was beginning to play tricks on me. It was not so much that I began to live in the past, as that the past began to take on more and more the clarity, the actual form of the present, and to intrude itself into my daytime thoughts. The present, on the contrary, seemed to grow a little hazy, to begin to slip away from me . . . so many things reminded me of her. And then I would be seized by memory so urgent that what I remembered seemed almost more real to me than what was before me.

Where others dreamed ahead that spring, toward the summer, I dreamed backward into the past. Sights, sounds, and smells, all served that journey well—the smell of scorching, the sound of wood—perhaps a shovel?—scraped along the pavement; the hoot of a tugboat in the river. At nightfall the shrill, sad voices of children, floating in through my window, brought back to

162

me another evening, in the mist, in the Park, and a child walking beside me down the long avenue of empty benches, skipping along on one foot, hopping over the chalk marks. . . . *"Do you know the game I like to play best? It's a wishing game."* Or on a sunny morning, beside the lake on which the boats were lazily drifting, I'd suddenly find myself entranced and motionless, seeing in front of me not the blue, dancing water, but the white, shining ice and the skaters, feeling the cold wind on my cheeks again, and Jennie's arm in mine, so firm and light. . . . Or coming home in the afternoon, I'd hurry up the stairs with a beating heart, because she might be there—remembering so clearly the first time she had come to see me, in her little velvet dress with the muff. *"I thought maybe you wanted me to come,"* she had said.

Such was my state of mind those early days of spring—neither happy nor unhappy; dreaming, and waiting. I didn't want very much, or hope for very much—just to see her again, and to be with her once more. I tried not to think about the summer, or, indeed, about the future at all;—how could I? I left that to her, just as I had left the past to her. Why we had met, or how it had come about, I did not know. I still do not know. I only know that we were meant to be together, that the strands of her life were woven in with mine; and that even time and the world could not part us altogether. Not then. Not ever.

What is it which makes a man and a woman know that they, of all other men and women in the world, belong to each other? Is it no more than chance and meeting? No more than being alive together in the world at the same time? Is it only a curve of the throat, a line of the chin, the way the eyes are set, a way of speaking? Or is it something deeper and stranger, something beyond meeting, something beyond chance and fortune? Are there others, in other times of the world, whom we would have loved, who would have loved us? Is there, perhaps, one soul among all others—among all who have lived, the endless generations, from world's end to world's end—who must love us or die? And whom we must love, in turn—whom we must seek all our lives long—headlong and home-sick—until the end?

By May I had no money left at all, and so I took the portrait down to Mr. Mathews. I hated to give it up, but there was no help for it; I needed money for rent, and for more paints, and canvas. I was still getting some of my meals at the Alhambra, although I had finished my work there; the picnic over the bar seemed to please the customers, and Mr. Moore didn't mind my having one free meal a day, as long as I didn't eat too much. As a matter of fact, he was thinking of getting up a fancy menu with an illustrated cover—possibly a picture of the restaurant, with himself standing in the doorway. Gus wanted me to get his cab into it, too. I didn't mind; an artist works for his meals one way or another.

Gus helped me bring the picture downtown in his cab, and went along with me to see that I wasn't cheated. We carried it into the gallery together, and set it up on the table in the office in the rear. Then we stepped aside, and let Mr. Mathews look at it.

He didn't say anything for a long while. At first I thought that he was disappointed, and my heart sank; but then I saw that he was really very much moved. He had grown a little pale; his eyes first widened, and then narrowed; and he kept stroking the palm of one hand with the fingers of the other. "Well," he said. "Well.

"Yes."

I began to feel excited, too. Up till then, I doubt if I had really looked at the picture myself with any sort of critical eye. There, in my room, it had been so much a part of me; I could still feel the brush strokes in my fingers . . . and besides, it was Jennie, it was all I had of her. . . . But here, in the gallery, seeing it as Mr. Mathews was seeing it, I could realize for the first time what I had done. It made me feel proud, and at the same time humble.

After a while Miss Spinney came in and joined us. She didn't say anything for a minute; and then she took a long breath. "Well, Adams," she said in a strangely gentle voice, "that's it, all right."

Mr. Mathews cleared his throat. "Yes," he said, "that's it. That's what I meant. It's . . . it's . . . " He seemed unable to continue. It was Gus who spoke up for him.

"She's a honey, Mack," he said. "I don't noways blame you."

And turning to Miss Spinney, he added in an easy tone,

"Treat him right, ma'am, on account of he's a friend of mine."

"I'll keep it in mind," said Miss Spinney.

She and Mr. Mathews went outside, to talk it over; and Gus edged up to me and gave me a nudge with his elbow. "I think they like it, Mack," he whispered.

"Yes," I said; "I think they do."

"Well, don't be too easy on them," he said. "Ask for fifty, right off."

"It's worth twice that," I said.

Gus' jaw dropped. "No," he croaked. "Go on. I wouldn't of believed it."

Mr. Mathews and Miss Spinney came back again, looking solemn; and Mr. Mathews settled down to business. "Mr. Adams," he began—

"Why so formal?" said Miss Spinney. "He's in the family."

"Well, then—Eben," said Mr. Mathews, swallowing, "I won't try to disguise my feelings from you. You have given me a great surprise. I am powerfully moved. This picture . . . well . . . I don't like to use the word masterpiece, but just the same . . . "

"Get on with it, Henry," said Miss Spinney.

"Yes," said Mr. Mathews hurriedly. "Quite. The point is, that we don't want to buy it. No," he said, holding up his hand as he saw my face fall—"it's not for the reason you think. The reason is, that I honestly don't know what it's worth."

"Well," I said, "what do you think it's worth?"

"That depends," he answered, "on who buys it. The

market isn't very good just at the moment, for individual collectors. But if a museum were to take it—"

"Yes?" I said.

"It might bring more than a thousand dollars," he said.

I heard Gus give a gulp beside me. "What I want to do," continued Mr. Mathews—"what we want to do—is to take it on consignment, and then do the very best we can for it. And as an advance—" he cleared his throat nervously—"as an advance, I can let you have two hundred dollars. . . . "

"Henry," said Miss Spinney ominously.

"Three hundred," amended Mr. Mathews unhappily.

Then Gus found his voice again. "Take it, Mack," he said hoarsely; and gave me a shove.

I went home in his cab, leaning back on the cushion, and looking out proudly at my city, which seemed to me to return my look with joy. Through the open window in front, I could see the back of Gus' head; I noticed that he had turned the flag down on his meter, and that the meter was ticking. Well, why not? I was a rich man. But just the same, I was surprised; and it surprised me that Gus wasn't saying anything. His silence wasn't natural; it wasn't like him.

As Eben realizes that his portrait is a success, what conflicting emotions does he feel?

He left me at my house, and took my fare without a word. When I tried to thank him for helping me, he looked away. "Forget it," he said. "It don't signify."

He took his hands off the wheel, and stared at them helplessly, as though in some way or other they had disappointed him. Then he let them drop again.

How does Gus react to Eben's success?

"I couldn't do nothing for you, Mack," he said. "And that's the truth."

Chapter XIII

Early next morning, in the bright spring sunshine, Jennie came back to me. I heard her voice in the hall, and had only time to slip into my coat, before she was up the stairs and in at the door. She had a little suitcase in her

166

hand; she dropped it just inside the doorway, and came flying across the room, and kissed me.

It was the most natural thing in the world. We held each other out at arm's length and looked at each other, smiling, and not saying anything. We couldn't have spoken. . . . The whole sunny, sweet-smelling spring morning had come in with her.

She was older—I saw that at once; a young lady now, dressed in a traveling suit; she even had gloves on. She was breathless, but only from running up the stairs, or from happiness; her brown eyes never faltered as they searched my face. I took a deep breath. "Jennie," I said; "I've missed you."

"I know," she answered. "I've missed you, too. And it's been longer for me." She drew her hands away from mine with sudden gravity. "I'm not in school any more," she said.

"I know," I said. "I can see."

She turned slowly on her heel, and looked around the room with simple joy. "How I've dreamed of this, Eben," she said; "I can't tell you. The nights I've lain awake, thinking of this room . . . "

"I know," I said.

"Do you?" she answered gently. "No, I don't think so."

She stood there, looking around her, and slowly taking off her gloves; and I looked around, too, and wished the room were more in order. I went over to smooth the bed a little, but she stopped me. "No," she said; "don't touch it. Do you remember how I wanted to tidy up for you once, when I was little? Let me do it now. And show me where the coffee is. . . . Poor Eben—I did get you up so early. Go and dress yourself, and then we'll have breakfast, and I'll tell you all that's happened."

"But, Jennie," I said, "if we have so little time . . . "

"We have a whole long day," she answered breathlessly. "And—and a little more."

I went along down the hall to the washroom, and left Jennie to tidy up, as she wanted. I thought I saw Mrs.

Jekes on the landing below, but I didn't pay much attention to her; I was too happy, the day was too lovely . . . a whole long day, and a little more. What did that mean—a little more? I cut myself twice, shaving.

Jennie had learned how to make a bed, and how to make coffee. I hardly knew my room when I got back to it: my work-table was laid with a clean towel, and my two cups, one of them with a broken handle, and the coffee pot, stood side by side, along with a pat of butter I'd had out on the window sill, and some bread she had toasted on a fork over the gas burner. There was a good smell in the air. We sat down together, hand in hand, to our breakfast.

I told her about the picture; and her fingers tightened on mine. "Oh, but that's grand," she cried. "That's wonderful, Eben. Aren't you happy?"

She was silent for a moment, thinking about something. "Eben," she said at last, "let's do something special—shall we? To celebrate? Because I haven't really very long to stay with you. You see . . . I'm being sent abroad—to France—to a finishing school—for two years."

"Jennie," I cried.

"I know," she said quickly. "I don't want to go; but I guess I have to. And anyhow—it won't seem very long. And then . . . "

"And then?" I asked.

"I'm going to hurry," she said earnestly. "And then some day I'll be as old as you."

About how old does Jennie seem now? What underlies Eben's acceptance of her present age and appearance?

"I'm twenty-eight, Jennie," I said gravely. She nodded her head.

"I know it," she replied. "And so will I be . . . then."

"But not when you come back from France," I said.

"No," she agreed. "There'll be a long time still, after that."

She held my hand tight. "I'm going to hurry, though," she said. "I've got to."

For a moment she seemed to be lost in thought, her head bent, her eyes hidden under their long lashes. Then

168

she roused herself, and sat up with a smile. "Let's go on a picnic, Eben," she said. "Somewhere in the country—for the whole day—

"It's something we've never done before."

Something we'd never done before—as though we'd ever done very much of anything. But she didn't have to urge me. A whole day in the country, in the warm spring weather, together . . . "Yes," I said, "yes. That's what we'll do." She could hardly wait for me to finish my coffee; we hurried down the stairs and out into the street, hand in hand; and the bright sunny morning fell on us like an armful of flowers.

Gus was in his cab, at the corner. When he saw me with Jennie, he took his hat off, and looked frightened. I don't believe he had ever thought she was real, or ever expected to see her. I went up to the cab, and opened the door. "Gus," I said, "we're going on a picnic. We're going out into the country for the day . . . somewhere . . . anywhere. I want you to take us. How much will it cost?"

Why does Gus respond with a look of fright?

He twisted his hat in his hands, and tried to smile; he seemed to be having some trouble in swallowing. "Now listen, Mack," he said; "now listen . . . "

"It doesn't matter what it costs," I said, and helped Jennie into the cab.

What was the good of being rich, if I couldn't do what I liked?

Gus looked back once or twice, as though to make sure that we were really there. "So it's a fact," he said finally, more to himself than to me; and in a kind of awe. "Well—

"Where do you want to go, Mack?"

I waved him forward. "Wherever it's green," I said. "Wherever it's country."

I don't know where we went, but it was green and lovely. It was somewhere north of the city—perhaps in Westchester. It took us about an hour to get there. We left the cab by the roadside, and climbed a fence, and ran across a field with a cow in it. The cow didn't notice us. We climbed a little hill, among some trees. Jennie was flushed and breathless, and full of laughter; she and I ran ahead, and Gus came after us.

At noon we sat together on a warm stone wall in the sun at the edge of a meadow, and near a little wood. There were yellow dandelions in the grass, and the air was sweet as honey. We had some sandwiches along—lettuce and bread for Jennie, sausage for Gus and me. We ate our sandwiches, and drank some beer out of cans. It was the first beer Jennie had ever tasted; she didn't like it; she said it tasted bitter.

Gus and Jennie did most of the talking. He told her how he had tried to find her once; and how he had helped me sell the picture; and she told him please to take good care of me, and not to let anything happen. I didn't talk very much; I felt drowsy in the sun; I kept wishing Arne were there, too; I kept thinking about what it would be like some day when we were all together.

Jennie sat on the wall beside me, her head against my shoulder. She had twined a yellow dandelion in her hair; it gave out a fresh, weedy fragrance. The sky was robin's egg blue; I heard a bird singing in the woods. I was happy—happier than I had ever been before, happier than I've ever been since.

Gus left us after lunch, and went back to the cab, to take a nap. Then Jennie, too, grew silent, resting against me, dreamy and content. After a while, I felt her stir, and draw a long, uneven breath. "What are you thinking, Jennie?" I asked.

She answered slowly and gently, "I'm thinking how beautiful the world is, Eben; and how it keeps on being beautiful—no matter what happens to us. The spring comes year after year, for us, or Egypt; the sun goes down in the same green, lovely sky; the birds sing . . . for us, or yesterday . . . or for tomorrow. It was never made for anything but beauty, Eben—whether we lived now, or long ago."

"Tomorrow," I said. "But when is tomorrow, Jennie?"

170

"Does it matter?" she asked. "It's always. This was tomorrow—once.

"Promise me you'll never forget."

I quoted softly:

"Where I come from
Nobody knows;
And where I'm going
Everything goes."

She took it up with a little cry of surprise:

"The wind blows,
The sea flows—
And God knows.

"I think He knows, Eben," she said.

And she lifted her lips, trusting and innocent, to mine.

Later we walked in the faint green of the woods, through the shadow of branches, over the ferns and the moss. We found a little brook, and violets hidden among their leaves. Jennie stopped to pick them; she made a tiny bunch, to carry home. "It's to remember today," she said.

The sun began to sink in the west; the shadows fell around us. It grew chilly; we turned, and started home.

Chapter XIV

I had one clear day of happiness, and I shall never forget it. Even the miserable ending to it cannot change its quality in my memory; for everything that Jennie and I did was good, and unhappiness came only from the outside. Not many—lovers or friends—can say as much. For friends and lovers are quick to wound, quicker than strangers, even; the heart that opens itself to the world, opens itself to sorrow.

Consider the way Jennie explains her ideas about "tomorrow." In what ways does it seem reasonable? unreasonable?

Note that the last line of the song has been changed from "And nobody knows" to "And God knows."

171

I don't think that we spoke of the question of where Jennie was to stay that night. She was sailing in the morning (on the *Mauretania*, I remember she told me—how strange it was to hear the old name again) and we both seemed to take it for granted that we'd stay together until then.

We had supper at the Alhambra, at a little table near the bar, where she could see my mural, and then we walked home together in the quiet evening. It was cool, the air was still, and in the green west the evening star hung like a lantern over the city.

Those are the scenes, the memories, with which I comfort myself. The spring comes year after year, she had said, and tomorrow is always. When at last there was no tomorrow any more, I remembered yesterday. Yesterday is always, too.

She told me that she had been at the gallery that day of the exhibition, when I thought I had seen her; and that she had been crying. "I don't know why," she said. "It was a picture of a river, and some little hills across on the other side—the Pamet, it was called. And all of a sudden I felt that I knew it, and that it was a sad place—and I found myself crying. I wanted to come to you, but I couldn't; I had to go back. I was unhappy for a while, and then I forgot it."

She put her hand in mine; it was trembling a little. "I'm sorry that you asked me," she said. "I didn't want to remember it."

I turned her hand over, and patted it. "It's a funny little river, Jennie," I said, "and not sad at all. It comes in from the bay, and it's not very deep. The children play there, and the bitterns croak in the reeds at night. And at low tide, everybody goes out and digs for clams."

She smiled uncertainly. "I know," she said. "I'm being silly. Don't let's talk about it any more. Tell me about Paris, instead—you were there, weren't you? Is it very lovely? My school is in Passy—is that near where you were? Tell me what to see, and what to do—so that some

172

day we'll have done it all together. . . . "

We sat on the edge of the bed, and talked for a long time. I told her about Arne, about the Atelier Dufoix, about the Clos des Lilas, where we used to go sometimes when we had money, and the little bistro on the Rue du Bac where we went when we didn't. She listened to me hungrily, seeing it all ahead of her. "Oh, Eben," she said; "it's going to be such fun."

We even planned what we'd do together. I remembered a room on the Île St. Louis, where a friend of mine had lived—a room like the prow of a ship, butting its way up the Seine, and the river pouring by on both sides, under the windows. I promised to take her to the Luxembourg, to the Quai des Marinières, and to the Fair at Neuilly—I promised to dance with her in the Place Pigalle on Bastille Day—and to take her out into the Forest of St. Cloud in the spring, to drink new wine under the trees. "It's going to be such fun," she said.

It was late when Mrs. Jekes knocked on the door. I think I shall remember the sound of it all my life. When death comes at last, I expect he'll sound like that, too.

Even before the door opened, I think I had an idea of what was coming. She stood in the doorway, a still, wintry figure, her hands folded, as always, across her stomach. "Oh no," she said; "oh no. Not in my house, not at night, you won't. There's a limit to everything, my friends. I've run a decent place all my life, and I mean to keep it so."

And pointing a white, shaking finger at Jennie, she cried suddenly,

"Get out."

I was too startled even to speak. I seemed to freeze up inside; perhaps it was just as well, for otherwise there's no telling what I might have done. Jennie got up from the bed, slowly, as though in a dream; she turned her frightened face away from me, so that I shouldn't see how ashamed she was. She went quietly over to the chair where she had laid her hat and coat.

"I'm sorry, Eben," she faltered. "I didn't think. . . . "

What explains Mrs. Jekes' behavior toward Jennie and Eben? Note that the terms "wintry figure" and "freeze up" repeat Arne's feelings on page 145 and Eben's feelings on page 105.

173

"Get out," said Mrs. Jekes.

I found my voice then. "Be still," I cried to her; and to Jennie: "Don't listen . . . don't listen to her."

But Jennie shook her head. "No," she said; "no—it's too late now: it's been said. It couldn't ever not be said again."

She took up her hat and coat, and stooped to pick up the little suitcase which lay by the door where she had dropped it that morning. Mrs. Jekes moved aside to let her pass. She went by her without a glance, but she turned in the doorway, and looked back at me—a look so full of longing, of love, and of trust, that it was like a hand laid for a moment against my cheek. It was that look, more than anything else, which kept me from rushing after her.

"Goodbye, Eben," she said clearly. "I'll be back again some day—but not like this. Not ever again like this. Not until we can be together always."

Mrs. Jekes watched her go. She followed her down the stairs; I heard her footsteps grow fainter and fainter down the stairs.

Chapter XV

I moved out of Mrs. Jekes' house after that; and since summer was not far off, I decided to join Arne on the Cape at once. Mr. Mathews and Miss Spinney said goodbye to me like old friends; Mr. Mathews gave me a little folding easel which had belonged to Fromkes, and Miss Spinney gave me a bottle of brandy—to keep, as she put it, the fog out of my fingers. "I want another flower-piece," she declared; "a two-and-a-half by four; and a church. I'm sort of fond of churches, the little white ones, with the big steeples. Goodbye, and God bless you. Don't drown yourself in the sea."

"What would I want to drown myself in the sea for?" I asked.

"I don't know," she answered. "Men are fools enough to do anything. Personally, I don't trust the sea. I wouldn't go within fifty miles of it."

"You're tough," I said. "The sea would never get you."

She looked at me with a strange expression; I saw the red start to creep up over her chin. "It's the tough ones drown easy," she said, and turned away.

Mr. Mathews walked to the door with me; he kept reaching up every now and then to pat me on the back. "Goodbye, my boy," he said, "goodbye. I'm glad you came to me; we'll do big things together. You've earned a rest; now enjoy it. But remember—no landscapes. Leave the dunes to Eastwood."

"I want to do the fishermen," I said.

"Fishermen," he echoed doubtfully; "well . . . "

"In the traps," I said, "in the early morning, with the fish churning in the nets."

Mr. Mathews looked at me gloomily. "Listen," he said; "there are enough fish in the world."

He sighed heavily. "But not enough women," he added.

Gus took me to my train. "Take care of yourself, Mack," he said. "Don't do anything I wouldn't do." I had Jennie's violets in a paper bag in my pocket; they were withered by now, but they still retained a little of their fragrance. My paints and canvases and my easel were in one bundle, and my clothes were in another. The train went at midnight, the great office buildings were dark as we drove down to the station. I kept thinking of how Jennie had been there in the cab with me only the day before.

I knew that I'd see her again, and I told Gus so. "Sure," he said; "sure. Why not? You don't want to be too wise in this world, Mack, because there's always something happens you don't expect. You take my own people, now—they thought they weren't going to get out of Egypt. But they got out all right. And why? So they could write the Bible.

"They couldn't have guessed that."

"They didn't have to guess it," I said.

"I know," said Gus; "you mean Somebody told them. Well—what did He tell them? That's what I want to know."

"I thought He made it clear," I said.

"Not to me," said Gus. "I'm still trying to figure it out. And the way I figure it, is like this: whatever it was, it was good news, on account of the only bad news would be that what we knew was all there was."

I started to pull out some money to pay him for the ride, but he waved it away. "Forget it," he said. "The flag wasn't down. You've done plenty for me."

"Goodbye, Gus," I said. "I'll see you in the fall."

"Sure," he agreed. "Drop me a postal."

I hesitated a moment before picking up my bags. "You think God is trying to tell me something?" I asked, half in earnest.

"I wouldn't put it past Him," said Gus.

"But what?" I cried.

He shook his head. "I wouldn't know," he said.

I came down into Provincetown the next afternoon. The moment we crossed the bridge at Bourne, and I breathed the warm, sunny fragrance of scrub pine and broom, I felt the old peace of summer flow into me. Lilac was out in the Yarmouth yards and doorways, and in Brewster the juice-pear and the wild plum had opened their blossoms, white as snow. The marshes at Wellfleet were all a silvery green; and beyond Truro, there was the bay, still and shining, bluer than a bluebird's wing, with Plymouth clear, dark, and distant on the horizon.

Arne was waiting for me; he had a room in the west end of town, down near Furtado's boatyard, and he took me there to wash up and get settled. I went to the window, and drew in a deep breath of the past. How well I remembered it. The old weedy, fishy smell rose from the tide; the gulls were circling and crying out in the harbor; and on the sand below, Manuel was hammering at the white hull of a lobsterman. The schooner *Mary P. Goulart* was in harbor, along with most of the fisheries' fleet; and

I saw John Worthington's tunaman, the *Bocage,* come chugging in across the blue water from the North Truro nets, kicking up a little foam at her bows. Slowly and peacefully sky and water deepened; the sun went down over Peaked Hill Bars, and the ruby light came on at Wood End, and the white light at the Point.

We walked down to the fish wharf, past Dyer's hardware store and Page's Garage, past the post office, and the little square with its great elms. The summer visitors hadn't begun to arrive yet, and the town was quiet, with only its own people in the streets. Dark-faced fishermen lounged in the doorways, talking together in their own language, half-argot and half-Portuguese; and the girls went by, two by two in the dusk, hatless and laughing. We stopped in at Taylor's for supper, and I ordered a chowder, the way they make it down there. I wanted to hear the Provincetown news: who was teaching that year, and how the classes were shaping up, whether Jerry Farnsworth had his old studio, and whether Tom Blakeman was going to take a class in etching again. And then, of course, Arne had to hear about the portrait. When I told him that Mr. Mathews hoped to sell it to a museum some day, he flung out his hands in horror.

"Don't have it, Eben," he thundered. "Never allow it. A museum? The death of the soul."

"Sure," I said. "Like Innes, or Chase."

"They're dead," he answered. "That's all past and done with."

"Is it?" I asked. "I'm not so sure."

"Good God," he bellowed earnestly; "the past is behind us. What?"

"There's still Rembrandt," I said, "and Van Gogh. We're not quite done with them yet. . . . The past isn't behind us, Arne—it's all around us. And down here, on the Cape, is where one ought to feel it more—where the years follow each other like tides in the Pamet, and the boats come in each day with the same fish they had before."

I smiled at him across the table. "I'm only beginning to think about things like that," I said.

"Well," he said unhappily, "I wish you wouldn't. The artist ought not to think so much, it's bad for his color sense."

And with that, we plunged into the old debate, and for the rest of the meal the talk was all of color and line, symbol, form, and mass. "I tell you," cried Arne, pulling at his beard, "we must be like little children again. We must bring back color into the world. That is what color is for, to look at. Do not think: paint. Like children."

He pounded the table, clutched his beard, and roared like a bull. He was perfectly happy. I asked him whether he expected the children to understand his paintings, and he gave me a look of scorn. "Only an artist," he declared, "can hope to understand what another artist is trying to do. That is why there is so little understanding of art among the masses.

"Just the same," he added inconsequentially, "the museums are always full of children."

It was always like that with Arne.

As we went out into the street again after supper, on our way home, he said to me in a hopeful way,

"Is this model of yours coming to the Cape this summer, Eben?"

I answered almost without thinking. "Yes," I said. "Some day." He nodded his great head thoughtfully. "Good," he said. "I shall do a portrait of her, myself."

It amused me, as I laughed quietly in the darkness. That would be something to see, that picture.

But it made me feel lonely all of a sudden. I wondered where Jennie was, and what she was doing—in what far-off place over which this velvet-blue and soft spring evening of ours had long since passed like a wind. Was she still at sea? Night was on the sea, the dark sweep of earth's shadow; but tomorrow's sun was already rising above the eastern slopes of the Urals. And yesterday's sun? Did it still shine on the low stone wall at the meadow's edge, near the little wood? It was still today, still noon on the Pacific, on the long, blue swells which washed Hawaii. Yesterday . . . tomorrow . . . where were they?

It would be a long time until Jennie came back to me. Not until we could be together always, she had said. A long summer . . . Hurry, I said to her, in my heart.

I knew that I could never explain it to Arne. I didn't try.

The damp sea air, salty and fresh from the flats, or suddenly pierced with spice from the flowering gardens of Provincetown, flowed around us as we wandered home under the white street lamps. In the harbor the riding lights of the *Mary P. Goulart* rocked gently in the gloom; the beams of the lighthouses at Long Point and Wood End, blinked at the bay; and the great white cross of High Land Light at North Truro swept like the spokes of a wheel through the heavens. The stars burned calmly overhead. . . . How many years ago had those metallic rays first leaped out across the empty spaces between their home and ours? Long, long ago; from beyond our furthest yesterday.

The gulls were sleeping out on the water, in the blue dark, silent and forgetful, ranged in rows along the decks of the empty fishing boats. The streets were quiet and deserted; we heard our footsteps following us home.

Chapter XVI

But I didn't want to stay in Provincetown for the summer. I still had more than two hundred dollars left of the money I had received for the portrait, and I decided to take a small house in Truro, on the Pamet. It was little more than a shack, really, up on the bluff above the water; the pines stood close, making a brown carpet of needles all around the house, and you looked down at the river through their branches. I could hear the waters of the bay endlessly sounding, and the wind in the pines,

179

not unlike the sound of the sea. The air was warm and sweet with the odor of earth and sun, and there was shelter from the easterly rains, and from the northwest wind, which soared up strong and cold over Cornhill behind me. I was right in the path of a southeast blow, or a smoky sou'wester, but that was an advantage; the winds from the south were fair-weather winds, and came in warm and soft.

At low tide the Pamet is no more than a trickle of water among the reeds; but at full moon, and with a full-course tide, it overflows the marshes, and one can imagine it as it once was, before the sand piled up at the harbor mouth—a wide, deep river on which as many as thirty whalers could ride to their moorings. But that was long ago. Today the little river pours in and out of a narrow channel to the bay, and wanders crookedly across the Cape between the bay and the ocean. Perhaps a hundred yards from where the Pamet rises among its springs, the low dunes begin; and just across them is the beach and the sea. It's not a long trip from ocean to bay; the Cape is narrow at that end, less than three miles wide.

The little houses nestle in the hollows, safe from the northwest winds which blow so hard in winter. There is pine, and scrub oak, locust, aspen, and elm, bearberry, gorse, wintergreen, beach plum, and cherry. Everything is on a small scale; the tiny hills and hollows, seen in perspective, have the appearance of mountains and valleys. The spires of the two old churches and the meeting house dominate everything; they rise on the highest ridge, and brood serene and lovely over the valleys.

Families still live in Truro from the old days: the Snows, the Dyers, the Atwoods, Atkinses, Cobbs, Paines, Riches. Old names, old families of Cape Cod . . . It is their country, their home, it belongs to them. They are quiet and kind, hard-working people.

I settled down to work, too. But for a week or so, the colors of the Cape made all my senses drowsy—the pale sand-yellow, the light green, and the faded blue of water and sky deepening off to violet in the distance. Birds on their way north were stopping off to visit; robins searched the lawns, finches darted like minnows in and out of the trees, a pair of orioles had built a nest in the elm tree back of my house.

By June the gorse was yellow, and the bearberries pink and white on the downs; bob-whites called to each other in the grass. I went down to swim in the river; it was swift and fresh, and the little green crabs fled away from me in the shallows. Some children were there already, playing in an old hulk drawn up on the shore. One, with hair the color of hay, was playing that he was a pirate. He had his crew ready for battle; they consisted of a cap pistol, and his sister. He could not find an enemy.

All summer the children play on the beaches. They are happy and friendly; as each wave sweeps in across the sand, the smaller ones turn their backs to the sea, and run sensibly away. When the water, edged with foam, draws back again, they go running after it, with an air of driving the ocean before them. But at the next wave, they flee as before, with shrill alarm, and fresh surprise. The sun warms their small brown legs, and they collect with enthusiasm bits of clam shell, sand dollars, and colored stones worn by the tide. The larger children plunge into the waves like little dolphins. The water is clear and cold.

Time stands still in Truro; the weeks slip by, one after another. In June there was a nor'easter, the wind came whistling in from the sea, driving the rain almost level before it; it blew for three days, doors swelled and stuck, bureau drawers wouldn't open, and a green mold appeared on some of my canvases. Even the pine logs which burned all day in the fireplace couldn't keep my little house warm or dry. Then the wind swung around to the west, the sun came out, and there was the summer again, the pale sand-yellow, the light green, and the faded blue.

I did a good deal of painting: I did a canvas of the

South Truro church for Miss Spinney, the old building, lonely and empty on the downs above the bay; and a watercolor of the sea from the end of Long Nook valley. It was a breezy day, with the wind northeast, the sea was dark, the wine-dark of the Greeks, with bands of green in it, darkening out to the horizon; and the sky was like the inside of a blue porcelain bowl with the light shining through it. I sent them both to Mr. Mathews. But the best thing I did was a painting of the men out in the traps in the early morning. I had to do it mostly from memory: the boats go out to the nets before it's light.

Everything is quiet and dark, the water comes in, in long swells out of the darkness. The boats head out into the swells . . . in the east the sky turns gray, and then pink; the dawn comes up slowly. The stars pale out, tones of blue begin to show in the sky. Far out from shore, one boat slips into the traps, drawing the nets up as it goes. The fish are down there; they pass backwards and forwards under the boat like shadows. The nets come higher; suddenly they break water in a rush of silver, and the fishermen begin scooping them in over the sides. The sun rises, the bay sparkles in the light, the fish are silver underfoot. Slowly and heavily one of the boats crosses the bay to Provincetown, while the other heads back again to the shore.

I wanted Arne to go with me, but he said there wasn't enough color in it for him. He was painting the Provincetown Electric Light and Power Plant; he said that it represented industry, and that industry represented the real world of today, and that it was this real world in which an artist should look for a subject worthy of him.

"Let us not fool ourselves, Eben," he exclaimed. "Beauty is only noble when it is useful. The symbol of the world today is a power plant; and if it appears ugly to us, that is only because we do not look at it in the right way."

But he came to Truro for the beach picnics in July. We lay on the sand at Cornhill, while the sun set, and the moon rose over the hill behind us, and men in corduroys and women with kerchiefs around their hair tended the fire of driftwood gathered on the beach. The sunset paled away into rose and green; the old blue night came down dim and hazy over the shore, and across the bay the lanterns of Provincetown twinkled in the dusk. Within the leaping yellow light of our fire the figures of our friends moved about; more wood was gathered, baskets unpacked, rugs laid down. As the flames burned lower toward the coals, steaks and sausages were broiled; a great bean pot was set beside the fire, a pail of mussels, a kettle of coffee. Afterwards we sang, sitting around the fire, while the moon sailed gently overhead, and the tide sent little ripples to break against the sand.... *"I dream of Jeannie with the light brown hair . . ."*

Or in the still, warm afternoons of August, we swam together in the sea, as the long rollers came lifting in, green and clear, to break in a bounce of foam, and slide hissing and dying up the beach. Far out, beyond the line of the horizon, beyond sight, over the world's rim, lay Europe, torn with her wars; but here all was peace, the empty shore curved away endlessly to the south under the summer sun, the light breeze stirred the grasses on the dunes, and only the shouts of children rose against the rolling thunder of the sea.

It was then that I longed for Jennie, at such times as these, when the world's beauty fell most upon my heart. And yet, in a way which I found hard to explain, I was not lonely; for I had a sense—as I have had ever since—of not being alone—a feeling that the world and Jennie and I were one, joined together in a unity for which there was no name, an inexpressible one-ness. Her very absence, not only from my sight, but from the slow-wheeling days around me, made them seem less real and solid to me; she was nowhere in the weather, the rains which fell across the Cape were not the rains which fell upon her little figure hurrying along somewhere—in what city, in what year?—yet for that reason all weathers seemed one weather to me, and the seasons of the past mingled in my

183

dreams with the summer all around me. For she was somewhere in the world; and wherever she was, there, too, was something of me.

She had said, "How beautiful the world is, Eben. It was never made for anything but beauty—whether we lived now, or long ago."

We had that beauty together. We never lost it.

Chapter XVII

Summer drained away into fall, but Jennie did not return. By September the bearberries were red, and people were picking beach plums in the fields along the roads, to make into jelly. The reeds in the river were silver-brown; and in the afternoons the sun slanted lower through the pines around my house. The birds which had been gone most of the summer, began to appear again, on their way south: red-headed woodpeckers, bluebirds, warblers, and grackles. Swallows swept nervously through the air, and sometimes at evening I saw a wedge of wild duck wavering southward against the sky.

I had received a good-sized check from Mr. Mathews, and decided to use some of it to rent a little sailboat from John Worthington's brother, Bill, who lived near the railroad bridge, close to where the Pamet emptied into the bay. I knew something about sailing, though not a great deal; but I didn't think I could get into much trouble. The boat, an eighteen-foot centerboard knock-about, was kept moored near the mouth of the river, in a small backwater to one side of the swiftly moving stream. It took a good bit of navigating to get out into the bay, through the narrow channel; tide and wind both had to be right, but the wind seemed almost always easterly that month, streaming back from the Bermuda high which stood like a formidable but invisible cloud somewhere out at sea; and with a stiff breeze behind me, I could usually manage to make out, even against the tide.

Coming back, I had to wait for the current, and then come in close-hauled. Arne constituted himself my crew; he sat forward, ducked the boom when we came about, and handled the jib sheets with a sort of wild solemnity. It was exciting to lean against the wind, and feel the boat fight back against it; to watch the green water slide by, and hear the current chuckle against the planking. It was good exercise, too; it made my arms ache, and put blisters on my hands.

We used to sail out into the bay, sometimes as far as the traps, once or twice as far as Provincetown. It was a world by itself, out there on the water, in the shine and sun-dazzle, a world of never-ending blue, of steady wind, of clear and arrowy distance; and I was happy there.

Late in September a hurricane was reported in the Caribbean. We thought little about it; it was the time of year for hurricanes; they either hit the Florida Keys or blew themselves out in the Atlantic. This one apparently was headed for Florida.

On the Cape we had a period of unusually clear weather—a weather breeder, Arne said. We made the most of it, for the season was drawing to an end; the line storm would be along soon, and after that it would be too cold and rough for sailing. We went out every day. The weather was warm—unnaturally so for that time of year —and the wind southeast. We waited for it to swing around into the north.

On Monday the report was that the storm had missed Florida, and was heading for the Carolinas. That meant rain and a southwest blow; but on Tuesday we heard that it had turned east again, and would lose itself out at sea. So we figured we still had a few days' good sailing weather left to us, and decided to make a long trip up the coast, camp overnight on Great Island off Wellfleet, and come home the next day. We left a little before noon on Tuesday; there was a steady breeze from the southeast, and we made a fair reach of it all the way.

We camped that night on the island, and built a fire at

the sand's edge. We talked for a long time in the firelight; the shadows danced in the scrub behind us, the pale sky, sown with its stars, lay like a great lake above us, and the little boat rocked quietly at its anchor, on the tide. I tried to tell Arne something of what was in my mind, about myself, and about the world. "We know so little," I said, "and there's so much to know. We live by taste and touch; we see only what is under our noses. There are solar systems up there above us, greater than our own; and whole universes in a drop of water. And time stretches out endlessly on every side. This earth, this ocean, this little moment of living, has no meaning by itself. . . . Yesterday is just as true as today; only we forget."

Arne yawned. "Yes," he said. "So it is. Go to sleep."

"And love," I said, "is endless, too; and today's little happiness is only part of it."

"Go to sleep," said Arne. "Tomorrow is another day."

That night, for the first time in my life, I dreamed of Jennie: I dreamed of our meeting, long ago, I dreamed it over again as it had happened; I saw her as the child, walking down the long empty row of benches in the Mall, and I heard her say as she had said then, "I wish you'd wait for me to grow up, but you won't, I guess." And in my dream, I remembered the words of her little tuneless song—

"The wind blows, the sea flows . ."

I woke with a sense of alarm, with a feeling that something was wrong. The wind was still blowing, warm and steadily southeast, but I thought a little stronger. There was a faint haze in the air, and a few strange-looking clouds passed by overhead. They seemed to be traveling fast. I leaned over and shook Arne by the shoulder. "Get up, Arne," I said. "We've got to get home."

We put the sail up and headed north for Truro. We didn't waste any time. Out on the water, the wind seemed even stronger; it was a little aft of us, and I let the sail take all it would. It was something of a job to hold the tiller, for a fair sea was running, and the boat yawed a good

Notice the juxtaposition of ideas as Eben remembers Jennie's song and wakes up with a sense of alarm.

186

deal. Arne said nothing; he kept watching the sky.

The haze deepened very slowly, but the clouds increased; they were at different levels, moving rapidly, and of a shape I'd never seen before—long cylinders, fog-like tentacles, smoky fingers. They were a different tone of white, too, like cotton gone a little dusty. I had made the main sheet fast, but I wondered if the sail would hold. "Arne," I called to him, "hadn't we better reef?"

He nodded without speaking, and I managed to bring the boat up into the wind. I noticed that my fingers were trembling, and I thought that Arne looked a little pale. There was a curious urgency in the wind. "We'd better get out of here," I said.

The boat went off with a rush under a single reef, and I tried to head up a little to windward, to get some shelter from the shore. The waves were running a good deal higher now, and breaking at the crests; I had to put all my weight on the tiller to hold her steady. I was feeling decidedly uneasy, and I wondered whether I oughtn't to try to make for shore directly, but there was nowhere except the Pamet at Truro where I could have found shelter for the boat. I had no idea how hard the wind was blowing, but I knew it was blowing hard. And there was a strange sound to it, from somewhere far away.

A little before noon I saw Arne point behind us, and followed his glance back over the stern. The horizon to the south had disappeared behind a gray haze. It wasn't altogether gray, but gray-yellow, like mud. I thought perhaps it was rain, but it didn't look like it. We've got to get out of this, I thought.

My arms and hands were aching from holding the tiller, and my legs were tired from bracing myself against the sides. I beckoned Arne to come aft and take over, while I went forward to bail some of the water that had come in, mostly over the stern. Down in the cockpit, the waves seemed higher than ever; we would tilt up at the stern, hang for a moment on a crest, and then rush down the slope after it, and slew around in the hollow, till Arne straightened us out. Each time the tip of the boom hit the water, I thought we'd go over. My throat was dry, but I didn't feel frightened, I didn't have time. I kept listening to the wind; it wasn't like anything I'd ever heard before.

A little after that we started to work in toward the Pamet. I went back to the tiller, and told Arne to take the sheet, and let it out whenever we got over too far. He snubbed it around a cleat as well as he could, but it took all his great strength to hold it. We lay out to windward on the deck, with our legs braced against the centerboard scabbard; the huge seas broke behind us, and then foamed up over the counter, and the dark-green water poured along the leeward deck up to the coaming. It seemed to me that we looked right down at the sea under our feet; it rose sometimes in a slice of wave and curled up over the cockpit; then I kicked the tiller, and we came up. We seemed half in and half out of the water most of the time, I couldn't tell which. "I think we'll make it, though," I said. Arne shook his head. "Maybe," he answered.

About two hundred yards from shore, the mainsail went out, torn loose near the peak; and a moment later, the jib. I thought we were done for then; but both sails caught in the rigging and snagged, and the boat eased. I saw that as long as they held, we had a sort of double reef; and we hadn't much further to go. "I think we'll make it, Arne," I said.

I could barely see the river mouth for the waves, which gave me an idea of how high the tide was running; but I set a course for the railroad bridge, and trusted to luck. We hit it right, and went in through a white fury of foam, on a roaring breaker which picked us up and ran us up the channel like a chip of wood, and flung us out on the sand a hundred yards from the bay. Arne was out first, but before he could get the mainsail down, the wind tore it out of his hands, and sent it ballooning across the river, with half the rigging attached to it. We got the anchor out, but I knew it wouldn't hold. The waves were booming in through the river mouth, six feet high, and coming up the channel like wild horses. "It's no good, Arne," I said. "The tide's coming in; she'll drag right down to the bridge, and lose her mast." There was nothing we could do. I hadn't figured on such a high tide.

Bill Worthington had seen us come in. He was waiting for us as we climbed up onto the road from what was left of the beach. "Well, by God," he said, "you boys were out in something."

I grinned back at him, but I felt pretty shaky. My legs were trembling, and I couldn't keep my teeth together. "I'm sorry about the boat, Bill," I said. "I didn't figure the storm would be so bad."

Bill looked at me, and shook his head. "Storm, hell," he said. "This one's a hurricane."

Chapter XVIII

Bill told us that hurricane signals were flying at High Land Light; he said it made him feel queer in the pit of his stomach. But it was still only the beginning; we all knew that.

We made the boat fast as well as we could, and then Bill drove us home to the north side of the river. We could hear the sand pit against the car whenever we crossed an exposed place in the road, and once or twice the car swerved sharply in a sudden gust. Bill left us at the house, and went back to watch the tide. His own house wasn't any too far above high water.

It was only then, as we started down the path to the shack, that I began to have an idea of what the wind was really like. Out there, on the water, I'd been too busy; and besides, in a sort of way, we had been part of it, moving with it, running before it. But here, facing the open sweep from the southeast, I caught it full and fair, and it hit me like a blow.

189

The wind was coming across the Pamet in a steady flow, almost like a river of air in flood. There was no letup to it; it came flowing over heavy and solid and fast; it had pushed the marsh grass down flat, and bent the pines over in a quarter circle. There was something unnatural about it; it seemed to be coming from far away, but all the time it was coming nearer, and I had a feeling that it was darkness itself coming, and a force that didn't belong on this earth. My heart was beating fast; I felt cold and excited. I could hear that strange sound I had heard out on the bay, a sort of roaring hum, high up and far off; and the yellow-gray wall was still down there to the south. Or had it come closer? I couldn't tell. I looked down the slope at the river; it was up over the marsh, and the water was brown, and streaked with yellow foam. "I'm glad we're here," I said to Arne, shouting against the wind. He smiled then, for the first time. "If the house holds," he said.

A branch from a locust down at the water's edge suddenly snapped, and sailed a few yards up the slope toward us. "Come on," I said; "let's go in."

We went around the back way to get out of the direct force of the wind. While we'd been gone, the grocer had left a box of eggs on the little back porch; they were all over the floor. I thought, that'll be a mess to clean up tomorrow, but I didn't stop. The wind picked us up, and swept us in through the door, and we had to lean back against it to close it. It was cold and still in the house, but I could hear the roaring in my ears, from those hours out on the bay. After a while the noise in my ears went away, and then I could hear the storm itself, and that high, far off, humming sound.

Arne made a fire, and I got out the whiskey. I took a big drink; I could feel it warm me all the way down. We stood in front of the fire, and looked at each other. I could feel the house shake every now and then, and I heard the windows rattle; I wondered if I ought to try to put up the shutters, I tried to remember what I'd read about hurricanes. But then I remembered that the house had no shutters. There didn't seem to be anything to do.

"I wonder if the boat will hold," I said.

"I wouldn't think so," said Arne.

"We were lucky, at that," I said.

I took another drink. "I wonder how they're making out in Provincetown," I said.

Arne shook his head gloomily. "It'll be bad, all right," he remarked.

The rain began about then. It wasn't much of a downpour, but it came in almost level. In ten minutes there was a fair-sized puddle just inside the door. I laid a towel along the lintel, to keep the water out.

The wind seemed to be getting stronger all the time; once or twice it shook the house so hard I thought the walls would go. There was nothing to do but just sit there and wait for something to happen; and after a while, Arne said he thought we ought to go out and have a look around. He said he wanted to see what a hurricane looked like. We went out the back way, and it took all our strength to get the door closed after us. But when we got around to the front of the house, we couldn't breathe; the wind tore the air right out of our mouths. "Boy," said Arne, holding his hands in front of his face, "I'm glad I'm not out on the bay now."

I tried to see the bay, but it was lost in weather, a gray smother of rain and spray and blowing sand. I saw that the telegraph poles beyond Cat Island were down, and I pointed at them. And then the big elm behind the house went.

It went over slowly, with a sort of sigh, taking a lot of ground with it. Arne didn't say anything, but his eyes had a wild look in them. He grabbed my arm, and pointed across the river. A moment later we saw Bill Worthington's old barn sag over on its side, and watched the wind worry it along toward the river. "Maybe we ought to go over and help him," I shouted, with my mouth close to Arne's ear. He made a gesture of helplessness. "How are we going to get there?" he shouted back.

We were still watching Bill's house, crouched together with our arms wrapped around one of the straining pines, when the coastguard truck came by. It stopped on the road behind us, and a guardsman came clumping over in boots and oilskins. "Jeez," he said, "what do you guys think you're doing?" We told him that we were watching Bill's barn being blown into the river. "Well," he said, "there'll be more than that in the river soon. The ocean's breaking through at Dune Hollow." He walked back to the truck, and they went on, toward Cat Island and John Rule's house out at the edge of the marsh.

We were pretty high above the water where we were, and I didn't think even the ocean would reach that far. At any rate, we didn't have long to wait; in about ten minutes we saw the wave coming down the valley toward us, from the sea. It didn't look very high—just a line of brown foam, with branches and sand in it, but it was scary. It passed under us, and then there wasn't any marsh left, just water, moving fast.

And a moment later, I saw her.

She was below me, and a little to the east, near the town landing, trying to get up the slope from the river. She seemed tired; and the wind was worrying her like a dog. While I watched, she lost her balance, and half fell; and then she began to slip backward toward the water again. Another wave was coming down the valley from the east; I could see it coming.

I don't know how I got down the hill to her, against the wind, but I did. I got my arm around her just in time, and pulled her up out of the way; the crest went by almost a foot below us. She lay back against me, white and spent, with closed eyes. "I was afraid I wouldn't get here, darling," she said.

I held her close. Even then, with that mad flood below us, I thought we'd make it all right. I put my face down against hers; her cheeks were deathly cold. She lifted her

192

hands slowly, as though they were a great weight, and put her arms around my neck. "I had to get back to you, Eben," she said.

"We'll have to hurry, Jennie," I told her. I tried to pull her along, up the slope, but she was like a dead weight, she seemed to have no strength left at all. She smiled at me piteously, and shook her head. "You go, Eben," she said; "I can't make it."

I tried to lift her, then, but she was too heavy for me; I couldn't find a foothold on the slippery ground. The water was higher, now, almost at our feet; a dark ripple washed in over my ankles. "Jennie," I cried, "for God's sake . . ."

"Let me look at you," she whispered. I couldn't hear her, but I knew what she was saying. She held my face in her hands, and looked at me for a moment with wide, dark eyes. "It's been a long time, darling," she said.

I didn't want to talk, I wanted to get out of there, I wanted to get her up the slope away from the water. "Look," I said, "if I could lift you up on my back . . ."

But she didn't seem to hear me. "Yes," she said, almost to herself; "I wasn't wrong."

"Jennie," I cried; "please . . ."

Her arms tightened around me for a moment. "Hold me close, Eben," she said. "We're together, now."

I held her close, but my mind was in a panic. I couldn't lift her, I couldn't get her away, and the ground where we were standing was beginning to give. "Arne," I shouted as loudly as I could; "Arne."

It was then I saw it coming.

It came in from the bay, a great brown wave, sweeping back up the valley toward the sea. There was no escape from it; we could never have climbed above it; it came in steady and very fast, with a strange sucking noise. Well, I thought, we'll go together, anyhow.

Bending over, I kissed her full on the lips. "Yes, Jennie," I said; "we're together now."

She knew what was coming. "Eben," she whispered, pressed against my cheek, "there's only one love . . .

nothing can change it. It's still all right, darling, whatever happens, because we'll always be together . . . somewhere. . . ."

"I know," I said.

And then the wave hit us. I tried to hold on to her, to go out with her, but it tore us apart. I felt her whirled out of my arms; the water drew me under, and rolled me over and over; I felt myself flung upwards, sucked down, and then flung upwards again. Then something crashed into me, and that was all I knew.

Arne found me sprawled in a tree half in and half out of the water, and dragged me back to safety. How he managed to carry me up the slope and back to the house in that wind, I don't know. He put me to bed, and made me drink almost a pint of whiskey; and he sat beside me all that night. He told me later that he had to hold me down in bed, that I kept trying to get back to the river. I don't remember much about it; it was all dark for me, all I remember is the dark.

It was a week before I could travel; but it made no difference, because the roads were out, and we couldn't have gotten through, anyway. I lay in bed, and ate what Arne gave me, and tried not to think about what had happened. Arne brought back the news from outside; he told me that there hadn't been as much damage in Truro as we'd thought; a lot of trees had gone over in Provincetown, and a fishing boat had been flung up on the rocks; John Worthington's nets were gone at North Truro, but except for the ocean breaking through into the Pamet, it hadn't been so bad. Even Bill's home had escaped, though the water had come up as high as the windows. The beach at Dune Hollow had started to build up again; pretty soon everything would be the same as before.

I came back to the city on a bright autumn day, deep blue and sun-yellow in the streets, and the great buildings rising clear and sharp in the keen, high air. Mr. Mathews was waiting for me at the gallery. "We worried

Beginning with Chapter XV consider the many ways the author has prepared the reader for this ending.

about you, Eben," he said. "Miss Spinney and I . . . we couldn't get any news for a long while."

He patted me awkwardly on the shoulder. "I'm glad to see you, my boy," he said. "I—I'm very glad. . . ."

Miss Spinney didn't say anything. She looked to me as though she had been crying.

It was Gus who gave me the little clipping from the newspaper. "I thought maybe you hadn't seen it, Mack," he said.

It was from the *Times,* of September 22nd. "The steamship *Latania,"* it read, "has reported by wireless today the loss of one of its passengers in the storm, a hundred miles off the Nantucket Lightship. Miss Jennie Appleton, who was returning to America after a stay of eight years abroad, was swept overboard by a wave which smashed a part of the bridge, and injured several of the passengers. Officials of the line are endeavoring to discover the whereabouts of Miss Appleton's relatives in this country."

Gus hesitated; he looked at me, and then he looked away. "I thought maybe you didn't know," he said. "I'm sorry, Mack."

I gave the clipping back to him. "No," I said, "I knew. "It's still all right," I said. "It's all right."

What events and insights has Eben had to accept in order to allow him to tell Gus "It's all right"?

SYNTHESIS

If Eben had met Jennie only as an adult young woman, do you think she would still have inspired the portrait?

Is the Jennie that Eben *paints* real or unreal? Is the Jennie that Eben *loves* real or unreal?

How would the story have been different if it had been told by Jennie? by Gus? by Mrs. Jekes?

How much time has elapsed between Eben's first and last encounters with Jennie? How has the sense of illusion been maintained?

Comment on the validity of these statements:
1. "Portrait of Jennie" is a story of space and time.
2. "Portrait of Jennie" is a romantic story.
3. "Portrait of Jennie" is an expression of truths about life that are independent of time and place.

When a writer gives the reader veiled hints of later developments in his story, he is using the literary device called *foreshadowing*. This technique is used to alert the reader's mind to the possibility of an event; its effect is mild suspense, vague mystery, or "shadowy" conjecture. The technique is recognized completely only when the reader is aware of the event that was hinted at—it demands a looking back. Discuss Nathan's use of foreshadowing in this story.

Contrast the treatment of love in "Portrait of Jennie," "The Canterville Ghost," and "The Diamond as Big as the Ritz."

COMMENT

Robert Nathan is an author of novels, plays, movie scripts, and poetry, as well as an illustrator and writer of children's books. His favorite theme is the power of love, and he even uses that theme as a satirical solution to the 1932 economic depression in his novel *One More Spring*.

"Portrait of Jennie" was published in 1940. It was made into a motion picture in 1948, starring Joseph Cotten, Jennifer Jones, David Wayne, and Ethel Barrymore; you may still be able to see it on television if you check your weekly TV movie listings.

THE GHOSTLY RENTAL

HENRY JAMES

I was in my twenty-second year, and I had just left college. I was at liberty to choose my career, and I chose it with much promptness. I afterward renounced it, in truth, with equal ardor, but I have never regretted those two youthful years of perplexed and excited but also of agreeable and fruitful experiment. I had a taste for theology, and during my college term I had been an admiring reader

Lucky young man, isn't he? Can you guess his social and economic status?

Dr. William E. Channing: U.S. Unitarian clergyman and writer (1780–1842). The "rose of faith" metaphor indicates that his theology emphasized love and de-emphasized sacrifice.

Cambridge, Massachusetts.

Friedrich Overbeck and **Ary Scheffer:** painters of religious subjects.

of Dr. Channing. This was theology of a grateful and succulent savor; it seemed to offer one the rose of faith delightfully stripped of its thorns. And then (for I rather think this had something to do with it), I had taken a fancy to the old Divinity School. I have always had an eye to the back scene in the human drama, and it seemed to me that I might play my part with a fair chance of applause (from myself at least) in that detached and tranquil home of mild casuistry, with its respectable avenue on one side and its prospect of green fields and contact with acres of woodland on the other.

Cambridge, for the lovers of woods and fields, has changed for the worse since those days, and the precinct in question has forfeited much of its mingled pastoral and scholastic quietude. It was then a College-hall in the woods—a charming mixture. What it is now has nothing to do with my story; and I have no doubt that there are still doctrine-haunted young seniors who, as they stroll near it in the summer dusk, promise themselves, later, to taste of its fine leisurely quality. For myself, I was not disappointed. I established myself in a great square, low-browed room, with deep window-benches; I hung prints from Overbeck and Ary Scheffer on the walls; I arranged my books, with great refinement of classification, in the alcoves beside the high chim-

ney-shelf, and I began to read Plotinus and
St. Augustine. Among my companions were
two or three men of ability and of good
fellowship with whom I occasionally brewed
a fireside bowl; and with adventurous reading, deep discourse, potations conscien-
tiously shallow, and long country walks, my
initiation into the clerical mystery pro-
gressed agreeably enough.

    With one of my comrades I formed an
especial friendship, and we passed a great
deal of time together. Unfortunately he had a
chronic weakness of one of his knees, which
compelled him to lead a very sedentary life,
and as I was a methodical pedestrian, this
made some difference in our habits. I used
often to stretch away for my daily ramble
with no companion but the stick in my hand
or the book in my pocket. But in the use of
my legs and the sense of unstinted open air I
have always found company enough. I
should, perhaps, add that in the enjoyment
of a very sharp pair of eyes I found something of a social pleasure. My eyes and I
were on excellent terms; they were indefati-
gable observers of all wayside incidents, and
so long as they were amused I was contented. It is, indeed, owing to their inquisi-
tive habits that I came into possession of this
remarkable story.

    Much of the country about the old
college town is pretty now, but it was prettier

Plotinus: Roman
philosopher.
St. Augustine: one of
the fathers in the early
Christian Church.

Isn't he a little smug
about his nosiness?

201

This story first appeared in 1876. How would these comments fit the present times?

thirty years ago. That multitudinous eruption of domiciliary pasteboard which now graces the landscape, in the direction of the low, blue Waltham Hills, had not yet taken place; there were no genteel cottages to put the shabby meadows and scrubby orchards to shame—a juxtaposition by which, in later years, neither element of the contrast has gained. Certain crooked crossroads then, as I remember them, were more deeply and naturally rural, and the solitary dwellings on the long grassy slopes beside them, under the tall, customary elm that curved its foliage in mid-air like the outward dropping ears of a girdled wheat-sheaf, sat with their shingled hoods well pulled down on their ears, and no prescience whatever of the fashion of French roofs—weather-wrinkled old peasant women, as you might call them, quietly wearing the native coif and never dreaming of mounting bonnets and indecently exposing their venerable brows.

That winter was what is called an "open" one; there was much cold, but little snow; the roads were firm and free, and I was rarely compelled by the weather to forego my exercise. One gray December afternoon I had sought it in the direction of the adjacent town of Medford, and I was retracing my steps at an even pace and watching the pale, cold tints—the transparent amber and faded rose-color—which curtained, in

202

wintry fashion, the western sky and reminded me of a skeptical smile on the lips of a beautiful woman. I came, as dusk was falling, to a narrow road which I had never traversed and which I imagined offered me a short cut homeward. I was about three miles away; I was late and would have been thankful to make them two. I diverged, walked some ten minutes, and then perceived that the road had a very unfrequented air. The wheel-ruts looked old; the stillness seemed peculiarly sensible. And yet down the road stood a house, so that it must in some degree have been a thoroughfare. On one side was a high, natural embankment, on the top of which was perched an apple-orchard whose tangled boughs made a stretch of coarse black lace-work hung across the coldly rosy west.

In a short time I came to the house, and I immediately found myself interested in it. I stopped in front of it gazing hard, I hardly knew why, but with a vague mixture of curiosity and timidity. It was a house like most of the houses thereabouts, except that it was decidedly a handsome specimen of its class. It stood on a grassy slope; it had its tall, impartially drooping elm beside it and its old black well-cover at its shoulder. But it was of very large proportions, and it had a striking look of solidity and stoutness of timber. It had lived to a good old age, too, for

Why "timidity"?

the wood-work on its doorway and under its eaves, carefully and abundantly carved, referred it to the middle, at the latest, of the last century. All this had once been painted white, but the broad back of time, leaning against the door-posts for a hundred years, had laid bare the grain of the wood. Behind the house stretched an orchard of apple-trees, more gnarled and fantastic than usual, and wearing, in the deepening dusk, a blighted and exhausted aspect.

All the windows of the house had rusty shutters, without slats, and these were closely drawn. There was no sign of life about it; it looked blank, bare and vacant, and yet, as I lingered near it, it seemed to have a familiar meaning—an audible eloquence. I have always thought of the impression made upon me at first sight, by that gray colonial dwelling, as a proof that induction may sometimes be near akin to divination; for after all, there was nothing on the face of the matter to warrant the very serious induction that I made. I fell back and crossed the road. The last red light of the sunset disengaged itself, as it was about to vanish, and rested faintly for a moment on the time-silvered front of the old house. It touched, with perfect regularity, the series of small panes in the fan-shaped window above the door and twinkled there fantastically. Then it died away and left the place more

The narrator assumes that he possesses a special ability to prophesy. Does this assumption fit his character?

intensely somber. At this moment, I said to myself with the accent of profound conviction—"The house is simply haunted!"

Somehow, immediately, I believed it, and so long as I was not shut up inside, the idea gave me pleasure. It was implied in the aspect of the house, and it explained it. Half an hour before, if I had been asked, I would have said, as befitted a young man who was explicitly cultivating cheerful views of the supernatural, that there were no such things as haunted houses. But the dwelling before me gave a vivid meaning to the empty words; it had been spiritually blighted.

The longer I looked at it, the intenser seemed the secret that it held. I walked all round it, I tried to peep here and there through a crevice in the shutters, and I took a puerile satisfaction in laying my hand on the door-knob and gently turning it. If the door had yielded, would I have gone in?—would I have penetrated the dusky stillness? My audacity, fortunately, was not put to the test. The portal was admirably solid, and I was unable even to shake it. At last I turned away, casting many looks behind me. I pursued my way, and, after a longer walk than I had bargained for, reached the high-road. At a certain distance below the point at which the long lane I have mentioned entered it, stood a comfortable, tidy dwelling, which might have offered itself as the model

What indications are there that the house is haunted? that the narrator hopes it is haunted?

of the house which is in no sense haunted—which has no sinister secrets and knows nothing but blooming prosperity. Its clean white paint stared placidly through the dusk, and its vine-covered porch had been dressed in straw for the winter. An old, one-horse chaise, freighted with two departing visitors, was leaving the door; and through the undraped windows, I saw the lamp-lit sitting-room and the table spread with the early "tea," which had been improvised for the comfort of the guests. The mistress of the house had come to the gate with her friends; she lingered there after the chaise had wheeled creakingly away, half to watch them down the road and half to give me, as I passed in the twilight, a questioning look. She was a comely, quick young woman with a sharp, dark eye, and I ventured to stop and speak to her.

"That house down that side-road," I said, "about a mile from here—the only one—can you tell me whom it belongs to?"

She stared at me a moment and, I thought, colored a little. "Our folks never go down that road," she said, briefly.

"But it's a short way to Medford," I answered.

She gave a little toss of her head. "Perhaps it would turn out a long way. At any rate, we don't use it."

This was interesting. A thrifty Yankee

household must have good reasons for this scorn of time-saving processes. "But you know the house, at least?" I said.

"Well, I have seen it."

"And to whom does it belong?"

She gave a little laugh and looked away as if she were aware that, to a stranger, her words might seem to savor of agricultural superstition. "I guess it belongs to them that are in it."

"But is there anyone in it? It is completely closed."

"That makes no difference. They never come out, and no one ever goes in." And she turned away.

But I laid my hand on her arm, respectfully. "You mean," I said, "that the house is haunted?"

She drew herself away, colored, raised her finger to her lips, and hurried into the house, where, in a moment, the curtains were dropped over the windows.

For several days I thought repeatedly of this little adventure, but I took some satisfaction in keeping it to myself. If the house was not haunted, it was useless to expose my imaginative whims, and if it was, it was agreeable to drain the cup of horror without assistance. I determined, of course, to pass that way again; and a week later—it was the last day of the year—I retraced my steps. I approached the house from the op-

What—except a belief in ghosts—might account for the woman's superstitious attitude toward the house?

207

Remember that this is the narrator's description. Note how his desire for adventure affects his interpretation.

posite direction and found myself before it at about the same hour as before. The light was failing, the sky low and gray; the wind wailed along the hard, bare ground and made slow eddies of the frost-blackened leaves. The melancholy mansion stood there, seeming to gather the winter twilight around it and mask itself in it, inscrutably. I hardly knew on what errand I had come, but I had a vague feeling that if this time the door-knob were to turn and the door to open, I should take my heart in my hands and let them close behind me. Who were the mysterious tenants to whom the good woman at the corner had alluded? What had been seen or heard—what was related? The door was as stubborn as before, and my impertinent fumblings with the latch caused no upper window to be thrown open, nor any strange, pale face to be thrust out. I ventured even to raise the rusty knocker and give it half-a-dozen raps, but they made a flat, dead sound and aroused no echo. Familiarity breeds contempt; I don't know what I should have done next if, in the distance, up the road (the same one I had followed), I had not seen a solitary figure advancing. I was unwilling to be observed hanging about this ill-famed dwelling, and I sought refuge among the dense shadows of a grove of pines near by, where I might peep forth and yet remain invisible.

How might a policeman interpret these "impertinent fumblings"?

208

Presently, the new-comer drew near, and I perceived that he was making straight for the house. He was a little, old man, the most striking feature of whose appearance was a voluminous cloak of a sort of military cut. He carried a walking-stick and advanced in a slow, painful, somewhat hobbling fashion, but with an air of extreme resolution. He turned off from the road and followed the vague wheel-track, and within a few yards of the house he paused. He looked up at it, fixedly and searchingly, as if he were counting the windows, or noting certain familiar marks. Then he took off his hat and bent over slowly and solemnly, as if he were performing an obeisance. As he stood uncovered, I had a good look at him. He was, as I have said, a diminutive old man, but it would have been hard to decide whether he belonged to this world or to the other. His head reminded me, vaguely, of the portraits of Andrew Jackson. He had a crop of grizzled hair, as stiff as a brush, a lean, pale, smooth-shaven face, and an eye of intense brilliancy, surmounted with thick brows, which had remained perfectly black. His face, as well as his cloak, seemed to belong to an old soldier; he looked like a retired military man of a modest rank; but he struck me as exceeding the classic privilege of even such a personage to be eccentric and grotesque.

Summarize his reactions to the appearance of this new character.

When he had finished his salute, he advanced to the door, fumbled in the folds of his cloak, which hung down much further in front than behind, and produced a key. This he slowly and carefully inserted into the lock, and then, apparently, he turned it. But the door did not immediately open; first he bent his head, turned his ear, and stood listening, and then he looked up and down the road. Satisfied or reassured, he applied his aged shoulder to one of the deep-set panels and pressed a moment. The door yielded—opening into perfect darkness. He stopped again on the threshold and again removed his hat and made his bow. Then he went in and carefully closed the door behind him.

Who in the world was he, and what was his errand? He might have been a figure out of one of Hoffmann's tales. Was he vision or a reality—an inmate of the house or a familiar, friendly visitor? What had been the meaning, in either case, of his mystic genuflexions, and how did he propose to proceed in that inner darkness? I emerged from my retirement and observed narrowly several of the windows. In each of them, at an interval, a ray of light became visible in the chink between the two leaves of the shutters. Evidently, he was lighting up; was he going to give a party—a ghostly revel? My curiosity grew intense, but I was quite at a loss how to

Hoffmann's tales: grotesque stories written by E.T.A. Hoffmann (1776–1822).

The narrator wants to find a ghost under every bush.

210

satisfy it. For a moment I thought of rapping peremptorily at the door; but I dismissed this idea as unmannerly and calculated to break the spell, if spell there was. I walked round the house and tried, without violence, to open one of the lower windows. It resisted, but I had better fortune, in a moment, with another. There was a risk, certainly, in the trick I was playing—a risk of being seen from within, or (worse) seeing, myself, something that I should repent of seeing. But curiosity, as I say, had become an inspiration, and the risk was highly agreeable.

It still seems a game, doesn't it?

Through the parting of the shutters I looked into a lighted room—a room lighted by two candles in old brass flambeaux placed upon the mantel-shelf. It was apparently a sort of back parlor, and it had retained all its furniture. This was a homely, old-fashioned pattern, and consisted of hair-cloth chairs and sofas, spare mahogany tables, and framed samplers hung upon the walls. But although the room was furnished, it had a strangely uninhabited look; the tables and chairs were in rigid positions, and no small, familiar objects were visible. I could not see everything, and I could only guess at the existence, on my right, of a large folding door. It was apparently open, and the light of the neighboring room passed through it. I waited for some time, but the room remained empty.

flambeaux (flam′bōz): large decorated candlesticks.

At last I became conscious that a large shadow was projected upon the wall opposite the folding door—the shadow, evidently, of a figure in the adjoining room. It was tall and grotesque and seemed to represent a person sitting perfectly motionless, in profile. I thought I recognized the perpendicular bristles and far-arching nose of my little old man. There was a strange fixedness in his posture; he appeared to be seated and looking intently at something. I watched the shadow a long time, but it never stirred. At last, however, just as my patience began to ebb, it moved slowly, rose to the ceiling, and became indistinct. I don't know what I should have seen next, but by an irresistible impulse I closed the shutter. Was it delicacy?—was it pusillanimity? I can hardly say. I lingered, nevertheless, near the house, hoping that my friend would reappear.

I was not disappointed; for he at last emerged, looking just as when he had gone in and taking his leave in the same ceremonious fashion. (The lights, I had already observed, had disappeared from the crevice of each of the windows.) He faced about before the door, took off his hat, and made an obsequious bow. As he turned away I had a hundred minds to speak to him, but I let him depart in peace. This, I may say, was pure delicacy;—you will answer, perhaps, that it came too late. It seemed to me that he

pusillanimity
(pyü′ sə lə nim′ə tē): cowardliness.

Note how easily the narrator assumes that the old man is a "friend" in this adventure.

212

had a right to resent my observation; though my own right to exercise it (if ghosts were in the question) struck me as equally positive. I continued to watch him as he hobbled softly down the bank and along the lonely road. Then I musingly retreated in the opposite direction. I was tempted to follow him, at a distance, to see what became of him; but this, too, seemed indelicate; and I confess, moreover, that I felt the inclination to coquet a little, as it were, with my discovery—to pull apart the petals of the flower one by one.

I continued to smell the flower, from time to time, for its oddity of perfume had fascinated me. I passed by the house on the cross-road again, but never encountered the old man in the cloak or any other wayfarer. It seemed to keep observers at a distance, and I was careful not to gossip about it: one inquirer, I said to myself, may edge his way into the secret, but there is no room for two. At the same time, of course, I would have been thankful for any chance side-light that might fall across the matter—though I could not well see whence it was to come. I hoped to meet the old man in the cloak elsewhere, but as the days passed by without his reappearing, I ceased to expect it. And yet I reflected that he probably lived in that neighborhood, inasmuch as he had made his pilgrimage to the vacant house on foot. If he had come from a distance, he would have

There is a conflict between the narrator's sense of good manners and his curiosity. How does he rationalize his actions?

An odd image!

213

been sure to arrive in some old deep-hooded gig with yellow wheels—a vehicle as venerably grotesque as himself.

One day I took a stroll in Mount Auburn cemetery—an institution at that period in its infancy and full of a sylvan charm which it has now completely forfeited. It contained more maple and birch than willow and cypress, and the sleepers had ample elbow room. It was not a city of the dead, but at the most a village, and a meditative pedestrian might stroll there without too importunate a reminder of the grotesque side of our claims to posthumous consideration.

I had come out to enjoy the first foretaste of Spring—one of those mild days of late winter when the torpid earth seems to draw the first long breath that marks the rupture of the spell of sleep. The sun was veiled in haze, and yet warm, and the frost was oozing from its deepest lurking-places. I had been treading for half an hour the winding ways of the cemetery, when suddenly I perceived a familiar figure seated on a bench against a southward-facing evergreen hedge. I call the figure familiar, because I had seen it often in memory and in fancy; in fact, I had beheld it but once. Its back was turned to me, but it wore a voluminous cloak, which there was no mistaking. Here, at last, was my fellow-visitor at the haunted house, and here was my chance, if I wished to approach him!

214

I made a circuit and came toward him from in front. He saw me, at the end of the alley, and sat motionless, with his hands on the head of his stick, watching me from under his black eyebrows as I drew near. At a distance these black eyebrows looked formidable; they were the only thing I saw in his face. But on a closer view I was reassured, simply because I immediately felt that no man could really be as fantastically fierce as this poor old gentleman looked. His face was a kind of caricature of martial truculence.

I stopped in front of him and respectfully asked leave to sit and rest upon his bench. He granted it with a silent gesture of much dignity, and I placed myself beside him. In this position I was able, covertly, to observe him. He was quite as much an oddity in the morning sunshine as he had been in the dubious twilight. The lines in his face were as rigid as if they had been hacked out of a block by a clumsy woodcarver. His eyes were flamboyant, his nose terrific, his mouth implacable. And yet, after a while, when he slowly turned and looked at me fixedly, I perceived that in spite of this portentous mask, he was a very mild old man. I was sure he even would have been glad to smile, but, evidently, his facial muscles were too stiff— they had taken a different fold, once and for all. I wondered whether he was demented, but I dismissed the idea; the fixed glitter in

What expectations of evil does the narrator bring to this meeting? Do these expectations match what he sees?

portentous: ominous; threatening.

his eye was not that of insanity. What his face really expressed was deep and simple sadness; his heart perhaps was broken, but his brain was intact. His dress was shabby but neat, and his old blue cloak had known half a century's brushing.

I hastened to make some observation upon the exceptional softness of the day, and he answered me in a gentle, mellow voice, which it was almost startling to hear proceed from such bellicose lips.

"This is a very comfortable place," he presently added.

"I am fond of walking in graveyards," I rejoined deliberately, flattering myself that I had struck a vein that might lead to something. I was encouraged; he turned and fixed me with his duskily glowing eyes. Then very gravely—"Walking, yes. Take all your exercise now. Someday you will have to settle down in a graveyard in a fixed position."

"Very true," said I. "But you know there are some people who are said to take exercise even after that day."

He had been looking at me still; at this he looked away.

"You don't understand?" I said, gently.

He continued to gaze straight before him.

"Some people, you know, walk about after death," I went on.

At last he turned and looked at me more portentously than ever. "You don't believe that," he said simply.

portentous seems to be one of Henry James' favorite words.

"How do you know I don't?"

"Because you are young and foolish." This was said without acerbity—even kindly, but in the tone of an old man whose consciousness of his own heavy experience made everything else seem light.

Would you agree?

"I am certainly young," I answered; "but I don't think that, on the whole, I am foolish. But say I don't believe in ghosts—most people would be on my side."

"Most people are fools!" said the old man.

I let the question rest and talked of other things. My companion seemed on his guard; he eyed me defiantly and made brief answers to my remarks, but I nevertheless gathered an impression that our meeting was an agreeable thing to him, and even a social incident of some importance. He was evidently a lonely creature, and his opportunities for gossip were rare. He had had troubles, and they had detached him from the world and driven him back upon himself; but the social chord in his antiquated soul was not entirely broken, and I was sure he was gratified to find that it could still feebly resound. At last, he began to ask questions himself; he inquired whether I was a student.

"I am a student of divinity," I answered.

"Of divinity?"

"Of theology. I am studying for the ministry."

At this he eyed me with peculiar intensity—after which his gaze wandered away again. "There are certain things you ought to know, then," he said at last.

"I have a great desire for knowledge," I answered. "What things do you mean?"

He looked at me again awhile, but without heeding my question.

"I like your appearance," he said. "You seem to me a sober lad."

"Oh, I am perfectly sober!" I exclaimed—yet departing for a moment from my soberness.

"I think you are fair-minded," he went on.

"I don't any longer strike you as foolish, then?" I asked.

"I stick to what I said about people who deny the power of departed spirits to return. They *are* fools!" And he rapped fiercely with his staff on the earth.

I hesitated a moment, and then, abruptly, "You have seen a ghost!" I said.

His hope comes true!

He appeared not at all startled.

"You are right, sir!" he answered with great dignity. "With me it's not a matter of cold theory—I have not had to pry into old

218

books to learn what to believe. *I know!* With these eyes I have beheld the departed spirit standing before me as near as you are!" And his eyes, as he spoke, certainly looked as if they had rested upon strange things.

How does the old man's attitude toward ghosts differ from the narrator's?

I was irresistibly impressed—I was touched with credulity.

"And was it very terrible?" I asked.

"I am an old soldier—I am not afraid!"

"When was it?—where was it?" I asked.

He looked at me mistrustfully, and I saw that I was going too fast.

"Excuse me from going into particulars," he said. "I am not at liberty to speak more fully. I have told you so much, because I cannot bear to hear this subject spoken of lightly. Remember in the future, that you have seen a very honest old man who told you—on his honor—that he had seen a ghost!" And he got up, as if he thought he had said enough. Reserve, shyness, pride, the fear of being laughed at, the memory, possibly, of former strokes of sarcasm—all this, on one side, had its weight with him; but I suspected that on the other, his tongue was loosened by the garrulity of old age, the sense of solitude, and the need of sympathy —and perhaps, also, by the friendliness which he had been so good as to express toward myself. Evidently it would be unwise

How does the narrator interpret the old man's reticence?

219

to press him, but I hoped to see him again.

"To give greater weight to my words," he added, "let me mention my name—Captain Diamond, sir. I have seen service."

"I hope I may have the pleasure of meeting you again," I said.

"The same to you, sir!" And brandishing his stick portentously—though with the friendliest intentions—he marched stiffly away.

I asked two or three persons—selected with discretion—whether they knew anything about Captain Diamond, but they were quite unable to enlighten me. At last, suddenly, I smote my forehead and, dubbing myself a dolt, remembered that I was neglecting a source of information to which I had never applied in vain. The excellent person at whose table I habitually dined, and who dispensed hospitality to students at so much a week, had a sister as good as herself and of conversational powers more varied. This sister, who was known as Miss Deborah, was an old maid in all the force of the term. She was deformed, and she never went out of the house; she sat all day at the window, between a bird-cage and a flower-pot, stitching small linen articles—mysterious bands and frills. She wielded, I was assured, an exquisite needle, and her work was highly prized. In spite of her deformity and her confinement, she had a little, fresh, round face and an imperturbable serenity of spirit. She had also a very quick little wit of her own, she was extremely observant, and she had a high relish for a friendly chat. Nothing pleased her so much as to have you—especially, I think, if you were a young divinity student—move your chair near her sunny window and settle yourself for twenty minutes' "talk." "Well, sir," she used always to say, "what is the latest monstrosity in Biblical criticism?"—for she used to pretend to be horrified at the rationalistic tendency of the age. But she was an inexorable little philosopher, and I am convinced that she was a keener rationalist than any of us, and that, if she had chosen, she could have propounded questions that would have made the boldest of us wince.

Try to paraphrase this section.

Her window commanded the whole town—or rather, the whole country. Knowledge came to her as she sat singing, with her little, cracked voice, in her low rocking-chair. She was the first to learn everything, and the last to forget it. She had the town gossip at her fingers' ends, and she knew everything about people she had never seen. When I asked her how she had acquired her learning, she said simply—"Oh, I observe!" "Observe closely enough," she once said, "and it doesn't matter where you are. You may be in a pitch-dark closet. All you want is something to start with; one thing leads to anoth-

What similarities are there between Miss Deborah and the narrator?

221

er, and all things are mixed up. Shut me up in a dark closet and I will observe after a while that some places in it are darker than others. After that (give me time) and I will tell you what the President of the United States is going to have for dinner." Once I paid her a compliment. "Your observation," I said, "is as fine as your needle, and your statements are as true as your stitches."

Of course Miss Deborah had heard of Captain Diamond. He had been much talked about many years before, but he had survived the scandal that attached to his name.

"What was the scandal?" I asked.

"He killed his daughter."

"Killed her?" I cried. "How so?"

Notice how unemotional they both are about the scandal. Is this in keeping with what you know about the narrator? Miss Deborah?

"Oh, not with a pistol, or a dagger, or a dose of arsenic! With his tongue. Talk of women's tongues! He cursed her—with some horrible oath—and she died!"

"What had she done?"

"She had received a visit from a young man who loved her, and whom he had forbidden the house."

"The house," I said—"ah yes! The house is out in the country, two or three miles from here, on a lonely cross-road."

Why the sharp look?

Miss Deborah looked sharply at me as she bit her thread. "Ah, you know about the house?" she said.

"A little," I answered; "I have seen it. But I want you to tell me more."

But here Miss Deborah betrayed an incommunicativeness which was most unusual. "You wouldn't call me superstitious, would you?" she asked.

"You?—you are the quintessence of pure reason."

"Well, every thread has its rotten place, and every needle its grain of rust. I would rather not talk about that house."

"You have no idea how you excite my curiosity!" I said.

"I can feel for you. But it would make me very nervous."

"What harm can come to you?" I asked.

"Some harm came to a friend of mine." And Miss Deborah gave a very positive nod.

"What had your friend done?"

"She had told me Captain Diamond's secret, which he had told her with a mighty mystery. She had been an old flame of his, and he took her into his confidence. He bade her tell no one and assured her that if she did, something dreadful would happen to her."

"And what happened to her?"

"She died."

"Oh, we are all mortal!" I said. "Had she given him a promise?"

"She had not taken it seriously; she had not believed him. She repeated the story

Note that an element
of mystery is
beginning to appear.

to me, and three days afterward she was taken with inflammation of the lungs. A month afterward, here where I sit now, I was stitching her grave-clothes. Since then I have never mentioned what she told me."

"Was it very strange?"

"It was strange, but it was ridiculous, too. It is a thing to make you shudder and to make you laugh, both. But you can't worry it out of me. I am sure that if I were to tell you, I should immediately break a needle in my finger and die the next week of lock-jaw."

I retired and urged Miss Deborah no further; but every two or three days, after dinner, I came and sat down by her rocking-chair. I made no further allusion to Captain Diamond; I sat silent, clipping tape with her scissors. At last, one day, she told me I was looking poorly. I was pale.

"I am dying of curiosity," I said. "I have lost my appetite. I have eaten no dinner."

Bluebeard's wife: in a French folktale Bluebeard warned his wife never to open a certain door in his castle. Her curiosity, however, led her to open the door. Inside she found the murdered bodies of his six previous wives.

"Remember Bluebeard's wife!" said Miss Deborah.

"One may as well perish by the sword as by famine!" I answered.

Still she said nothing, and at last I rose with a melodramatic sigh and departed. As I reached the door, she called me and pointed to the chair I had vacated. "I never was hard-hearted," she said. "Sit down, and if we are to perish, may we at least perish

224

together." And then, in very few words, she communicated what she knew of Captain Diamond's secret. "He was a very high-tempered old man, and though he was very fond of his daughter, his will was law. He had picked out a husband for her and given her due notice. Her mother was dead, and they lived alone together. The house had been Mrs. Diamond's own marriage portion; the Captain, I believe, hadn't a penny. After his marriage they had come to live there, and he had begun to work the farm. The poor girl's lover was a young man with whiskers, from Boston. The Captain came in one evening and found them together; he collared the young man and hurled a terrible curse at the poor girl. The young man cried that she was his wife, and he asked her if it was true. She said, No! Thereupon Captain Diamond, his fury growing fiercer, repeated his imprecation, ordered her out of the house, and disowned her forever. She swooned away, but her father went raging off and left her.

"Several hours later, he came back and found the house empty. On the table was a note from the young man telling him that he had killed his daughter, repeating the assurance that she was his own wife and declaring that he himself claimed the sole right to commit her remains to earth. He had carried the body away in a gig! Captain Diamond wrote him a dreadful note in answer, saying that he didn't believe his daughter was dead, but that, whether or no, she was dead to him. A week later, in the middle of the night, he saw her ghost. Then, I suppose, he was convinced. The ghost reappeared several times, and finally began regularly to haunt the house. It made the old man very uncomfortable, for little by little his passion had passed away and he was given up to grief. He determined at last to leave the place, and tried to sell it or rent it; but meanwhile the story had gone abroad, the ghost had been seen by other persons, the house had a bad name, and it was impossible to dispose of it. With the farm, it was the old man's only property, and his only means of subsistence; if he could neither live in it nor rent it he was beggared. But the ghost had no mercy, as he had had none. He struggled for six months, and at last he broke down. He put on his old blue cloak and took up his staff and prepared to wander away and beg his bread. Then the ghost relented and proposed a compromise. 'Leave the house to me!' it said. 'I have marked it for my own. Go off and live elsewhere. But to enable you to live, I will be your tenant, since you can find no other. I will hire the house of you and pay you a certain rent.' And the ghost named a sum. The old man consented, and he goes every quarter to collect his rent!"

I laughed at this recital, but I confess I shuddered, too, for my own observation had exactly confirmed it. Had I not been witness of one of the Captain's quarterly visits, had I not all but seen him sit watching his spectral tenant count out the rent-money, and when he trudged away in the dark, had he not a little bag of strangely gotten coin hidden in the folds of his old blue cloak? I imparted none of these reflections to Miss Deborah, for I was determined that my observations should have a sequel, and I promised myself the pleasure of treating her to my story in its full maturity. "Captain Diamond," I asked, "has no other known means of subsistence?"

"None whatever. He toils not, neither does he spin—his ghost supports him. A haunted house is valuable property!"

"And in what coin does the ghost pay?"

"In good American gold and silver. It has only this peculiarity—that the pieces are all dated before the young girl's death. It's a strange mixture of matter and spirit!"

"And does the ghost do things handsomely; is the rent large?"

"The old man, I believe, lives decently, and has his pipe and his glass. He took a little house down by the river; the door is sidewise to the street, and there is a little garden before it. There he spends his days, and has an old colored woman to do for him.

What is there about the way Miss Deborah tells the story that makes the narrator laugh?

Does this add an ominous note to the otherwise lighthearted conversation?

227

Some years ago he used to wander about a good deal, he was a familiar figure in the town, and most people knew his legend. But of late he has drawn back into his shell; he sits over his fire, and curiosity has forgotten him. I suppose he is falling into his dotage. But I am sure, I trust," said Miss Deborah in conclusion, "that he won't outlive his faculties or his powers of locomotion, for, if I remember rightly, it was part of the bargain that he should come in person to collect his rent."

Is there a note of disappointment?

We neither of us seemed likely to suffer any especial penalty for Miss Deborah's indiscretion; I found her, day after day, singing over her work, neither more nor less active than usual. For myself, I boldly pursued my observations. I went again, more than once, to the great graveyard, but I was disappointed in my hope of finding Captain Diamond there. I had a prospect, however, which afforded me compensation. I shrewdly inferred that the old man's quarterly pilgrimages were made upon the last day of the old quarter. My first sight of him had been on the 31st of December, and it was probable that he would return to his haunted home on the last day of March. This was near at hand; at last it arrived. I betook myself late in the afternoon to the old house on the cross-road, supposing that the hour of twilight was the appointed season. I

228

was not wrong. I had been hovering about for a short time, feeling very much like a restless ghost myself, when he appeared in the same manner as before and wearing the same costume. I again concealed myself and saw him enter the house with the ceremonial which he had used on the former occasion. A light appeared successively in the crevice of each pair of shutters, and I opened the window which had yielded to my importunity before. Again I saw the great shadow on the wall, motionless and solemn. But I saw nothing else. The old man reappeared at last, made his fantastic salaam before the house, and crept away into the dusk.

One day, more than a month after this, I met him again at Mount Auburn. The air was full of the voice of spring; the birds had come back and were twittering over their winter's travels, and a mild west wind was making a thin murmur in the raw verdure. He was seated on a bench in the sun, still muffled in his enormous mantle, and he recognized me as soon as I approached him. He nodded at me as if he were an old bashaw giving the signal for my decapitation, but it was apparent that he was pleased to see me.

bashaw (bə shô′): Turkish official.

"I have looked for you here more than once," I said. "You don't come often."

"What did you want of me?" he asked.

"I wanted to enjoy your conversation.

229

I did so greatly when I met you here before."

"You found me amusing?"

"Interesting!" I said.

"You didn't think me cracked?"

"Cracked? My dear sir—!" I protested.

"I'm the sanest man in the country. I know that is what insane people always say; but generally they can't prove it. I can!"

"I believe it," I said. "But I am curious to know how such a thing can be proved."

He was silent awhile.

"I will tell you. I once committed, unintentionally, a great crime. Now I pay the penalty. I give up my life to it. I don't shirk it; I face it squarely, knowing perfectly what it is. I haven't tried to bluff it off; I haven't begged off from it; I haven't run away from it. The penalty is terrible, but I have accepted it. I have been a philosopher!

"If I were a Catholic, I might have turned monk and spent the rest of my life in fasting and praying. That is no penalty; that is an evasion. I might have blown my brains out—I might have gone mad. I wouldn't do either. I would simply face the music, take the consequences. As I say, they are awful! I take them on certain days, four times a year. So it has been these twenty years; so it will be as long as I last. It's my business; it's my avocation. That's the way I feel about it. I call that reasonable!"

"Admirably so!" I said. "But you fill me with curiosity and with compassion."

"Especially with curiosity," he said, cunningly.

"Why," I answered, "if I know exactly what you suffer I can pity you more."

What do you think of this for an answer?

"I'm much obliged. I don't want your pity; it won't help me. I'll tell you something, but it's not for myself; it's for your own sake." He paused a long time and looked all round him, as if for chance eavesdroppers. I anxiously awaited his revelation, but he disappointed me. "Are you still studying theology?" he asked.

"Oh, yes," I answered, perhaps with a shade of irritation. "It's a thing one can't learn in six months."

"I should think not, so long as you have nothing but your books. Do you know the proverb, 'A grain of experience is worth a pound of precept'? I'm a great theologian."

"Ah, you have had experience," I murmured sympathetically.

"You have read about the immortality of the soul; you have seen Jonathan Edwards and Dr. Hopkins chopping logic over it and deciding, by chapter and verse, that it is true. But I have seen it with these eyes; I have touched it with these hands!" And the old man held up his rugged old fists and shook them portentously. "That's better!" he went on; "but I have bought it dearly. You had

231

better take it from the books—evidently you always will. You are a very good young man; you will never have a crime on your conscience."

I answered, with some juvenile fatuity, that I certainly hoped I had my share of human passions, good young man and prospective Doctor of Divinity as I was.

"Ah, but you have a nice, quiet little temper," he said. "So have I—now! But once I was very brutal—very brutal. You ought to know that such things are. I killed my own child."

"Your own child?"

"I struck her down to the earth and left her to die. They could not hang me, for it was not with my hand I struck her. It was with foul and damnable words. That makes a difference; it's a grand law we live under! Well, sir, I can answer for it that *her* soul is immortal. We have an appointment to meet four times a year, and then I catch it!"

"She has never forgiven you?"

"She has forgiven me as the angels forgive! That's what I can't stand—the soft, quiet way she looks at me. I'd rather she twisted a knife about in my heart—O Lord, Lord, Lord!" and Captain Diamond bowed his head over his stick, and leaned his forehead on his crossed hands.

I was impressed and moved, and his attitude seemed for the moment a check to further questions. Before I ventured to ask him anything more, he slowly rose and pulled his old cloak around him. He was unused to talking about his troubles, and his memories overwhelmed him. "I must go my way," he said; "I must be creeping along."

"I shall perhaps meet you here again," I said.

"Oh, I'm a stiff-jointed old fellow," he answered, "and this is rather far for me to come. I have to reserve myself. I have sat sometimes a month at a time smoking my pipe in my chair. But I should like to see you again." And he stopped and looked at me, terribly and kindly. "Someday, perhaps, I shall be glad to be able to lay my hand on a young, unperverted soul. If a man can make a friend, it is always something gained. What is your name?"

I had in my pocket a small volume of Pascal's *Thoughts,* on the fly-leaf of which were written my name and address. I took it out and offered it to my old friend. "Pray keep this little book," I said. "It is one I am very fond of, and it will tell you something about me."

He took it and turned it over slowly, then looking up at me with a scowl of gratitude, "I'm not much of a reader," he said; "but I won't refuse the first present I shall have received since—my troubles; and the last. Thank you, sir!" And with the little

Pascal: seventeenth-century French philosopher.

233

book in his hand he took his departure.

I was left to imagine him for some weeks after that sitting solitary in his arm-chair with his pipe. I had not another glimpse of him. But I was awaiting my chance, and on the last day of June, another quarter having elapsed, I deemed that it had come. The evening dusk in June falls late, and I was impatient for its coming. At last, toward the end of a lovely summer's day, I revisited Captain Diamond's property. Every-thing now was green around it save the blighted orchard in its rear, but its own immitigable grayness and sadness were as striking as when I had first beheld it beneath a December sky. As I drew near it, I saw that I was late for my purpose, for my purpose had simply been to step forward on Captain Diamond's arrival and bravely ask him to let me go in with him. He had preceded me, and there were lights already in the windows. I was unwilling, of course, to disturb him during his ghostly interview, and I waited till he came forth. The lights disappeared in the course of time; then the door opened and Captain Diamond stole out. That evening he made no bow to the haunted house, for the first object he beheld was his fair-minded young friend planted, modestly but firmly, near the door-step. He stopped short, look-ing at me, and this time his terrible scowl was in keeping with the situation.

"I knew you were here," I said. "I came on purpose."

He seemed dismayed, and looked round at the house uneasily.

"I beg your pardon if I have ventured too far," I added, "but you know you have encouraged me."

Is this true?

"How did you know I was here?"

"I reasoned it out. You told me half your story, and I guessed the other half. I am a great observer, and I had noticed this house in passing. It seemed to me to have a mystery. When you kindly confided to me that you saw spirits, I was sure that it could only be here that you saw them."

"You are mighty clever," cried the old man. "And what brought you here this evening?"

I was obliged to evade this question.

"Oh, I often come; I like to look at the house—it fascinates me."

He turned and looked up at it himself. "It's nothing to look at outside." He was evidently quite unaware of its peculiar outward appearance, and this odd fact, communicated to me thus in the twilight, and under the very brow of the sinister dwelling, seemed to make his vision of the strange things within more real.

Note how Captain Diamond rejects the narrator's impressions of the house as mysterious.

"I have been hoping," I said, "for a chance to see the inside. I thought I might find you here and that you would let me go in with you. I should like to see what you see."

He seemed confounded by my boldness, but not altogether displeased. He laid his hand on my arm. "Do you know what I see?" he asked.

"How can I know, except as you said the other day, by experience? I want to have the experience. Pray, open the door and take me in."

Captain Diamond's brilliant eyes expanded beneath their dusky brows, and after holding his breath a moment, he indulged in the first and last apology for a laugh by which I was to see his solemn visage contorted. It was profoundly grotesque, but it was perfectly noiseless. "Take you in?" he softly growled. "I wouldn't go in again before my time's up for a thousand times that sum." And he thrust out his hand from the folds of his cloak and exhibited a small agglomeration of coin, knotted into the corner of an old silk pocket-handkerchief. "I stick to my bargain, no less but no more!"

"But you told me the first time I had the pleasure of talking with you that it was not so terrible."

"I don't say it's terrible—now. But it's damned disagreeable!"

This adjective was uttered with a force that made me hesitate and reflect. While I did so, I thought I heard a slight movement

Is "damned" used merely as an expletive?

236

of one of the window-shutters above us. I looked up, but everything seemed motionless. Captain Diamond, too, had been thinking; suddenly he turned toward the house. "If you will go in alone," he said, "you are welcome."

"Will you wait for me here?"

"Yes, you will not stop long."

"But the house is pitch dark. When you go you have lights."

He thrust his hand into the depths of his cloak and produced some matches. "Take these," he said. "You will find two candlesticks with candles on the table in the hall. Light them, take one in each hand, and go ahead."

"Where shall I go?"

"Anywhere—everywhere. You can trust the ghost to find you."

I will not pretend to deny that by this time my heart was beating. And yet I imagine I motioned the old man with a sufficiently dignified gesture to open the door. I had made up my mind that there was in fact a ghost. I had conceded the premise. Only I had assured myself that once the mind was prepared and the thing was not a surprise, it was possible to keep cool. Captain Diamond turned the lock, flung open the door, and bowed low to me as I passed in. I stood in the darkness, and heard the door close behind me. For some moments I stirred neither

Is he getting nervous?

finger nor toe; I stared bravely into the impenetrable dusk. But I saw nothing and heard nothing, and at last I struck a match. On the table were two old brass candlesticks rusty from disuse. I lighted the candles and began my tour of exploration.

A wide staircase rose in front of me, guarded by an antique balustrade of that rigidly delicate carving which is found so often in old New England houses. I postponed ascending it, and turned into the room on my right. This was an old-fashioned parlor, meagerly furnished, and musty with the absence of human life. I raised my two lights aloft and saw nothing but its empty chairs and its blank walls. Behind it was the room into which I had peeped from without and which, in fact, communicated with it, as I had supposed, by folding doors. Here, too, I found myself confronted by no menacing specter.

I crossed the hall again and visited the rooms on the other side; a dining-room in front, where I might have written my name with my finger in the deep dust of the great square table; a kitchen behind with its pots and pans eternally cold. All this was hard and grim, but it was not formidable. I came back into the hall and walked to the foot of the staircase, holding up my candles; to ascend required a fresh effort, and I was scanning the gloom above. Suddenly, with an inexpressible sensation, I became aware that this gloom was animated; it seemed to move and gather itself together. Slowly—I say slowly, for to my tense expectancy the instants appeared ages—it took the shape of a large, definite figure, and this figure advanced and stood at the top of the stairs. I frankly confess that by this time I was conscious of a feeling to which I am in duty bound to apply the vulgar name of fear. I may poetize it and call it Dread, with a capital letter; it was at any rate the feeling that makes a man yield ground. I measured it as it grew, and it seemed perfectly irresistible; for it did not appear to come from within but from without, and to be embodied in the dark image at the head of the staircase. After a fashion I reasoned—I remember reasoning. I said to myself, "I had always thought ghosts were white and transparent; this is a thing of thick shadows, densely opaque." I reminded myself that the occasion was momentous, and that if fear were to overcome me I should gather all possible impressions while my wits remained.

Contrast what the narrator really feels with what he thinks he should feel.

I stepped back, foot behind foot, with my eyes still on the figure and placed my candles on the table. I was perfectly conscious that the proper thing was to ascend the stairs resolutely, face to face with the image, but the soles of my shoes seemed suddenly to have been transformed into

At what point does his pose as a detached onlooker become affected by real fear? Why doesn't he run?

leaden weights. I had got what I wanted; I was seeing the ghost. I tried to look at the figure distinctly so that I could remember it and fairly claim, afterward, not to have lost my self-possession. I even asked myself how long it was expected I should stand looking and how soon I could honorably retire. All this, of course, passed through my mind with extreme rapidity, and it was checked by a further movement on the part of the figure. Two white hands appeared in the dark perpendicular mass, and were slowly raised to what seemed to be the level of the head. Here they were pressed together, over the region of the face, and then they were removed, and the face was disclosed. It was dim, white, strange, in every way ghostly. It

Do you accept what the narrator says his reactions were to the ghost?

looked down at me for an instant, after which one of the hands was raised again, slowly, and waved to and fro before it. There was something very singular in this gesture; it seemed to denote resentment and dismissal, and yet it had a sort of trivial, familiar motion. Familiarity on the part of the haunting Presence had not entered into my calculations, and did not strike me pleasantly. I agreed with Captain Diamond that it was "damned disagreeable." I was pervaded by

Again, is "damned" merely an expletive? Remember that the narrator is a divinity student and that the subject he is dealing with is ghosts.

an intense desire to make an orderly and, if possible, a graceful retreat. I wished to do it gallantly, and it seemed to me that it would be gallant to blow out my candles. I turned

240

and did so, punctiliously, and then I made my way to the door, groped a moment, and opened it. The outer light, almost extinct as it was, entered for a moment, played over the dusty depths of the house, and showed me the solid shadow.

Standing on the grass, bent over his stick, under the early glimmering stars, I found Captain Diamond. He looked up at me fixedly for a moment, but asked no questions, and then he went and locked the door. This duty performed, he discharged the other—made his obeisance like the priest before the altar—and then without heeding me further, took his departure.

A few days later I suspended my studies and went off for the summer's vacation. I was absent for several weeks, during which I had plenty of leisure to analyze my impressions of the supernatural. I took some satisfaction in the reflection that I had not been ignobly terrified; I had not bolted nor swooned—I had proceeded with dignity. Nevertheless, I was certainly more comfortable when I had put thirty miles between me and the scene of my exploit, and I continued for many days to prefer the daylight to the dark. My nerves had been powerfully excited; of this I was particularly conscious when, under the influence of the drowsy air of the seaside, my excitement began slowly to ebb. As it disappeared, I attempted to take a sternly rational view of my experience. Certainly I had seen *something*—that was not fancy; but what had I seen? I regretted extremely now that I had not been bolder, that I had not gone nearer and inspected the apparition more minutely. But it was very well to talk; I had done as much as any man in the circumstances would have dared; it was indeed a physical impossibility that I should have advanced. Was not this paralyzation of my powers in itself a supernatural influence? Not necessarily, perhaps, for a sham ghost that one accepted might do as much execution as a real ghost. But why had I so easily accepted the sable phantom that waved its hand? Why had it so impressed itself? Unquestionably, true or false, it was a very clever phantom. I greatly preferred that it should have been true—in the first place because I did not care to have shivered and shaken for nothing, and in the second place because to have seen a well-authenticated goblin is, as things go, a feather in a quiet man's cap. I tried, therefore, to let my vision rest and to stop turning it over. But an impulse stronger than my will recurred at intervals and set a mocking question on my lips. Granted that the apparition was Captain Diamond's daughter; if it was she, it certainly was her spirit. But was it not her spirit and something more?

The middle of September saw me

What contradictions are apparent in his attitude toward the ghost?

242

again established among the theologic shades, but I made no haste to revisit the haunted house.

The last of the month approached—the term of another quarter with poor Captain Diamond—and found me indisposed to disturb his pilgrimage on this occasion; though I confess that I thought with a good deal of compassion of the feeble old man trudging away, lonely, in the autumn dusk, on his extraordinary errand. On the thirtieth of September, at noonday, I was drowsing over a heavy octavo when I heard a feeble rap at my door. I replied with an invitation to enter, but as this produced no effect, I repaired to the door and opened it. Before me stood an elderly Negro with her head bound in a scarlet turban and a white handkerchief folded across her bosom. She looked at me intently and in silence; she had that air of supreme gravity and decency which aged persons of her race so often wear. I stood interrogative and at last, drawing her hand from her ample pocket, she held up a little book. It was the copy of Pascal's *Thoughts* that I had given to Captain Diamond.

"Please, sir," she said, very mildly, "do you know this book?"

"Perfectly," said I, "my name is on the fly-leaf."

"It is your name—no other?"

In what ways does the time of the story affect characterization?

"I will write my name if you like, and you can compare them," I answered.

She was silent a moment and then, with dignity—"It would be useless, sir," she said; "I can't read. If you will give me your word, that is enough. I come," she went on, "from the gentleman to whom you gave the book. He told me to carry it as a token—a token—that is what he called it. He is right down sick, and he wants to see you."

"Captain Diamond—sick?" I cried. "Is his illness serious?"

"He is very bad—he is all gone."

I expressed my regret and sympathy, and offered to go to him immediately, if his sable messenger would show me the way.

Note the narrator's tendency to introduce overtones of exotic mystery into fairly common situations.

She assented deferentially, and in a few moments I was following her along the sunny streets, feeling very much like a personage in the Arabian Nights, led to a postern gate by an Ethiopian slave. My own conductress directed her steps toward the river and stopped at a decent little yellow house in one of the streets that descend to it. She quickly opened the door and led me in, and I very soon found myself in the presence of my old friend. He was in bed, in a darkened room, and evidently in a very feeble state. He lay back on his pillow, staring before him, with his bristling hair more erect than ever and his intensely dark and bright old eyes touched with the glitter of fever. His apartment was humble and scrupulously neat, and I could see that my dusky guide was a faithful servant. Captain Diamond, lying there rigid and pale on his white sheets, resembled some ruggedly carved figure on the lid of a Gothic tomb. He looked at me silently, and my companion withdrew and left us alone.

"Yes, it's you," he said, at last, "it's you, that good young man. There is no mistake, is there?"

"I hope not; I believe I'm a good young man. But I am very sorry you are ill. What can I do for you?"

"I am very bad, very bad; my poor old bones ache so!" and, groaning portentously, he tried to turn toward me.

I questioned him about the nature of his malady and the length of time he had been in bed, but he barely heeded me; he seemed impatient to speak of something else. He grasped my sleeve, pulled me toward him, and whispered quickly:

"You know my time's up!"

"Oh, I trust not," I said, mistaking his meaning. "I shall certainly see you on your legs again."

"God knows!" he cried. "But I don't mean I'm dying; not yet a bit. What I mean is, I'm due at the house. This is rent-day."

"Oh, exactly! But you can't go."

"I can't go. It's awful. I shall lose my

money. If I am dying, I want it all the same. I want to pay the doctor. I want to be buried like a respectable man."

"It is this evening?" I asked.

"This evening at sunset, sharp."

He lay staring at me, and, as I looked at him in return, I suddenly understood his motive in sending for me. Morally, as it came into my thought, I winced. But I suppose I looked unperturbed, for he continued in the same tone. "I can't lose my money. Someone else must go. I asked Belinda, but she won't hear of it."

"You believe the money will be paid to another person?"

"We can try, at least. I have never failed before and I don't know. But, if you say I'm as sick as a dog, that my old bones ache, that I'm dying, perhaps she'll trust you. She don't want me to starve!"

"You would like me to go in your place, then?"

"You have been there once; you know what it is. Are you afraid?"

I hesitated.

Why does he hesitate?

"Give me three minutes to reflect," I said, "and I will tell you." My glance wandered over the room and rested on the various objects that spoke of the threadbare, decent poverty of its occupant. There seemed to be a mute appeal to my pity and my resolution in their cracked and faded sparseness. Meanwhile, Captain Diamond continued, feebly, "I think she'd trust you, as I have trusted you; she'll like your face; she'll see there is no harm in you. It's a hundred and thirty-three dollars, exactly. Be sure you put them into a safe place."

"Yes," I said at last, "I will go, and, so far as it depends upon me, you shall have the money by nine o'clock tonight."

Why does he decide to go to the house?

He seemed greatly relieved; he took my hand and faintly pressed it, and soon afterward I withdrew. I tried for the rest of the day not to think of my evening's work, but, of course, I thought of nothing else. I will not deny that I was nervous; I was, in fact, greatly excited, and I spent my time in alternately hoping that the mystery should prove less deep than it appeared, and yet fearing that it might prove too shallow. The hours passed very slowly, but, as the afternoon began to wane, I started on my mission. On the way I stopped at Captain Diamond's modest dwelling to ask how he was doing, and to receive such last instructions as he might desire to lay upon me. The old Negro, gravely and inscrutably placid, admitted me, and, in answer to my inquiries, said that the Captain was very low; he had sunk since the morning.

"You must be right smart," she said, "if you want to get back before he drops off."

A glance assured me that she knew of

my projected expedition, though, in her own opaque black pupil, there was not a gleam of self-betrayal.

"But why should Captain Diamond drop off?" I asked. "He certainly seems very weak; but I cannot make out that he has any definite disease."

"His disease is old age," she said, sententiously.

"But he is not so old as that; sixty-seven or sixty-eight, at most."

She was silent a moment.

"He's worn out; he's used up; he can't stand it any longer."

"Can I see him a moment?" I asked; upon which she led me again to his room.

He was lying in the same way as when I had left him, except that his eyes were closed. But he seemed very "low," as she had said, and he had very little pulse. Nevertheless, I further learned that the doctor had been there in the afternoon and professed himself satisfied. "He don't know what's been going on," said Belinda, curtly.

The old man stirred a little, opened his eyes, and after some time recognized me.

"I'm going, you know," I said. "I'm going for your money. Have you anything more to say?" He raised himself slowly, and with a painful effort, against his pillows; but he seemed hardly to understand me. "The house, you know," I said. "Your daughter."

He rubbed his forehead, slowly, awhile, and at last his comprehension awoke. "Ah, yes," he murmured, "I trust you. A hundred and thirty-three dollars. In old pieces—all in old pieces." Then he added more vigorously, and with a brightening eye, "Be very respectful—be very polite. If not—if not—" and his voice failed again.

"Oh, I certainly shall be," I said, with a rather forced smile. "But, if not?"

"If not, I shall know it!" he said, very gravely. And with this, his eyes closed and he sunk down again.

I took my departure and pursued my journey with a sufficiently resolute step. When I reached the house, I made a propitiatory bow in front of it, in emulation of Captain Diamond. I had timed my walk so as to be able to enter without delay; night had already fallen. I turned the key, opened the door, and shut it behind me. Then I struck a light, and found the two candlesticks I had used before standing on the tables in the entry. I applied a match to both of them, took them up, and went into the parlor. It was empty, and though I waited awhile, it remained empty. I passed then into the other rooms on the same floor, and no dark image rose before me to check my steps. At last, I came out into the hall again and stood weighing the question of going upstairs. The staircase had been the scene of my discomfi-

Is there an element of fear, threat, or both, in the Captain's statement "If not, I shall know it!"?

ture before, and I approached it with profound mistrust. At the foot, I paused, looking up, with my hand on the balustrade. I was acutely expectant, and my expectation was justified. Slowly, in the darkness above, the black figure that I had seen before took shape. It was not an illusion; it was a figure, and the same. I gave it time to define itself, and watched it stand and look down at me with its hidden face. Then, deliberately, I lifted up my voice and spoke:

Compare this reaction to the ghost with his previous one.

"I have come in place of Captain Diamond, at his request," I said. "He is very ill; he is unable to leave his bed. He earnestly begs that you will pay the money to me; I will immediately carry it to him." The figure stood motionless, giving no sign. "Captain Diamond would have come if he were able to move," I added, in a moment, appealingly; "but he is utterly unable."

At this the figure slowly unveiled its face and showed me a dim, white mask; then it began slowly to descend the stairs. Instinctively, I fell back before it, retreating to the door of the front sitting-room. With my eyes still fixed on it, I moved backward across the threshold; then I stopped in the middle of the room and set down my lights. The figure advanced; it seemed to be that of a tall woman, dressed in vaporous black crepe. As it drew near, I saw that it had a perfectly human face, though it looked extremely pale and sad. We stood gazing at each other; my agitation had completely vanished; I was only deeply interested.

"Is my father dangerously ill?" said the apparition.

At the sound of its voice—gentle, tremulous, and perfectly human—I started forward; I felt a rebound of excitement. I drew a long breath, I gave a sort of cry, for what I saw before me was not a disembodied spirit, but a beautiful woman, an audacious actress. Instinctively, irresistibly, by the force of reaction against my credulity, I stretched out my hand and seized the long veil that muffled her head. I gave it a violent jerk, dragged it nearly off, and stood staring at a large fair person of about five-and-thirty. I comprehended her at a glance; her long black dress, her pale, sorrow-worn face painted to look paler, her very fine eyes—the color of her father's—and her sense of outrage at my movement.

This is the narrator's only admission of impulsive, or improper, behavior in the story. What does he offer as an excuse for it? Can you think of any other reasons?

"My father, I suppose," she cried, "did not send you here to insult me!" and she turned away rapidly, took up one of the candles, and moved toward the door. Here she paused, looked at me again, hesitated, and then drew a purse from her pocket and flung it down on the floor. "There is your money!" she said, majestically.

I stood there, wavering between amazement and shame, and saw her pass out into the hall. Then I picked up the purse. The next moment, I heard a loud shriek and a crash of something dropping, and she came staggering back into the room without her light.

"My father—my father!" she cried; and with parted lips and dilated eyes, she rushed toward me.

"Your father—where?" I demanded.

"In the hall, at the foot of the stairs."

I stepped forward to go out, but she seized my arm. "He is in white," she cried, "in his shirt. It's not he!"

"Why, your father is in his house, in his bed, extremely ill," I answered.

She looked at me fixedly, with searching eyes.

"Dying?"

"I hope not," I stuttered.

She gave a long moan and covered her face with her hands.

How does Henry James leave the actual appearance of the ghost in question for the reader?

"Oh, heavens, I have seen his ghost!" she cried.

She still held my arm; she seemed too terrified to release it. "His ghost!" I echoed, wondering.

"It's the punishment of my long folly!" she went on.

Why does each assume personal responsibility for the ghost's appearance?

"Ah," said I, "it's the punishment of my indiscretion—of my violence!"

"Take me away, take me away!" she cried, still clinging to my arm. "Not there"

—as I was turning toward the hall and the front door—"not there, for pity's sake! By this door—the back entrance." And snatching the other candles from the table, she led me through the neighboring room into the back part of the house. Here was a door opening from a sort of scullery into the orchard. I turned the rusty lock, and we passed out and stood in the cool air beneath the stars. Here my companion gathered her black drapery about her and stood for a moment, hesitating. I had been infinitely flurried, but my curiosity touching her was uppermost. Agitated, pale, picturesque, she looked, in the early evening light, very beautiful.

"You have been playing all these years a most extraordinary game," I said.

She looked at me somberly and seemed disinclined to reply. "I came in perfect good faith," I went on. "The last time— three months ago—you remember?—you greatly frightened me."

"Of course it was an extraordinary game," she answered at last. "But it was the only way."

"Had he not forgiven you?"

"So long as he thought me dead, yes. There have been things in my life he could not forgive."

I hesitated and then—"And where is your husband?" I asked.

"I have no husband—I have never had a husband."

She made a gesture which checked further questions and moved rapidly away. I walked with her round the house to the road, and she kept murmuring—"It was he—it was he!" When we reached the road, she stopped and asked me which way I was going. I pointed to the road by which I had come, and she said—"I take the other. You are going to my father's?" she added.

"Directly," I said.

"Will you let me know tomorrow what you have found?"

"With pleasure. But how shall I communicate with you?"

She seemed at a loss and looked about her. "Write a few words," she said, "and put them under that stone." And she pointed to one of the lava slabs that bordered the old well. I gave her my promise to comply, and she turned away. "I know my road," she said. "Everything is arranged. It's an old story."

She left me with a rapid step, and as she receded into the darkness, resumed, with the dark flowing lines of her drapery, the phantasmal appearance with which she had at first appeared to me. I watched her till she became invisible, and then I took my own leave of the place. I returned to town at a swinging pace and marched straight to the little yellow house near the river. I took the liberty of entering without a knock and, encountering no interruption, made my way to Captain Diamond's room. Outside the door, on a low bench, with folded arms, sat the sable Belinda.

"How is he?" I asked.

"He's gone to glory."

"Dead?" I cried.

She rose with a sort of tragic chuckle.

"He's as big a ghost as any of them now!"

I passed into the room and found the old man lying there irredeemably rigid and still. I wrote that evening a few lines which I proposed on the morrow to place beneath the stone, near the well; but my promise was not destined to be executed. I slept that night very ill—it was natural—and in my restlessness left my bed to walk about the room. As I did so, I caught sight, in passing my window, of a red glow in the north-western sky. A house was on fire in the country, and evidently burning fast. It lay in the same direction as the scene of my evening's adventures, and as I stood watching the crimson horizon, I was startled by a sharp memory. I had blown out the candle which lighted me, with my companion, to the door through which we escaped, but I had not accounted for the other light, which she had carried into the hall and dropped—heaven knew where—in her consternation. The next day I walked out with my folded letter and turned into the familiar cross-road. The haunted house was a mass of charred beams and smoldering ashes; the well-cover had been pulled off, in quest of water, by the few neighbors who had had the audacity to contest what they must have regarded as a demon-kindled blaze, the loose stones were completely displaced, and the earth had been trampled into puddles.

What remains unresolved in this story?

SYNTHESIS

Consider what the narrator reveals about himself when he announces at the beginning of the story that he first chose a career as a clergyman and then renounced it. (The matter of religion is an interesting thread to follow throughout this story.)

What does Captain Diamond's willingness to participate in this "Ghostly Rental" indicate about his character? his feelings of guilt? his love for his daughter? How would he have judged her if he had become aware of the deception before he died?

Discuss the contradiction in the daughter's feelings for and behavior toward her father. How would you explain this contradiction? How would she have expected her father to act if he had become aware of the deception?

256

Which parts of this story are beyond the *Edges of Reality?* In what details does this story resemble "The Canterville Ghost"? Compare the overall effects of both ghost stories.

At the end of each of their stories Henry James and F. Scott Fitzgerald have the major element in their settings destroyed. Consider what purpose this destruction serves. Who does the destroying? What are the reactions of the survivors?

COMMENT

Henry James, who usually wrote copious notes about his stories, made no specific comment on "The Ghostly Rental." Many years after its publication, he suggested that it echoed people and places he had become familiar with during his brief stay at Harvard in 1862–63.

This story is from *Henry James: Stories of the Supernatural*. The book contains eighteen tales, including the psychological-horror classic "The Turn of the Screw," which has been dramatized, made into an opera by English composer Benjamin Britten (1954), and filmed under the title, "The Innocents."

THE COUNTRY OF THE BLIND

H.G. WELLS

Three hundred miles and more from Chimborazo, one hundred from the snows of Cotopaxi, in the wildest wastes of Ecuador's Andes, there lies that mysterious mountain valley, cut off from the world of men, the Country of the Blind. Long years ago that valley lay so far open to the world that men might come at last through frightful gorges and over an icy pass into its equable meadows; and thither indeed men came, a family or so of Peruvian half-breeds fleeing from the lust and tyranny of an

"The Country of the Blind" by H.G. Wells from THE COMPLETE SHORT STORIES OF H.G. WELLS. Reprinted by permission of A. P. Watt & Son for The Estate of H.G. Wells.

Mindobamba:
imaginary volcano in
the Andes.

evil Spanish ruler. Then came the stupendous outbreak of Mindobamba, when it was night in Quito for seventeen days, and the water was boiling at Yaguachi and all the fish floating dying even as far as Guayaquil; everywhere along the Pacific slopes there were landslips and swift thawings and sudden floods, and one whole side of the old Arauca crest slipped and came down in thunder, and cut off the Country of the Blind forever from the exploring feet of men. But one of these early settlers had chanced to be on the hither side of the gorges when the world had so terribly shaken itself, and he perforce had to forget his wife and his child and all the friends and possessions he had left up there, and start life over again in the lower world. He started it again but ill; blindness overtook him, and he died of punishment in the mines; but the story he told begot a legend that lingers along the length of the Cordilleras of the Andes to this day.

He told of his reason for venturing back from that fastness, into which he had first been carried lashed to a llama, beside a vast bale of gear, when he was a child. The valley, he said, had in it all that the heart of man could desire—sweet water, pasture, an even climate, slopes of rich brown soil with tangles of a shrub that bore an excellent fruit, and on one side great hanging forests of pine that held the avalanches high. Far overhead, on three sides, vast cliffs of grey-green rock were capped by cliffs of ice; but the glacier stream came not to them but flowed away by the farther slopes, and only now and then huge ice masses fell on the valley side. In this valley it neither rained nor snowed, but the abundant springs gave a rich green pasture that irrigation would spread over all the valley space. The settlers did well indeed there. Their beasts did well and multiplied, and but one thing marred their happiness. Yet it was enough to mar it greatly. A strange disease had come upon them, and had made all the children born to them there—and indeed, several older children also—blind. It was to seek some charm or antidote against this plague of blindness that he had with fatigue and danger and difficulty returned down the gorge. In those days, in such cases, men did not think of germs and infections but of sins; and it seemed to him that the reason of this affliction must lie in the negligence of these priestless immigrants to set up a shrine so soon as they entered the valley. He wanted a shrine—a handsome, cheap, effectual shrine—to be erected in the valley; he wanted relics and such-like potent things of faith, blessed objects and mysterious medals and prayers. In his wallet he had a bar of native silver for which he would not account; he insisted there was none in the valley, with something of the insistence of an inexpert liar. They had all clubbed their money and ornaments together, having little need for such treasure up there, he said, to buy them holy help against their ill. I figure this dim-eyed young mountaineer, sunburnt, gaunt, and anxious, hat-brim clutched feverishly, a man all unused to the ways of the lower world, telling this story to some keen-eyed, attentive priest before the great convulsion; I can picture him presently seeking to return with pious and infallible remedies against that trouble, and the infinite dismay with which he must have faced the tumbled vastness where the gorge had once come out. But the rest of his story of mischances is lost to me, save that I know of his evil death after

Is the narrator sympathetic to the mountaineer?

261

several years. Poor stray from that remoteness! The stream that had once made the gorge now bursts from the mouth of a rocky cave, and the legend his poor, ill-told story set going developed into the legend of a race of blind men somewhere "over there" one may still hear today.

And amidst the little population of that now isolated and forgotten valley the disease ran its course. The old became groping and purblind, the young saw but dimly, and the children that were born to them saw never at all. But life was very easy in that snow-rimmed basin, lost to all the world, with neither thorns nor briars, with no evil insects nor any beasts save the gentle breed of llamas they had lugged and thrust and followed up the beds of the shrunken rivers in the gorges up which they had come. The seeing had become purblind so gradually that they scarcely noted their loss. They guided the sightless youngsters hither and thither until they knew the whole valley marvellously, and when at last sight died out among them the race lived on. They had even time to adapt themselves to the blind control of fire, which they made carefully in stoves of stone. They were a simple strain of people at the first, unlettered, only slightly touched with the Spanish civilisation, but with something of a tradition of the arts of old Peru and of its lost philosophy. Generation followed generation. They forgot many things; they devised many things. Their tradition of the greater world they came from became mythical in colour and uncertain. In all things save sight they were strong and able; and presently the chance of birth and heredity sent one who had an original mind and who could talk and persuade among them, and then afterwards anoth-

Describe the role of the "one who had an original mind." Is a Biblical connection possible?

er. These two passed, leaving their effects, and the little community grew in numbers and in understanding, and met and settled social and economic problems that arose. Generation followed generation. There came a time when a child was born who was fifteen generations from that ancestor who went out of the valley with a bar of silver to seek God's aid, and who never returned. Thereabouts it chanced that a man came into this community from the outer world. And this is the story of that man.

He was a mountaineer from the country near Quito, a man who had been down to the sea and had seen the world, a reader of books in an original way, an acute and enterprising man, and he was taken on by a party of Englishmen who had come out to Ecuador to climb mountains, to replace one of their three Swiss guides who had fallen ill. He climbed here and he climbed there, and then came the attempt on Parascotopetl, the Matterhorn of the Andes, in which he was lost to the outer world. The story of the accident has been written a dozen times. Pointer's narrative is the best. He tells how the party worked their difficult and almost vertical way up to the very foot of the last and greatest precipice, and how they built a night shelter amidst the snow upon a little shelf of rock, and, with a touch of real dramatic power, how presently they found Núñez had gone from them. They shouted, and there was no reply; shouted and whistled, and for the rest of that night they slept no more.

As the morning broke they saw the traces of his fall. It seems impossible he could have uttered a sound. He had slipped eastward towards the unknown side of the mountain; far below he had

What does "in an original way" add to this characterization?

Parascotopetl (pär äs-ko′tə pet′əl): this fictitious peak of the Andes is compared to the Matterhorn in the Alps, still one of the most difficult mountains in the world to climb.

Núñez (nü′nyās).

263

struck a steep slope of snow, and ploughed his way down it in the midst of a snow avalanche. His track went straight to the edge of a frightful precipice, and beyond that everything was hidden. Far, far below, and hazy with distance, they could see trees rising out of a narrow, shut-in valley—the lost Country of the Blind. But they did not know it was the lost Country of the Blind, nor distinguish it in any way from any other narrow streak of upland valley. Unnerved by this disaster, they abandoned their attempt in the afternoon, and Pointer was called away to the war before he could make another attack. To this day Parascotopetl lifts an unconquered crest, and Pointer's shelter crumbles unvisited amidst the snows.

What is accomplished by this one-sentence paragraph?

And the man who fell survived.

At the end of the slope he fell a thousand feet, and came down in the midst of a cloud of snow upon a snow slope even steeper than the one above. Down this he was whirled, stunned and insensible, but without a bone broken in his body; and then at last came to gentler slopes, and at last rolled out and lay still, buried amidst a softening heap of the white masses that had accompanied and saved him. He came to himself with a dim fancy that he was ill in bed; then realised his position with a mountaineer's intelligence, and worked himself loose, and after a rest or so, out until he saw the stars. He rested flat upon his chest for a space, wondering where he was and what had happened to him.

He explored his limbs, and discovered that several of his buttons were gone and his coat turned over his head. His knife had gone from his pocket and his hat was lost, though he had tied it under his

264

chin. He recalled that he had been looking for loose stones to raise his piece of the shelter wall. His ice-axe had disappeared.

He decided he must have fallen, and looked up to see, exaggerated by the ghastly light of the rising moon, the tremendous flight he had taken. For a while he lay, gazing blankly at that vast pale cliff towering above, rising moment by moment out of a subsiding tide of darkness. Its phantasmal mysterious beauty held him for a space, and then he was seized with a paroxysm of sobbing laughter. . . .

After a great interval of time he became aware that he was near the lower edge of the snow. Below, down what was now a moonlit and practicable slope, he saw the dark and broken appearance of rock-strewn turf. He struggled to his feet, aching in every joint and limb, got down painfully from the heaped loose snow about him, went downward until he was on the turf, and there dropped rather than lay beside a boulder, drank deep from the flask in his inner pocket, and instantly fell asleep. . . .

He was awakened by the singing of birds in the trees far below.

He sat up and perceived he was on a little alp at the foot of a vast precipice that was grooved by the gully down which he and his snow had come. Over against him another wall of rock reared itself against the sky. The gorge between these precipices ran east and west and was full of the morning sunlight, which lit to the westward the mass of fallen mountain that closed the descending gorge. Below him it seemed there was a precipice equally steep, but behind the snow in the gully he found a sort of chimney-cleft dripping with snow-water down which a desperate man might venture. He

Is this response believable?

265

found it easier than it seemed, and came at last to another desolate alp, and then after a rock climb of no particular difficulty to a steep slope of trees. He took his bearings and turned his face up the gorge, for he saw it opened out above upon green meadows, among which he now glimpsed quite distinctly a cluster of stone huts of unfamiliar fashion. At times his progress was like clambering along the face of a wall, and after a time the rising sun ceased to strike along the gorge, the voices of the singing birds died away, and the air grew cold and dark about him. But the distant valley with its houses was all the brighter for that. He came presently to a talus, and among the rocks he noted—for he was an observant man—an unfamiliar fern that seemed to clutch out of the crevices with intense green hands. He picked a frond or so and gnawed its stalk and found it helpful.

talus: sloping pile of rock fragments at the foot of a cliff.

About midday he came at last out of the throat of the gorge into the plain and the sunlight. He was stiff and weary; he sat down in the shadow of a rock, filled up his flask with water from a spring and drank it down, and remained for a time resting before he went on to the houses.

They were very strange to his eyes, and indeed the whole aspect of that valley became, as he regarded it, queerer and more unfamiliar. The greater part of its surface was lush green meadow, starred with many beautiful flowers, irrigated with extraordinary care, and bearing evidence of systematic cropping piece by piece. High up and ringing the valley about was a wall, and what appeared to be a circumferential water-channel, from which the little trickles of water that fed the meadow plants came, and on the higher slopes above this flocks of llamas cropped the scanty herbage. Sheds, apparently shelters or feeding-places for the llamas, stood against the boundary wall here and there. The irrigation streams ran together into a main channel down the centre of the valley, and this was enclosed on either side by a wall breast high. This gave a singularly urban quality to this secluded place, a quality that was greatly enhanced by the fact that a number of paths paved with black and white stones, and each with a curious little kerb at the side, ran hither and thither in an orderly manner. The houses of the central village were quite unlike the casual and higgledy-piggledy agglomeration of the mountain villages he knew; they stood in a continuous row on either side of a central street of astonishing cleanness; here and there their parti-coloured façade was pierced by a door, and not a solitary window broke their even frontage. They were parti-coloured with extraordinary irregularity; smeared with a sort of plaster that was sometimes grey, sometimes drab, sometimes slate-coloured or dark brown; and it was the sight of this wild plastering that first brought the word *blind* into the thoughts of the explorer. "The good man who did that," he thought, "must have been as blind as a bat."

He descended a steep place, and so came to the wall and channel that ran about the valley, near where the latter spouted out its surplus contents into the deeps of the gorge in a thin and wavering thread of cascade. He could now see a number of men and women resting on piled heaps of grass, as if taking a siesta, in the remoter part of the meadow, and nearer the village a number of recumbent children, and then nearer at hand three men carrying pails on yokes along a little path that ran from the encircling wall towards the houses. These latter were clad in garments of llama cloth and boots and belts of leather, and they wore caps of cloth with back and ear flaps. They followed one another in single file, walking slowly and yawning as they walked, like men who have been up all night. There was something so reassuringly prosperous and respectable in their bearing that after a moment's hesitation Núñez stood forward as conspicuously as possible upon his rock, and gave vent to a mighty shout that echoed round the valley.

The three men stopped, and moved their heads as though they were looking about them. They turned their faces this way and that, and Núñez gesticulated with freedom. But they did not appear to see him for all his gestures, and after a time, directing themselves towards the mountains far away to the right, they shouted as if in answer. Núñez bawled again, and then once more, and as he gestured ineffectually the word *blind* came up to the top of his thoughts. "The fools must be blind," he said.

What quick changes are already apparent in Núñez's attitude toward the blind people?

When at last, after much shouting and wrath, Núñez crossed the stream by a little bridge, came through a gate in the wall, and approached them, he was sure that they were blind. He was sure that this was the Country of the Blind of which the legends told. Conviction had sprung upon him, and a sense of great and rather enviable adventure. The three stood side by side, not looking at him, but with their ears directed towards him, judging him by his unfamiliar steps. They stood close together like men a little afraid, and he could see their

268

eyelids closed and sunken, as though the very balls beneath had shrunk away. There was an expression near awe on their faces.

"A man," one said, in hardly recognisable Spanish—"a man it is—a man or a spirit—coming down from the rocks."

But Núñez advanced with the confident steps of a youth who enters upon life. All the old stories of the lost valley and the Country of the Blind had come back to his mind, and through his thoughts ran this old proverb, as if it were a refrain—

"In the Country of the Blind the One-eyed Man Is King."

"In the Country of the Blind the One-eyed Man Is King."

And very civilly he gave them greeting. He talked to them and used his eyes.

"Where does he come from, brother Pedro?" asked one.

"Down out of the rocks."

"Over the mountains I come," said Núñez, "out of the country beyond there—where men can see. From near Bogotá, where there are a hundred thousands of people, and where the city passes out of sight."

"Sight?" muttered Pedro. "Sight?"

"He comes," said the second blind man, "out of the rocks."

The cloth of their coats, Núñez saw, was curiously fashioned, each with a different sort of stitching.

They startled him by a simultaneous movement towards him, each with a hand outstretched. He stepped back from the advance of these spread fingers.

Could Wells appropriately have written, "He talked to them and used his *ears*"?

269

"Come hither," said the third blind man, following his motion and clutching him neatly.

And they held Núñez and felt him over, saying no word further until they had done so.

"Carefully," he cried, with a finger in his eye, and found they thought that organ, with its fluttering lids, a queer thing in him. They went over it again.

"A strange creature, Correa," said the one called Pedro. "Feel the coarseness of his hair. Like a llama's hair."

"Rough he is as the rocks that begot him," said Correa, investigating Núñez's unshaven chin with a soft and slightly moist hand. "Perhaps he will grow finer." Núñez struggled a little under their examination, but they gripped him firm.

"Carefully," he said again.

"He speaks," said the third man. "Certainly he is a man."

"Ugh!" said Pedro, at the roughness of his coat.

"And you have come into the world?" asked Pedro.

"Out of the world. Over mountains and glaciers; right over above there, halfway to the sun. Out of the great big world that goes down, twelve days' journey to the sea."

They scarcely seemed to heed him. "Our fathers have told us men may be made by the forces of Nature," said Correa. "It is the warmth of things and moisture, and rottenness—rottenness."

"Let us lead him to the elders," said Pedro.

"Shout first," said Correa, "lest the children be afraid. This is a marvellous occasion."

So they shouted, and Pedro went first and took Núñez by the hand to lead him to the houses.

He drew his hand away. "I can see," he said.

Which words expose the conflict in viewpoint?

"See?" said Correa.

"Yes, see," said Núñez, turning towards him, and stumbled against Pedro's pail.

"His senses are still imperfect," said the third blind man. "He stumbles, and talks unmeaning words. Lead him by the hand."

Is there justification for the blind men's judgment of Núñez?

"As you will," said Núñez, and was led along, laughing.

It seemed they knew nothing of sight.

Well, all in good time he would teach them.

He heard people shouting, and saw a number of figures gathering together in the middle roadway of the village.

He found it taxed his nerve and patience more than he had anticipated, that first encounter with the population of the Country of the Blind. The place seemed larger as he drew near to it, and the smeared plasterings queerer, and a crowd of children and men and women (the women and girls, he was pleased to note, had, some of them, quite sweet faces, for all that their eyes were shut and sunken) came about him, holding on to him, touching him with soft, sensitive hands, smelling at him, and listening at every word he spoke. Some of the maidens and children, however, kept aloof as if afraid, and indeed his voice seemed coarse and rude beside their softer notes. They mobbed him. His three guides kept close to him with an effect of proprietorship, and said again and again, "A wild man out of the rocks."

"Bogotá," he said. "Bogotá. Over the mountain crests."

"A wild man—using wild words," said Pedro. "Did you hear that—*Bogotá?* His mind is hardly formed yet. He has only the beginnings of speech."

271

A little boy nipped his hand. "Bogotá!" he said mockingly.

"Ay! A city to your village. I come from the great world—where men have eyes and see."

"His name's Bogotá," they said.

"He stumbled," said Correa, "stumbled twice as we came hither."

"Bring him to the elders."

And they thrust him suddenly through a doorway into a room as black as pitch, save at the end there faintly glowed a fire. The crowd closed in behind him and shut out all but the faintest glimmer of day, and before he could arrest himself he had fallen headlong over the feet of a seated man. His arm, out-flung, struck the face of someone else as he went down; he felt the soft impact of features and heard a cry of anger, and for a moment he struggled against a number of hands that clutched him. It was a one-sided fight. An inkling of the situation came to him, and he lay quiet.

"I fell down," he said; "I couldn't see in this pitchy darkness."

There was a pause as if the unseen persons about him tried to understand his words. Then the voice of Correa said, "He is but newly formed. He stumbles as he walks and mingles words that mean nothing with his speech."

Others also said things about him that he heard or understood imperfectly.

"May I sit up?" he asked, in a pause. "I will not struggle against you again."

They consulted and let him rise.

The voice of an older man began to question him, and Núñez found himself trying to explain the great world out of which he had fallen, and the sky and mountains and sight and such-like marvels, to these elders who sat in darkness in the Country of the Blind. And they would believe and understand nothing whatever he told them, a thing quite outside his expectation. They would not even understand many of his words. For fourteen generations these people had been blind and cut off from all the seeing world; the names for all the things of sight had faded and changed; the story of the outer world was faded and changed to a child's story; and they had ceased to concern themselves with anything beyond the rocky slopes above their circling wall. Blind men of genius had arisen among them and questioned the shreds of belief and tradition they had brought with them from their seeing days, and had dismissed all these things as idle fancies, and replaced them with new and saner explanations. Much of their imagination had shrivelled with their eyes, and they had made for themselves new imaginations with their ever more sensitive ears and finger-tips. Slowly Núñez realised this; that his expectation of wonder and reverence at his origin and his gifts was not to be borne out; and after his poor attempt to explain sight to them had been set aside as the confused version of a new-made being describing the marvels of his incoherent sensations, he subsided, a little dashed, into listening to their instruction. And the eldest of the blind men explained to him life and philosophy and religion, how that the world (meaning their valley) had been first an empty hollow in the rocks, and then had come, first, inanimate things without the gift of touch, and llamas and a few other creatures that had little sense, and then men, and at last angels, whom one could hear singing and making fluttering

Consider how the "blind men of genius" discriminate between "idle fancies" and "saner explanations."

273

sounds, but whom no one could touch at all, which puzzled Núñez greatly until he thought of the birds.

He went on to tell Núñez how this time had been divided into the warm and the cold, which are the blind equivalents of day and night, and how it was good to sleep in the warm and work during the cold, so that now, but for his advent, the whole town of the blind would have been asleep. He said Núñez must have been specially created to learn and serve the wisdom they had acquired, and for that all his mental incoherency and stumbling behaviour he must have courage and do his best to learn, and at that all the people in the doorway murmured encouragingly. He said the night—for the blind call their day night—was now far gone, and it behooved everyone to go back to sleep. He asked Núñez if he knew how to sleep, and Núñez said he did, but that before sleep he wanted food.

They brought him food—llama's milk in a bowl, and rough salted bread—and led him into a lonely place to eat out of their hearing, and afterwards to slumber until the chill of the mountain evening roused them to begin their day again. But Núñez slumbered not at all.

Instead, he sat up in the place where they had left him, resting his limbs and turning the unanticipated circumstances of his arrival over and over in his mind.

Every now and then he laughed, sometimes with amusement, and sometimes with indignation.

"Unformed mind!" he said. "Got no senses yet! They little know they've been insulting their heaven-sent king and master. I see I must bring them to reason. Let me think—let me think."

He was still thinking when the sun set.

What is wrong with Núñez's aims? with the assumptions he makes about the blind people and himself?

274

Núñez had an eye for all beautiful things, and it seemed to him that the glow upon the snowfields and glaciers that rose about the valley on every side was the most beautiful thing he had ever seen. His eyes went from that inaccessible glory to the village and irrigated fields, fast sinking into the twilight, and suddenly a wave of emotion took him, and he thanked God from the bottom of his heart that the power of sight had been given him.

He heard a voice calling to him from out of the village. "Ya ho there, Bogotá! Come hither!"

At that he stood up smiling. He would show these people once and for all what sight would do for a man. They would seek him, but not find him.

"You move not, Bogotá," said the voice.

He laughed noiselessly, and made two stealthy steps aside from the path.

"Trample not on the grass, Bogotá; that is not allowed." Núñez had scarcely heard the sound he made himself. He stopped, amazed.

The owner of the voice came running up the piebald path towards him.

He stepped back into the pathway. "Here I am," he said.

"Why did you not come when I called you?" said the blind man. "Must you be led like a child? Cannot you hear the path as you walk?"

Núñez laughed. "I can see it," he said.

"There is no such word as *see*," said the blind man, after a pause. "Cease this folly, and follow the sound of my feet."

Núñez followed, a little annoyed.

"My time will come," he said.

"You'll learn," the blind man answered. "There is much to learn in the world."

"Has no one told you, 'In the Country of the Blind the One-eyed Man Is King'?"

"What is blind?" asked the blind man carelessly over his shoulder.

Four days passed, and the fifth found the King of the Blind still incognito, as a clumsy and useless stranger among his subjects.

Note the sarcasm. At whom is it directed?

It was, he found, much more difficult to proclaim himself than he had supposed, and in the meantime, while he meditated his *coup d'état,* he did what he was told and learned the manners and customs of the Country of the Blind. He found working and going about at night a particularly irksome thing, and he decided that that should be the first thing he would change.

coup d'état
(kü´ dā tä´): sudden and forcible seizure of ruling power by a minority (French).

They led a simple, laborious life, these people, with all the elements of virtue and happiness, as these things can be understood by men. They toiled, but not oppressively; they had food and clothing sufficient for their needs; they had days and seasons of rest; they made much of music and singing, and there was love among them, and little children.

It was marvellous with what confidence and precision they went about their ordered world. Everything, you see, had been made to fit their needs; each of the radiating paths of the valley area had a constant angle to the others, and was distinguished by a special notch upon its kerbing; all obstacles and irregularities of path or meadow had long since been cleared away; all their methods and procedure arose naturally from their special needs. Their senses had become marvellously acute; they could hear and judge the slightest gesture of a man a dozen paces away—could hear the very beating of his heart. Intonation had long replaced expression with them, and touches gesture, and their work with hoe and spade and fork was as free and confident as garden work can be. Their sense of smell was extraordinarily fine; they could distinguish individual differences as readily as a dog can, and they went about the tending of the llamas, who lived among the rocks above and came to the wall for food and shelter, with ease and confidence. It was only when at last Núñez sought to assert himself that he found how easy and confident their movements could be.

He rebelled only after he had tried persuasion.

He tried at first on several occasions to tell them of sight. "Look you here, you people," he said. "There are things you do not understand in me."

Once or twice one or two of them attended to him; they sat with faces downcast and ears turned intelligently towards him, and he did his best to tell them what it was to see. Among his hearers was a girl, with eyelids less red and sunken than the others, so that one could almost fancy she was hiding eyes, whom especially he hoped to persuade. He spoke of the beauties of sight, of watching the mountains, of the sky and the sunrise, and they heard him with amused incredulity that presently became condemnatory. They told him there were indeed no mountains at all, but that the end of the rocks where the llamas grazed was indeed the end of the world; thence sprang a cavernous roof of the universe, from which the dew and the avalanches fell; and when he maintained stoutly that the world had neither end nor roof such as they supposed, they said his thoughts were wicked. So far as he could describe sky and clouds and stars to

Which words indicate the blind people's changing reactions to Núñez's explanations?

277

them it seemed to them a hideous void, a terrible blankness in the place of the smooth roof to things in which they believed—it was an article of faith with them that the cavern roof was exquisitely smooth to the touch. He saw that in some manner he shocked them, and gave up that aspect of the matter altogether, and tried to show them the practical value of sight. One morning he saw Pedro in the path called Seventeen and coming towards the central houses, but still too far off for hearing or scent, and he told them as much. "In a little while," he prophesied, "Pedro will be here." An old man remarked that Pedro had no business on Path Seventeen, and then, as if in confirmation, that individual as he drew near turned and went transversely into Path Ten, and so back with nimble paces towards the outer wall. They mocked Núñez when Pedro did not arrive, and afterwards, when he asked Pedro questions to clear his character, Pedro denied and outfaced him, and was afterwards hostile to him.

Then he induced them to let him go a long way up the sloping meadows towards the wall with one complaisant individual, and to him he promised to describe all that happened among the houses. He noted certain goings and comings, but the things that really seemed to signify to these people happened inside of or behind the windowless houses—the only things they took note of to test him by—and of these he could see or tell nothing; and it was after the failure of this attempt, and the ridicule they could not repress, that he resorted to force. He thought of seizing a spade and suddenly smiting one or two of them to earth, and so in fair combat showing the advantage of eyes. He went so

Why are they "shocked"?

Invent other tests that might have helped Núñez prove he had sight. If he had convinced the villagers, how would you have expected them to regard this power?

278

far with that resolution as to seize his spade, and then he discovered a new thing about himself, and that was that it was impossible for him to hit a blind man in cold blood.

He hesitated, and found them all aware that he snatched up the spade. They stood alert, with their heads on one side, and bent ears towards him for what he would do next.

"Put that spade down," said one, and he felt a sort of helpless horror. He came near obedience.

Then he thrust one backwards against a house wall, and fled past him and out of the village.

He went athwart one of their meadows, leaving a track of trampled grass behind his feet, and presently sat down by the side of one of their ways. He felt something of the buoyancy that comes to all men in the beginning of a fight, but more perplexity. He began to realise that you cannot even fight happily with creatures who stand upon a different mental basis to yourself. Far away he saw a number of men carrying spades and sticks come out of the street of houses, and advance in a spreading line along the several paths towards him. They advanced slowly, speaking frequently to one another, and ever and again the whole cordon would halt and sniff the air and listen.

The first time they did this Núñez laughed. But afterwards he did not laugh.

One struck his trail in the meadow grass, and came stooping and feeling his way along it.

For five minutes he watched the slow extension of the cordon, and then his vague disposition to do something forthwith became frantic. He stood up, went a pace or so towards the circumferential wall, turned, and went back a little way. There they all

Is this always true? What does it tell you about Núñez?

279

stood in a crescent, still and listening.

He also stood still, gripping his spade very tightly in both hands. Should he charge them?

The pulse in his ears ran into the rhythm of "In the Country of the Blind the One-eyed Man Is King!"

Should he charge them?

He looked back at the high and unclimbable wall behind—unclimbable because of its smooth plastering, but withal pierced with many little doors—and at the approaching line of seekers. Behind these, others were now coming out of the street of houses.

Should he charge them?

"Bogotá!" called one. "Bogotá! where are you?"

He gripped his spade still tighter, and advanced down the meadows towards the place of habitations, and directly he moved they converged upon him. "I'll hit them if they touch me," he swore; "by Heaven, I will. I'll hit." He called aloud, "Look here, I'm going to do what I like in this valley. Do you hear? I'm going to do what I like and go where I like!"

They were moving in upon him quickly, groping, yet moving rapidly. It was like playing blindman's buff, with everyone blindfolded except one. "Get hold of him!" cried one. He found himself in the arc of a loose curve of pursuers. He felt suddenly he must be active and resolute.

"You don't understand," he cried in a voice that was meant to be great and resolute, and which broke. "You are blind, and I can see. Leave me alone!"

"Bogotá! Put down that spade, and come off the grass!"

The last order, grotesque in its urban familiarity, produced a gust of anger.

"I'll hurt you," he said, sobbing with emotion. "By Heaven, I'll hurt you. Leave me alone!"

He began to run, not knowing clearly where to run. He ran from the nearest blind man, because it was a horror to hit him. He stopped, and then made a dash to escape from their closing ranks. He made for where a gap was wide, and the men on either side, with a quick perception of the approach of his paces, rushed in on one another. He sprang forward, and then saw he must be caught, and *swish!* the spade had struck. He felt the soft thud of hand and arm, and the man was down with a yell of pain, and he was through.

Through! And then he was close to the street of houses again, and blind men, whirling spades and stakes, were running with a sort of reasoned swiftness hither and thither.

He heard steps behind him just in time, and found a tall man rushing forward and swiping at the sound of him. He lost his nerve, hurled his spade a yard wide at his antagonist, and whirled about and fled, fairly yelling as he dodged another.

He was panic-stricken. He ran furiously to and fro, dodging when there was no need to dodge, and in his anxiety to see on every side of him at once, stumbling.

For a moment he was down and they heard his fall. Far away in the circumferential wall a little doorway looked like heaven, and he set off in a wild rush for it. He did not even look round at his pursuers until it was gained, and he had stumbled across the bridge, clambered a little way among the rocks, to the surprise and dismay of a young llama, who went leaping out of sight, and lay down sobbing for breath.

And so his *coup d'état* came to an end.

He stayed outside the wall of the valley of the Blind for two nights and days without food or shelter, and meditated upon the unexpected. During these meditations he repeated very frequently and always with a profounder note of derision the exploded proverb: "In the Country of the Blind the One-eyed Man Is King." He thought chiefly of ways of fighting and conquering these people, and it grew clear that for him no practicable way was possible. He had no weapons, and now it would be hard to get one.

canker: something that causes decay. Is this meant to be sarcastic?

The canker of civilisation had got to him even in Bogotá, and he could not find it in himself to go down and assassinate a blind man. Of course, if he did that, he might then dictate terms on the threat of assassinating them all. But—sooner or later he must sleep! . . .

He tried also to find food among the pine trees, to be comfortable under pine boughs while the frost fell at night, and—with less confidence—to catch a llama by artifice in order to try to kill it—perhaps by hammering it with a stone—and so finally, perhaps, to eat some of it. But the llamas had a doubt of him and regarded him with distrustful brown eyes, and spat when he drew near. Fear came on him the second day and fits of shivering. Finally he crawled down to the wall of the Country of the Blind and tried to make terms. He crawled along by the stream, shouting, until two blind men came out to the gate and talked to him.

In what other ways has civilization "got to him"?

"I was mad," he said. "But I was only newly made."

They said that was better.

He told them he was wiser now, and repented of all he had done.

Then he wept without intention, for he was very weak and ill now, and they took that as a favourable sign.

They asked him if he still thought he could "see."

"No," he said. "That was folly. The word means nothing—less than nothing!"

They asked him what was overhead.

"About ten times ten the height of a man there is a roof above the world—of rock—and very, very smooth." He burst again into hysterical tears. "Before you ask me any more, give me some food or I shall die."

He expected dire punishments, but these blind people were capable of toleration. They regarded his rebellion as but one more proof of his general idiocy and inferiority; and after they had whipped him they appointed him to do the simplest and heaviest work they had for anyone to do, and he, seeing no other way of living, did submissively what he was told.

Is "whipping" your idea of toleration?

He was ill for some days, and they nursed him kindly. That refined his submission. But they insisted on his lying in the dark, and that was a great misery. And blind philosophers came and talked to him of the wicked levity of his mind, and reproved him so impressively for his doubts about the lid of rock that covered their cosmic casserole that he almost doubted whether indeed he was not the victim of hallucination in not seeing it overhead.

How would you illustrate this image of a "cosmic casserole"?

So Núñez became a citizen of the Country of the Blind, and these people ceased to be a generalised people and became individualities and familiar to

283

Why have the
people become
"individualities" to
Núñez now?

Medina-saroté
(mä ᴛнē nä sä rō tā′).

Note these standards
of beauty. Why are
they appropriate?

How does she
"observe" him? Is
there a better word?

him, while the world beyond the mountains became more and more remote and unreal. There was Yacob, his master, a kindly man when not annoyed; there was Pedro, Yacob's nephew; and there was Medina-saroté, who was the youngest daughter of Yacob. She was little esteemed in the world of the Blind, because she had a clear-cut face, and lacked that satisfying, glossy smoothness that is the blind man's ideal of feminine beauty; but Núñez thought her beautiful at first, and presently the most beautiful thing in the whole creation. Her closed eyelids were not sunken and red after the common way of the valley, but lay as though they might open again at any moment; and she had long eyelashes, which were considered a grave disfigurement. And her voice was strong, and did not satisfy the acute hearing of the valley swains. So that she had no lover.

There came a time when Núñez thought that, could he win her, he would be resigned to live in the valley for all the rest of his days.

He watched her; he sought opportunities of doing her little services, and presently he found that she observed him. Once at a rest-day gathering they sat side by side in the dim starlight, and the music was sweet. His hand came upon hers and he dared to clasp it. Then very tenderly she returned his pressure. And one day, as they were at their meal in the darkness, he felt her hand very softly seeking him, and as it chanced the fire leaped then and he saw the tenderness of her face.

He sought to speak to her.

He went to her one day when she was sitting in the summer moonlight spinning. The light made her a thing of silver and mystery. He sat down at her feet and told her he loved her, and told her how beautiful she seemed to him. He had a lover's voice, he spoke with a tender reverence that came near to awe, and she had never before been touched by adoration. She made him no definite answer, but it was clear his words pleased her.

After that he talked to her whenever he could take an opportunity. The valley became the world for him, and the world beyond the mountains where men lived in sunlight seemed no more than a fairy tale he would someday pour into her ears. Very tentatively and timidly he spoke to her of sight.

Sight seemed to her the most poetical of fancies, and she listened to his description of the stars and the mountains and her own sweet white-lit beauty as though it was a guilty indulgence. She did not believe, she could only half understand, but she was mysteriously delighted, and it seemed to him that she completely understood.

His love lost its awe and took courage. Presently he was for demanding her of Yacob and the elders in marriage, but she became fearful and delayed. And it was one of her elder sisters who first told Yacob that Medina-saroté and Núñez were in love.

There was from the first very great opposition to the marriage of Núñez and Medina-saroté; not so much because they valued her as because they held him as a being apart, an idiot, incompetent thing below the permissible level of a man. Her sisters opposed it bitterly as bringing discredit on them all; and old Yacob, though he had formed a sort of liking for his clumsy, obedient serf, shook his head and said the thing could not be. The young men were all angry at the idea of corrupting the race, and one went so far as to revile and strike

Why is she afraid to believe in his sight?

Núñez. He struck back. Then for the first time he found an advantage in seeing, even by twilight, and after that fight was over no one was disposed to raise a hand against him. But they still found his marriage impossible.

Old Yacob had a tenderness for his last little daughter, and was grieved to have her weep upon his shoulder.

"You see, my dear, he's an idiot. He has delusions; he can't do anything right."

"I know," wept Medina-saroté. "But he's better than he was. He's getting better. And he's strong, dear Father, and kind—stronger and kinder than any other man in the world. And he loves me—and, Father, I love him."

Old Yacob was greatly distressed to find her inconsolable, and, besides—what made it more distressing—he liked Núñez for many things. So he went and sat in the windowless council-chamber with the other elders and watched the trend of the talk, and said, at the proper time, "He's better than he was. Very likely, someday, we shall find him as sane as ourselves."

Then afterwards one of the elders, who thought deeply, had an idea. He was the great doctor among these people, their medicine-man, and he had a very philosophical and inventive mind, and the idea of curing Núñez of his peculiarities appealed to him. One day when Yacob was present he returned to the topic of Núñez.

"I have examined Bogotá," he said, "and the case is clearer to me. I think very probably he might be cured."

"That is what I have always hoped," said old Yacob.

"His brain is affected," said the blind doctor.

The elders murmured assent.

"Now, *what* affects it?"

"Ah!" said old Yacob.

"This," said the doctor, answering his own question. "Those queer things that are called the eyes, and which exist to make an agreeable soft depression in the face, are diseased, in the case of Bogotá, in such a way as to affect his brain. They are greatly distended, he has eyelashes, and his eyelids move, and consequently his brain is in a state of constant irritation and distraction."

"Yes?" said old Yacob. "Yes?"

"And I think I may say with reasonable certainty that, in order to cure him completely, all that we need do is a simple and easy surgical operation—namely, to remove these irritant bodies."

"And then he will be sane?"

"Then he will be perfectly sane, and a quite admirable citizen."

"Thank Heaven for science!" said old Yacob, and went forth at once to tell Núñez of his happy hopes.

Consider the satire in Yacob's remark.

But Núñez's manner of receiving the good news struck him as being cold and disappointing.

"One might think," he said, "from the tone you take, that you did not care for my daughter."

It was Medina-saroté who persuaded Núñez to face the blind surgeons.

"You do not want me," he said, "to lose my gift of sight?"

She shook her head.

"My world is sight."

Her head drooped lower.

"There are the beautiful things, the beautiful little things—the flowers, the lichens among the

287

rocks, the lightness and softness on a piece of fur, the far sky with its drifting down of clouds, the sunsets and the stars. And there is *you*. For you alone it is good to have sight, to see your sweet, serene face, your kindly lips, your dear, beautiful hands folded together. . . . It is these eyes of mine you won, these eyes that hold me to you, that these idiots seek. Instead, I must touch you, hear you, and never see you again. I must come under that roof of rock and stone and darkness, that horrible roof under which your imagination stoops. . . . No; you would not have me do that?"

A disagreeable doubt had arisen in him. He stopped, and left the thing a question.

"I wish," she said, "sometimes——" She paused.

"Yes?" said he, a little apprehensively.

"I wish sometimes—you would not talk like that."

"Like what?"

"I know it's pretty—it's your imagination. I love it, but *now*——"

He felt cold. *"Now?"* he said faintly.

She sat still.

"You mean—you think—I should be better, better perhaps——"

He was realising things very swiftly. He felt anger, indeed, anger at the dull course of fate, but also sympathy for her lack of understanding—a sympathy near akin to pity.

"Dear," he said, and he could see by her whiteness how intensely her spirit pressed against the things she could not say. He put his arms about her, he kissed her ear, and they sat for a time in silence.

"If I were to consent to this?" he said at last, in a voice that was very gentle.

She flung her arms about him, weeping wildly. "Oh, if you would," she sobbed, "if only you would!"

For a week before the operation that was to raise him from his servitude and inferiority to the level of a blind citizen, Núñez knew nothing of sleep, and all through the warm sunlit hours, while the others slumbered happily, he sat brooding or wandered aimlessly, trying to bring his mind to bear on his dilemma. He had given his answer, he had given his consent, and still he was not sure. And at last work-time was over, the sun rose in splendour over the golden crests, and his last day of vision began for him. He had a few minutes with Medina-saroté before she went apart to sleep.

"Tomorrow," he said, "I shall see no more."

"Dear heart!" she answered, and pressed his hands with all her strength.

"They will hurt you but little," she said; "and you are going through this pain—you are going through it, dear lover, for *me*. . . . Dear, if a woman's heart and life can do it, I will repay you. My dearest one, my dearest with the tender voice, I will repay."

He was drenched in pity for himself and her.

He held her in his arms, and pressed his lips to hers, and looked on her sweet face for the last time. "Good-bye!" he whispered at that dear sight, "good-bye!"

And then in silence he turned away from her.

She could hear his slow retreating footsteps, and something in the rhythm of them threw her into a passion of weeping.

He had fully meant to go to a lonely place where the meadows were beautiful with white narcissus, and there remain until the hour of his sacrifice should come, but as he went he lifted up his eyes and saw the morning, the morning like an angel in golden armour, marching down the steeps. . . .

It seemed to him that before this splendour he, and this blind world in the valley, and his love, and all, were no more than a pit of sin.

Núñez thinks of the valley as a "pit of sin." Why?

He did not turn aside as he had meant to do, but went on, and passed through the wall of the circumference and out upon the rocks, and his eyes were always upon the sunlit ice and snow.

He saw their infinite beauty, and his imagination soared over them to the things beyond he was now to resign forever.

In what ways does Núñez think that Bogotá is a "great free world"? Is he right or wrong?

He thought of that great free world he was parted from, the world that was his own, and he had a vision of those further slopes, distance beyond distance, with Bogotá, a place of multitudinous stirring beauty, a glory by day, a luminous mystery by night, a place of palaces and fountains and statues and white houses, lying beautifully in the middle distance. He thought how for a day or so one might come down through passes, drawing ever nearer and nearer to its busy streets and ways. He thought of the river journey, day by day, from great Bogotá to the still vaster world beyond, through towns and villages, forest and desert places, the rushing river day by day, until its banks receded and the big steamers came splashing by, and one had reached the sea—the limitless sea, with its thousand islands, its thousands of islands, and its ships seen dimly far away in their incessant journeyings round and about that greater world. And there, unpent by mountains, one saw the sky—the sky, not such a disc as one saw it here, but an arch of immeasurable blue, a deep of deeps in which the circling stars were floating. . . .

If Núñez had proclaimed his sight as a divine revelation, how might the blind people have reacted?

290

His eyes scrutinised the great curtain of the mountains with a keener inquiry.

For example, if one went so, up that gully and to that chimney there, then one might come out high among those stunted pines that ran round in a sort of shelf and rose still higher and higher as it passed above the gorge. And then? That talus might be managed. Thence perhaps a climb might be found to take him up to the precipice that came below the snow; and if that chimney failed, then another farther to the east might serve his purpose better. And then? Then one would be out upon the amber-lit snow there, and halfway up to the crest of those beautiful desolations.

He glanced back at the village, then turned right round and regarded it steadfastly.

He thought of Medina-saroté, and she had become small and remote.

He turned again towards the mountain wall, down which the day had come to him.

Then very circumspectly he began to climb.

When sunset came he was no longer climbing, but he was far and high. He had been higher, but he was still very high. His clothes were torn, his limbs were blood-stained, he was bruised in many places, but he lay as if he were at his ease, and there was a smile on his face.

From where he rested the valley seemed as if it were in a pit and nearly a mile below. Already it was dim with haze and shadow, though the mountain summits around him were things of light and fire. The mountain summits around him were things of light and fire, and the little details of the rocks near at hand were drenched with subtle beauty—a vein of green mineral piercing the grey, the flash of crystal faces here and there, a minute, minutely beautiful orange lichen close beside his face. There were deep mysterious shadows in the gorge, blue deepening into purple, and purple into a luminous darkness, and overhead was the illimitable vastness of the sky. But he heeded these things no longer, but lay quite inactive there, smiling as if he were satisfied merely to have escaped from the valley of the Blind in which he had thought to be King.

The glow of the sunset passed, and the night came, and still he lay peacefully contented under the cold stars.

Is Wells suggesting that it is not important whether or not Núñez escaped physically? In what sense *did* Núñez escape?

SYNTHESIS

The blind elders of the village are censors who seek to control the ideas of Núñez. Discuss the reasons for this need to control Núñez and the methods used to make him conform.

What prevents both Núñez and the blind people from understanding each other? Consider the proverb "In the Country of the Blind, the One-eyed Man Is King." Does it have any validity? What does it suggest about the responsibilities as well as the powers of being king? Was Núñez aware of both aspects of the proverb?

Compare the setting of "The Country of the Blind" with the setting of "The Diamond as Big as the Ritz," and contrast Núñez's adventures with John Unger's. In what ways are both characters changed by their experiences?

What one basic technique does Wells use to move the reader over the *Edges of Reality?* How does this shift in scene prepare the reader to accept Wells' social commentary without suspicion or defensiveness?

COMMENT

Herbert George Wells is famous for his many realistic science-fiction stories. "The Country of the Blind" was written in 1904 and presents a theme about which Wells cared deeply: the importance of an individual's freedom of thought and expression. Wells feared a growing tendency to suppress individual liberty in the interests of mass societies, and he felt that this suppression could destroy civilization.

Wells' pessimism increased at the onset of World War II, and in 1939, when he was asked to update "The Country of the Blind," he revised the ending to reflect his despair. In the new conclusion Wells allowed Núñez to escape from the valley only to discover that the mountain wall had split open and would soon bury the entire valley. Núñez was unable to save the blind villagers from the disaster he saw approaching, but he did save himself and Medina-saroté.

The new ending then focused on Medina-saroté. Although her life had been saved by her husband's sight, she had no wish to see. The world of vision "may be beautiful," she said, "but it must be terrible to *see*," and she kept the simple, protective illusions of blindness for the rest of her life.

The revision was never popular, and the original version used here is considered by many critics to be Wells' finest short story.

Pronunciation Key

The pronunciations given are shown in this way: **abbreviate** (ə brē′vē āt). The letters and signs used are pronounced as in the words below. The mark ′ is placed after a syllable with primary or heavy accent, as in the example above. The mark ′ after a syllable shows a secondary or lighter accent, as in **abbreviation** (ə brē′vē ā′shən).

a	hat, cap	i	it, pin	p	paper, cup	v	very, save
ā	age, face	ī	ice, five	r	run, try	w	will, woman
ä	father, far			s	say, yes	y	young, yet
		j	jam, enjoy	sh	she, rush	z	zero, breeze
b	bad, rob	k	kind, seek	t	tell, it	zh	measure, seizure
ch	child, much	l	land, coal	th	thin, both		
d	did, red	m	me, am	ᴛʜ	then, smooth		
		n	no, in			ə	represents:
e	let, best	ng	long, bring				a in about
ē	equal, be			u	cup, butter		e in taken
ėr	term, learn	o	hot, rock	ů	full, put		i in pencil
		ō	open, go	ü	rule, move		o in lemon
f	fat, if	ô	order, all				u in circus
g	go, bag	oi	oil, voice				
h	he, how	ou	house, out				

This pronunciation key is taken from the Thorndike-Barnhart school dictionaries.

1 2 3 4 5 6 7 8 9 10 11 12 13 14 15 16 17 18 19 20 21 22 23 24 25   80 79 78 77 76 75 74 73 72